P9-ECZ-472

JIMMY STEWART

Other titles by Michael Munn

Frank Sinatra: The Untold Story
John Wayne: The Man Behind The Myth
The Hollywood Connection: The True Story of Organized Crime
in Hollywood

JIMMY STEWART

THE TRUTH BEHIND THE LEGEND

MICHAEL MUNN

Skyhorse Publishing
A Herman Graf Book

Copyright © 2006, 2013 by Michael Munn

All Rights Reserved. No part of this book may be reproduced in any manner without the express written consent of the publisher, except in the case of brief excerpts in critical reviews or articles. All inquiries should be addressed to Skyhorse Publishing, 307 West 36th Street, 11th Floor, New York, NY 10018.

Skyhorse Publishing books may be purchased in bulk at special discounts for sales promotion, corporate gifts, fund-raising, or educational purposes. Special editions can also be created to specifications. For details, contact the Special Sales Department, Skyhorse Publishing, 307 West 36th Street, 11th Floor, New York, NY 10018 or info@skyhorsepublishing.com.

Skyhorse® and Skyhorse Publishing® are registered trademarks of Skyhorse Publishing, Inc.®, a Delaware corporation.

Visit our website at www.skyhorsepublishing.com.

10 9 8 7 6 5 4 3 2

Library of Congress Cataloging-in-Publication Data is available on file.

ISBN: 978-1-62636-094-5

Printed in the United States of America

I am dedicating this book to
my sister Judy
who bought me the soundtrack to *Exodus*
and opened up a whole new world of wonderful music,
and to my brother Peter
who took me to a flea-pit called the Tolmer to see *The Vikings*
and opened up another new world of Saturday afternoon cinema.
They both have a lot to answer for.

Contents

Foreword

James Stewart didn't hear a word I said, and told me, 'You'll hafta speak up.'

I'd not been told how deaf he was. He was, after all, sixty-seven – although as I later found out, he'd been losing his hearing for many years.

So there I was, in his dressing room at London's Prince of Wales Theatre, where he was performing *Harvey* in 1975, shouting questions at him. I was still a green young film journalist, twenty-two years old, nervous at meeting a screen legend and desperate not to sound like an idiot. Sensing my anxiety, Stewart smiled and said, very slowly, 'It's okay, son . . . this is only an interview, not a cross-examination. You ask the questions and . . . I'll do my damnedest to give you an intelligent answer.'

He also said, 'You don't hafta shout. Just . . . just speak *up*.'

I discovered in later years that he was quite good at lip-reading, although he wouldn't have admitted to it. He may even have been wearing a hearing aid, but I didn't notice. I never have been observant about surroundings, or clothing, or colour schemes. I am always aware, though, of people, and what they say. And I was aware that James Stewart was remarkably composed considering he would soon be going on stage to play Elwood P Dowd, the amiable drunk who believes he's got a six-foot white rabbit called Harvey as a friend. An hour later, I had the remarkable experience of seeing the play and watching Jimmy Stewart perform live on stage. The play was, as Stewart told me, much better than the famous 1950 film version.

My second interview with Stewart took place a few years after the first. For a long time I was convinced it had been in 1980, until, while researching this book, I came across the published interview in *Photoplay* and discovered it was actually 1979.

This time I met Stewart in a London hotel. I think it was the Dorchester, but again I have poor recollection of such details; I interviewed countless movie stars in countless hotels, countless restaurants, countless studios, countless bars, on countless outside locations, and after so many years the specifics of those places have often faded in my memory. But the memories of the stars – and some of those who never quite achieved stardom – are indelibly imprinted in my memory banks. And when it came to James Stewart – his mannerisms, his stories and his folksy persona – all of it is unforgettable.

It was on the day of that second meeting that I began to get to know Jimmy Stewart and his wife, Gloria. I'd begun the interview by being chatty, saying, 'I understand you're on your way from the Paris air show.' I'd forgotten how deaf he was; he tapped his ear and said, 'You'll hafta speak up . . . I'm a little . . .' and his words trailed off; I think he hated to use the word 'deaf'.

So I repeated my question, and he replied, 'Waall . . . I've been trying to get there for the past twenty years.'

'Why did it take so long?' I asked.

'I don't know really . . . I guess mostly my work. Over the years you get . . . you know . . . awful busy, and I've just never been able to . . . er . . . make it.' I'd also forgotten just how slowly Stewart talked, and how much he punctuated his sentences with pauses. He truly was the Jimmy Stewart the world had come to love and know.

But there was so much more to Jimmy Stewart than what he publicly revealed. He even had secrets; something I was to find out all about because of a brief interruption to the interview. About halfway through, the front door to his hotel suite flew open and in breezed a woman bursting with vitality and enthusiasm that almost overwhelmed the legendary laconic presence of James Stewart. 'This, young man,' he said to me as he rose out of his chair, 'is my wife Gloria.'

'I just did the museum – the Natural History,' she said. 'They've got two new exhibits there. Fascinating. One is on ecology, the other on dinosaurs. Certainly an improvement on those old cages with all those stuffed animals. They all look so *dead*.'

Stewart kissed her and said, 'But they *are* dead.'

She said, 'I know. But God, they needn't look *that* dead. Now I'm going for a bite to eat.'

Stewart told her, 'See you later, dear,' and she breezed out.

When the interview was over, I went down to the lobby and spotted Mrs Stewart, his wife of thirty years, having tea. She caught sight of me, and beckoned me over. 'Have some tea with me,' she said. 'Keep me company.'

So I did. We talked, and somehow it ended up with me volunteering to take her the next day to the British Museum, where I'd spent hundreds of hours as a child. We also took in other London sights, with me as her tour guide. To achieve this, I took a day off sick, and spent it touring London with Gloria Stewart in a taxi, walking around museums and exploring St Paul's Cathedral where I refused to go up into the dome.

'Why ever not?' she asked.

'Because I have an extreme fear of heights.'

'Oh,' she laughed, 'you must have *loved* Jim's film *Vertigo*.'

So I patiently waited until she came down again.

At the end of the day she invited me back to the hotel to have dinner with her and Jimmy – or Jim, as I was told to call him. Over dinner, I got to know a whole lot more about the real Jimmy Stewart.

I often found myself in a position to discover more about the real lives of stars when my trusty tape recorder was off, because I was not a hard-nosed journalist only on the hunt for a good story, and it obviously showed. I had been working in the film business since 1969, starting as a messenger boy and graduating to a publicist until I accidentally became a journalist in 1974. I was in search of a career as a film director and screenwriter, and was also making tentative steps towards being an actor. This meant that I always had a lot more to talk about with movie stars and directors and writers than just seeking answers that were the staple diet of fan magazines. It explains why and how I came to know so much about the big stars of Hollywood, and especially James Stewart.

I only had to mention that I'd spent a week with John Wayne in 1974 when he came to London to make *Brannigan*, or that I'd spent a day with Henry Fonda when he visited the city in 1976 to play *Clarence Darrow* on stage, or that I'd worked for John Huston for a time in 1974 (as well as dropping names like litter at every opportunity), to open the door for Jim and Gloria to be at ease with me.

Gloria insisted I spend a second day showing her more of the London sights, followed by dinner with the Stewarts again. There followed a third day of sightseeing, and by then I was Gloria's new best friend – or it seemed that way to me. I was just twenty-six and as everyone, including John Wayne, told me, I was 'a nice kid'.

Before I said goodbye to Jim and Gloria they gave me their home phone number, and I gave them mine. I never expected to see them again. But I did, just a couple of years later when they were back in London. I can't remember why they were over as by then I was winding down my journalistic career and was trying to make it as an actor, or a screenwriter, or a director, so I wasn't interested in doing an interview.

I saw them a couple more times during the 1980s, the last occasion being when Jim had some kind of reunion at his old Second World War air base at Tibenham in East Anglia. I lived in East Anglia at that time, and an American Air Force friend of mine drove me to the reunion. When Gloria saw me, I was made to feel like a long-lost friend – or maybe it was more like a son. Jim was typically more laconic, shaking my hand and saying, 'Sure is good to see ya, Mike.'

Jim always called me Mike. Gloria called me Michael. Perhaps it was because one of her own sons from her first marriage was called Michael. Perhaps she saw something in me that reminded her of him – or of the other son, Ronald, who had been killed while on active service in Vietnam in 1969. Jim even introduced me to a couple of the surviving members of his old squadron as 'my good friend Mike'.

I relate all this, not to elevate myself, but to try to explain the relationship I had developed with Jim and Gloria. A couple of times Gloria called to tell me she and Jim would be in England. I often telephoned them. Usually it was Gloria who answered, and she spent more hours than I could afford on a transatlantic phone call giving me all the latest news.

When Jim spoke, it was usually, 'Nice to hear from ya, Mike . . . hope you're well . . . we're doin' just fine . . . okay, bye now.' I always had to remind myself that when Jim spoke, you had to make sure he'd finished before you said anything. The pauses he put into his speech often fooled you into believing he had come to the end of whatever he was saying . . . and then he'd add a little bit more. Like the time I asked him if he'd sign a photograph for me in 1979. He said, slowly, 'I'm afraid I . . . er . . . don't . . . er,' and being convinced he was saying 'I'm afraid I don't sign autographs,' I answered, 'That's all right.' But then he finished his sentence: '. . . have a photograph to sign.' It was not a problem as I had brought a still from *How the West Was Won*. That was the first film I ever saw starring (or in that case *featuring*) James Stewart, along with a couple of dozen other big stars. It has always been a favourite movie of mine; it was filmed in Cinerama, a film process whereby film that was shot with a camera with three lenses and three strips of film running through it, was projected onto a giant curved screen using three projectors, creating the first virtual-reality cinema experience. The still showed Jim hugging Carroll Baker standing under a tree, and he immediately launched into a story about that picture (which is included in the pages of this book).

Getting to know the Stewarts was an exhilarating experience. It also held surprises: during those London tours with Gloria in 1979, she told me how Jim had worked for J Edgar Hoover, Director of the FBI, during the infamous Communist witch-hunts of the late 1940s and early 1950s. It was quite a story, and one that she told because she was confident I was not going to write any articles about it; it was a confidence I never betrayed because I was more interested in getting help and advice in my search for a career in films.

I don't think Jim ever knew she confided in me. And as I think back, I believe the only reason she did confide in me was because I first told her about a story John Wayne had related to me concerning his run-in with the Communists. Gloria, a staunch right-wing conservative like Jim and Duke Wayne, wanted me to know that Jim had played *his* part in serving his country by becoming what she described as 'an undercover *undercover* agent' for the FBI.

She also wanted me to know how he had served his country during the Second World War, a subject Jim hardly ever spoke about. The only time he talked of it, and then only briefly, was when I saw him at Tibenham. When I told him I wanted to write a book about the men and women of the film industry who served in the war, Gloria urged him to open up. And he did, if only barely.

Before she died in 1994, Gloria faxed me details of Jim's war record. It came too late to include in the book I had just written (called *Stars at War*), so now I have the opportunity to write about it in this book – as well as the fascinating story of how Jim came to be a secret agent. I write about it now because, regardless of the rights and wrongs of the witch-hunts – and I've heard both sides and have my own opinions – it illustrates that Jimmy Stewart was a man who believed passionately in his country and did his duty as he saw it. But while Hoover enlisted him to help round up Hollywood's Communists, for Jim it was more to do with the battle against an evil he felt was a greater threat than Communism. That was organised crime.

It would be impossible for me to write a biography of James Stewart without including these details, because they fill in the gaps both in the stories he told himself and those related by others. Though I didn't know it at the time, Henry Fonda, when I talked to him in 1976, was holding back such details. I believe he was the only person, apart from Gloria, who knew. That knowledge caused a deep rift in the legendary Fonda–Stewart friendship, and it must have taught Jim to keep his secrets in their place.

When Gloria told me about such things, she was also letting me know that Jim was a man of many dimensions. People seem to think he really is like the Mr Smith who went to Washington, or the George Bailey who had a wonderful life, or the Elwood P Dowd who was just crazy enough to think he had a six-foot white rabbit as a friend. He is also thought of as a wily old raconteur who, in the 1970s, told wonderful tall – and lengthy – tales on television chat shows. And, of course, a lot of people think Jimmy Stewart was somehow perfect. Too many books have presented him as something of a saint. He was a good man, true. But he had flaws. Don't we all, though? Why should Jimmy Stewart be any different to the rest of us? For instance, he had a temper, which he had to learn to control but which still occasionally surfaced. He had a slightly quirky streak. He was something of a ladies' man. And below the surface, he had a racist spirit which he tried to subdue. He was simply a Presbyterian from Pennsylvania who tried to do the best he could, never meaning to offend anyone.

He was also a far better actor than people seem to remember. While I was writing this book, a friend of mine, who has to be in the minority of humankind, said, 'I don't like James Stewart. He always played the same character.' In fact, Jim worked hard at his technique – a lot of which he taught to me. He strove (though not always) to create characters that were *unlike* himself – although they often had vestiges of his own personality, which would be true of all actors and their roles. You only have to watch *Mr. Smith Goes to Washington* and then *The Naked Spur*, or *Call Northside 777* and *Anatomy of a Murder*, to see an actor with a wider range than he was ever given credit for. In fact, Jim hated it when people, a lot of them critics, called him a 'natural' actor, as they often did. He worked hard to learn his craft, and a lot of today's generation of film actors would do well to study him.

When writing this book I became aware of a huge gap in the cultural knowledge of today's generation of film fans. It comes as a shock to discover that most young people have never heard of James Stewart. People of my generation and those who are older must encourage the youngsters of today to watch old movies and to get to know the great movie stars, even if some of their films were in black and white and didn't have spectacular computer-generated special effects.

It was a privilege for my generation to get to know Jimmy Stewart on the silver screen. It was a privilege for me to get to know him in life. And it was a hoot getting to know Gloria.

1

How the Stewarts
Won the West

'It's kinda hard to believe, but when I was a baby I was a good
round shape,' James Stewart once told me. 'I was eight pounds
when I was born but . . . somewhere on the way . . . through the
years . . . I got kinda thin!'

The round, bouncing baby boy named James Maitland Stewart
was born on 20 January 1908 in Indiana, Pennsylvania, to
Alexander and Bessie Stewart. Alexander – better known to all as
Alex – came from a large family of pioneers that settled in
Pennsylvania.

'The history of my family was like something out of *How the
West Was Won*,' Jim told me when we talked about that particular
favourite film of mine. 'In fact, when Henry Hathaway [one of three
directors who made that film] said he wanted me to play the mountain man [Linus Rawlins] in his segment of *How the West Was Won*,
I said, "You know, Henry, let's throw away the script and start a
new one, based on my family history." He said, "Damnit, Jim, why
didn't you say so before? John Ford and George Marshall are
shooting their episodes now, so it's too late. But if you ever want to
sit down and write a screenplay based on *your* family history, let me
know and we'll make *How the West Was Won by James Stewart and*

1

His Family of Presbyterian Pioneers." Anyway, Henry asked me to tell him about my family and . . . I guess he wished he hadn't asked because there were an awful lot of fellas in my family who shared names. But one evening I set out to tell him about how the Stewarts had won the West.'

William Stewart, his heavily pregnant wife, Margaret Gettys, and baby boy Archibald left Belfast in Northern Ireland in the fall of 1785. During the lengthy Atlantic crossing on the *Congress* passenger ship, Margaret gave birth to her second son, John Kerr Stewart.

Margaret had family who had already settled in America, in southern Pennsylvania, which was where William Stewart set himself up as a storekeeper. Three more children were born to the Stewarts – Martha, Alexander and William. But William Senior felt unsettled, and in 1794, he uprooted his family and spent the next few years moving from one town to another before finally establishing a home in Armstrong Township, just six miles west of Indiana. William Stewart Senior died in 1810, just fifty-six years of age.

His second son, John Kerr Stewart, married Elizabeth Hindman Armstrong, who came from a family with both English and Scottish blood, on 16 March 1815. John and Elizabeth established a homestead several miles to the north of Indiana. They had ten children – five sons and five daughters. Jim told me, 'To us, that may sound like a lot of babies to be having. But it took twenty-three years for all the babies to be had.'

The last to be born to John and Elizabeth was James Maitland Stewart, in 1839 (his grandson and namesake would become James Stewart the movie star). James Maitland was to become one of the best educated of the Stewarts, graduating from Dayton Academy and then from Westminster College, both in Pennsylvania. He grew up with a sound sense of business.

Archibald – the child born to William and Margaret in Belfast – had grown up to become a devout Presbyterian, but had never married. He devoted much of his life to fundraising for new hospitals, and he was also a founding member of the American Bible Society. When he went into partnership with a local family, the Suttons, to run a hardware store in 1851, he acquired the services of two of his brother John's sons, Alexander and Archibald, to help run the store, which became known throughout the Indiana region as the Big Warehouse. Religion had made its mark on many of the Stewarts, and both Alexander and Archibald shared their Uncle Archibald's religious fervour. Archibald the younger eventually left the Big Warehouse to become a justice of the peace, leaving Uncle Archibald and Alexander to run the store.

(About this far into Jim's story of his family history, Henry Hathaway had said, 'Goddamnit, Jim, there's been an awful lot of homesteading, having children, Bible reading and store-running – but no one's killed an Indian or an outlaw or anything much else exciting. That's not winning the West. That's *breeding* the West.' To which Jim said, 'Now hold on just a minute, Henry. I'm just coming to the best part – the Civil War.')

During the Civil War, which tore America apart between 1861 and 1865, justice of the peace Archibald and his youngest brother James Maitland enlisted in the Union Army. Seven of John Kerr Stewart's grandsons also fought in the war between the states. 'When my grandfather and other members of the family enlisted in the Civil War,' Jim told me, 'it began a strong tradition of military duty in the Stewarts.' This was a tradition that would eventually drive James Stewart to abandon films and join the US Army Air Force at the onset of the Second World War. Archibald and James Maitland appear to have been among Jim's greatest heroes.

Archibald had enlisted as a private in the 40th Regiment of the 11th Reserve of the Pennsylvania Volunteers in April 1861. Within just a few months, he had been promoted to second lieutenant because of his extraordinary leadership qualities. Two years later, he was promoted to first lieutenant. He fell at Spotsylvania, Virginia, in May 1864. One of his own nephews also died in the same battle. Another nephew was killed during the march through the South by General Sherman. Jim's grandfather, James Maitland Stewart, was a sergeant in the Signal Corps, who saw action at Winchester, Cedar Creek, Fisher's Hill and Richmond.

(Henry Hathaway was impressed with the Civil War stories and conceded that 'it would make a good picture *if* Civil War pictures made for good box office. But they're poison.' Whether Jim told Hathaway the rest of the family history, I have no idea – but he did tell me.)

James Maitland returned from the war to marry Virginia Kelly, whose father had died fighting in the Mexican War of 1847. Her grandfather had been a state senator, and her great-grandfather had fought in the Revolutionary War of Independence. James and Virginia had two sons – Alexander and Ernest; the latter was born with a leg deformity.

James went to work at the Big Warehouse, which continued to be managed by his older brother Alexander. However, Uncle Archibald, now in his mid-eighties and officially retired, maintained control of the store, and he considered the well-educated James Maitland a far better businessman than Alexander. (Uncle Archibald died in 1877 at the age of ninety-three.) James Maitland knew there would be a boom in building materials following the devastation of the Civil War, and taking advantage of the store's location close to the Penn Railroad, he succeeded in acquiring contracts for building materials and tools that boosted the success of the Big Warehouse.

James Maitland was popular with customers; he had a far more amiable personality than Alexander, and he rewarded his customers for their loyalty by throwing in occasional extra items with their orders. He had, in fact, what today we might call a good sense of marketing. One of his most popular giveaways was a penknife. He even sent one to President Calvin Coolidge and received a letter of thanks from the White House, which raised the esteem the locals had for James Maitland ever higher. He bought a booklet called *101 Famous Poems* in bulk just for the purpose of giving it to people he felt needed a little cheer in their lives, and he knew his regular customers well enough to be able to tell when any of them was burdened or troubled.

If anyone should have been troubled in his life, it was James Maitland. He lost Virginia to an illness at an early age, and a second wife also died before her time. His religious convictions were put to the test, but he seemed to emerge each time with a stronger faith. Such blows to his life did, however, dent his geniality, and he seemed to experience moments of bitterness and resentment.

His son Alex (who would be James Stewart's father) had been well educated, attending the best schools his father could afford, including Mercersburg Academy in the Cumberland Valley of southern Pennsylvania, and Princeton, a university that had strong connections with the Presbyterian Church. Then, suddenly, in April 1898, just weeks before receiving his Science degree, he took off to fight in the Spanish-American War with the Pennsylvanian Volunteers.

Alex's experiences during that war long remained a matter of conjecture, even for his son Jim. 'What I do know is that he spent seven months in the war at San Juan, the capital of Puerto Rico. He might have been in the battle for San Juan Hill in Cuba – people said he was, and he never denied it. But he never could quite confirm it either.'

Alex's penchant for tall tales rubbed off on to Jim, according to Gloria. There were, she said, the stories Jim told journalists and on television for pure entertainment, and then there was the truth. She added, however, that much of the truth was just as entertaining as the 'tall stories'. Gloria became a reliable guide as to the authenticity of the many tales Jim told me. Actor Burgess Meredith, a long-time friend of Jim's, also testified to Stewart's yarn-spinning: 'He's a gifted storyteller, and he can launch into one of his tales . . . and then he stumbles – that is, he undergoes some misfortune – just at the right spot. It's perfect timing, really, because it's the stumble and the pause that precedes the misfortune that makes it a crowd-pleaser, so to speak. And the reason Jimmy stumbles in his stories is to make his own misfortune the punch line. He satirises himself.' Jim's yarns, from my observation, ranged from the factual to the exaggerated, to the occasional bit of amusing fiction. For instance, Jim liked to tell how, when he became a cowboy star, he would talk to his horse, Pie, giving it strict instructions. He insisted that Pie followed his instructions to the letter. With Jim, you could guess when he was pulling your leg, but you were never completely sure.

Alex returned after serving his seven months in the war, and wore his uniform proudly to receive his belated graduation at Princeton. His father, James Maitland, had considered Alex's sudden departure from Princeton as irrational. His once gentle humour now honed with a sometimes cruel edge, James Maitland was heard to remark, 'I have one son with a crippled leg and another with a crippled head.'

Alex went on to prove that he was anything but crippled in the head. The esteem and respect in which he (and Jim) held James Maitland was never dented by the old man's sour demeanour. Alex had always been expected to work in the Big Warehouse, and Alex did not disappoint his father. He worked as his father's employee for several years until 1905 when he was able to buy a one-third investment in the store, a sound business move that more than satisfied James Maitland.

He also got engaged, to Elizabeth (Bessie) Ruth Jackson. Like Alex, she had been well educated, which for a woman of her time was a rarity. Her father was a man of means and good standing in the community, having founded a steel company and a bank, and he was able to afford to send her to Wilson College in Chambersburg which, like Princeton, had strong Presbyterian links. There she excelled in music and art.

Although Alex carried on the religious traditions of his father, he enjoyed the company of drinking men and explored numerous alcoholic sprees. His father had been unable to dissuade him from such carousing, but Bessie laid down the law: either he gave up his wicked ways or there would be no marriage. Alex at first took the ultimatum as a joke, but when he realised that she was deadly serious, he did as he was told. 'He didn't quit drinking,' said Jim, 'but he sure cut down his intake.'

Jim described his parents thus: 'Dad was a colourful character and had the common touch which appealed to many of the customers. Mom was a cultured, elegant and refined woman. They weren't much like each other at all, really. But they had love and respect – and they *liked* each other.'

Alex and Bessie married on 19 December 1906, and two years later, on 20 January 1908, the first of their three children arrived – James Maitland Stewart. The second child, a daughter, Mary Wilson (named from Bessie's side of the family), arrived on 12 January 1912, and on 29 October 1914 Virginia Kelly (named after her father's mother) was born. They lived close to the store, on Philadelphia Street, but when the family was complete, Alex moved them to 104 North Seventh Street in the Vinegar Hill district. Jim recalled, 'My folks lived there for the rest of their lives – and to me it was always home, even when I didn't live there much later in life. It was *always* home.'

The store, too, was a place that forever marked young James Stewart. He said:

'The store was the centre of my universe for many years. Certainly through my boyhood years . . . and it was always the place I could come back to and feel at home. I was . . . grounded there. As was my father. But what I came to realise . . . much later . . . was that the thing that made the store the centre of my life was not the store itself . . . but my father. That store *was* my father . . . and *he* was the centre of my life.

'My mother called me Jimsey . . . which was a name I wouldn't want anyone else calling me . . . so *don't*. But it was such an affectionate name coming from my Mom. [The way Jim used the words 'Dad' and 'Mom' always made them sound as though they required a capital 'D' and 'M', as though they were like any real name.] She had a sweet talent for music. She played the piano just . . . *beautifully*. She'd give recitals . . . Beethoven, Schubert . . . she could play all the classics. And she could sing too. Sang in the choir. And she encouraged me to appreciate music and to want to play . . . though I never was as good on the piano as she was. More important than anything, Mom was the rock of our family. She kept us all in line . . . including my father.'

In one of our many conversations between 1979 and 1994, Gloria told me, 'Jim's mother had a lifelong hearing problem which Jim inherited by the time he was middle-aged. Bessie had a slow way of speaking – very methodical, so she would make sure she was being understood. And Jim thought it was her way of compensating for her loss of hearing. She'd really strive to speak slowly and deliberately. As Jim grew, he found himself copying her speech patterns, and that's how Jim came to speak in his familiar drawl. People think it's because he's slow thinking at times. Well, that he *isn't*. He's dead sharp. But when he speaks you can almost see him thinking ahead, so it slows his speech down. And as he's got older and he's lost a lot of his hearing, it's become more pronounced, so the public now [in the late 1970s and 1980s] have the James Stewart they love and know. The cynics think it's an act.

The ignorant think he's not that bright. They've got it *so* wrong.'

Of his parents, Jim recalled, 'They were strict with us kids . . . but not in a harsh way. They believed in discipline, but they were never strict in a way that made you feel miserable. In fact, they made you feel more secure, because they laid down the rules of good behaviour . . . and you just kinda *knew* exactly where you stood. You knew what was right and wrong, and somehow my folks were able to instil that in us without terrorising us.'

Like many of the Stewarts before him, Jim was always a man with a strong faith in God, instilled in him from birth: 'Religion was an important part of our lives. We used to go to church a lot. The Presbyterian Church. My mother played the organ and my father sang in the choir.

'There was a minister . . . the Reverend Frederick Hinitt who kinda made a name for himself because he didn't just quote the Bible at you. He studied everything that was going on in the country, politically and socially . . . he read *all* the newspapers . . . and he would deliver these sermons that basically told people to be *better* people . . . not just because the Bible said so but because it was the *human* thing to do. He talked about all sorts of things from racial prejudice to social deprivation . . . not just moral deprivation. And I'd have to say that Reverend Hinitt was a big inspiration to me.

'But it wasn't just a one-day-a-week religion. At mealtimes we'd hold hands and give thanks for the food we had. Sunday evenings we'd sing hymns at home. As children my sisters and I didn't have religion force-fed to us. It was just a part of family life.'

This aspect of his family life is what made Jimmy Stewart a man not just admired as a movie star but loved as a human being by millions around the world. Said Gloria, in 1979, 'There's no doubt that Jim's religious background helped to bring out his virtues which he still has today. It's what makes him a decent, honourable and patriotic human being.'

It's possible, too, that the teaching of the Reverend Hinitt on racial tolerance prevented Jim from growing up into a bigot. Pennsylvania had a history of racial intolerance and was long a favourite state for the Ku Klux Klan to gather, but the Reverend's warnings must have helped Jim to contain his own prejudice.

Alex and Bessie also instilled in their children a curiosity about the world. Said Jim, 'My father loved organising family outings so we'd see something outside of our home town. Both my folks were *interested* in the world, and their curiosity to explore rubbed off on to my sisters and myself. It seems that wherever we went my father did his research so he'd know about the places we would visit, and when we'd arrive, he'd tell us about this and that, and we'd learn . . . and we'd want to go to other places and learn more. We would make regular visits to Pittsburgh. Before we had a car we'd go by train. Every summer we went further . . . to places like Yellowstone Park and Washington . . . and up to Canada. My parents were folks who wanted their kids to know more about the world. And the more we knew, the more we *wanted* to know.'

Alex Stewart was well known in Indiana, not just because he was a colourful, good-natured man, or because he ran the Big Warehouse, but also because he got involved with everything he felt a good citizen of any town *should* get involved with. He was a member of the Masonic lodge, of the Indiana Rotary Club, and of the Salvation Army's advisory board. But what excited Jim was that his father was a volunteer fire-fighter. Jim recalled:

'The town we lived in caught fire with alarming regularity . . . which was not surprising as most of the houses were built the previous century and were made a lot from wood. So my father was kept pretty busy.

'Our house was very close to the siren that would go off with a loud wailing to call the fire-fighters. Didn't matter where my father was, if the siren went off, he dropped everything and was soon driving the fire engine . . . and sometimes I'd go with him. Driving those ladder trucks was kind of precarious, and it made for an exciting ride.

'Of course, I couldn't go if the siren went off while we were at church, but my father would simply stand up in the choir loft and quickly leave with all eyes of the congregation upon him . . . because it could be any one of *their* houses that was on fire. But nobody dared leave church, and everyone would wait until my father came back. I could hear a sort of uneasy silence as everybody held their breath until my father calmly took his seat in the choir loft. Even the minister would stop and wait . . . and then my father would look to the congregation and nod to indicate that all was well . . . and then there was a huge collective sigh of relief.'

2

Beat the Kaiser

While many who become actors grow up with that burning ambition to tread the boards or grace the silver screen, Jim never did: 'I never had any ambition to be an actor when I was a boy. It never entered my head.

'Like all children, I liked to put on shows. It was all part of *playing* . . . just as a kid. When I was five I used to like playing with hand puppets . . . I'd sneak them into church and put on my own show. Mom was at the organ and Dad was in the choir, so I was on my own with my sisters . . . we were trusted to behave. My puppets used to join in the prayers and the hymns, and we'd have little conversations among ourselves. I didn't do it for the benefit of others. It was all for *me*.'

Even watching movies had no effect upon young Jim other than providing a means of being entertained. He said, 'I don't know that watching movies back then had much of an impact on anyone's ambitions. They were just flickering pictures you saw at the nickelodeons. I think people who wanted to become actors in those days did so because they'd go to the theatre and feel the thrill of performing to an audience.

'When you watched a movie back then, it didn't inspire you.

Well, it didn't inspire *me*. The movies were just a means of escape
from the real world. It was the cliff-hanging serials I enjoyed . . .
like *The Perils of Pauline*. Seeing a serial like that made you go to
the movie theatre every week because you didn't want to miss an
episode.'

Those flickering pictures did, however, provide Jim with his first
female fantasy figure: 'There was an actress called Ruth Roland . . .
she was one of the silent screen's great heroines in a whole succession of serials. I guess you could say she was my first fantasy
woman. She was my favourite actress. She may not have been the
best actress who ever lived but she was *my* favourite movie star.

'She was Pearl White's closest rival, but I thought she had a
more exciting personality on the screen than Pearl White, who was
always the more popular and is still better remembered. But Ruth
Roland's films had more style. The studio spent more money on
them. During the 1920s she was known as "Queen of the Thriller".
I remember watching one of her pictures, and she was in mortal
danger, and I got so excited and frightened that this would be the
end of Ruth, I jumped out of my seat . . . and my friends had to hold
me back from rushing at the screen to help her. *That* was the magic
of pictures back then. You weren't sophisticated then . . . you
didn't know anything about movie stars and their real lives. You just
saw their pictures and you got caught up in them . . . you *believed*
them. You'd forget you were just watching something that was
being *acted*.

'When I first got to Hollywood, I met her. I was just so thrilled
to meet this beautiful woman who had given me so much pleasure
. . . and I mean that in an innocent way. She was still young . . . just
in her thirties. I asked her if she really did all those stunts herself.
And they were really dangerous stunts. And she said she did. I
thought that was just incredible. And shortly after that she died. I'd
only just met her . . . and not long after I heard she was dead.' Ruth
Roland was just forty-five when she died of cancer in 1937.

Another great source of entertainment in those days was the
circus:

'My father used to love the arrival of the circus that came to town
twice a year. Dad would want to go and see them as their wagons

drove in just before dawn. And he'd wake me up and take me with him . . . and I got to thinking I'd like to run away with the circus. It was just such a thrill. When I turned eight I was allowed to help unload the wagons and my reward was being able to feed the animals. The elephants were always my favourites.

'The circus folk usually asked for credit to purchase supplies from the store, and Dad figured that if they needed credit, they also needed feeding, so he'd sometimes invite some of the circus folk to our house for an evening meal. I remember there was a certain smell about them . . . and you could tell they worked with the animals. Mom wasn't too keen on the smell, and she was even less keen on the conversation, which tended to be kind of *racy* . . . but Dad loved it, and so did us kids.

'When the circus artists were broke, they offered to pay Dad back with circus merchandise. There was one fella who played the accordion, and when he couldn't pay his bill, he gave Dad the accordion . . . and Dad gave it to me and said, "Here, son, learn to play the accordion." I knew how to play the piano a little, so I could pick out the keys, and then it was a case of figuring out how to squeeze the thing. It took a long time, but I taught myself to play the accordion . . . and I really came to *love* playing that instrument. Still do. At first I could only play it in the key of C. But I could play a tune, and that pleased my mother.

'Another time, some circus fella couldn't pay and he asked Dad what he'd like in return. Waall . . . Dad chose a fourteen-foot python, which arrived at the store in a wooden crate. Dad thought he could put the python in the window where it would be safe behind glass, and it would attract customers. And it sure did because everyone came to the store to see what the snake was doing. The python seemed to take a dislike to two spinsters who were looking at the snake, which suddenly struck at them . . . which didn't do the snake any good because he hit his nose on the window. But one of the spinsters fainted.

'Later, the police turned up and charged Dad with being in charge of a snake that was a threat to life and limb. So the snake had to be removed, but when Dad asked for a volunteer among his staff to get it from behind the glass, nobody stepped forward. So Dad got his friend, Doc Torrance, to come with him to the store late one

Sunday night, and they chloroformed the snake so they could remove it. Well, it took the two of them to grab the snake, hold it down and get the chloroform over its face, and what Dad later told me but nobody else was that he and the Doc almost chloroformed themselves in the process.

'That was the kind of fella my father was. He was a good churchgoer, but he liked adventure, he liked to live it up a little . . . and he was my hero. He used to ride horses at harness races in country fairs. I got to sit on 'em a bit but it was a while later before Dad taught me to ride . . . but I got to spend a lot of time cleaning out the stables. Can't say it was the most fun I ever had but it did give me something that would be important when I started making Westerns . . . which was a lack of fear of horses. They're big creatures, and they can scare a small child. But I learned not to be afraid of them.'

In all of Jim's tales about his childhood, little was ever said about his sisters, Mary (who everyone called Dotie) and Virginia. 'Sisters were little more than pests to a boy,' he once said. 'When Mom and Dad went out I had to babysit them 'cos they were younger than me. That was a cruel thing to do to a boy.' Jim much preferred the company of his dog to that of his sisters:

'I had a dog called Bounce. By God, I loved that dog. Then a neighbour's dog killed him, and I was so angry that I vowed to kill that dog. I just wanted revenge, and every day I'd tell my father I was going to kill it. I was actually aware that I was screaming for blood . . . and I used that emotion – that rage – later in the Westerns I made in the fifties. Anyway, Dad said to me, "So you really want to kill the dog?" and I said, "Yes, I sure do." And he said, "Right, let's go and do it."

'He took me to the store and we went down the alley by the side of the building, and I discovered he'd already got the dog and had it tied up there. He went into the store and came out with a huge deer rifle, put it in my hands, stepped back and said, "Okay, son, do your bloody work."

'I aimed the rifle at the dog, barely able to hold it . . . and this dog . . . he just looked at me through big brown eyes . . . and his tail started to wag . . . and I couldn't squeeze the trigger with him looking at me like that. Finally, the gun was too heavy to hold any longer, and I put it down. Then the dog started licking my hand.

'Then Dad untied the dog, and the three of us walked home. Dad didn't say a word to me. He'd taught me I wasn't a killer. He also taught me it was all right to say what was on my mind and get it off my chest. It was *okay* to be angry. But what you do about it is another matter.'

As Gloria once said to me, 'People think Jim is always this slow and *gentle* man – and mostly he is. But he can get as mad as any man. He has this terrible rage. But he has learned to contain it so it doesn't show very often. He has a rage that is as frightening as anything I have ever seen. But he controls it better than anyone I have ever known.'

Perhaps somewhat urged on by Alex's encouragement that the children seek adventure and learn about the world, Jim, before reaching his teens, came to the decision to seek greater thrills. He recalled:

'When I was ten I made the momentous decision to go on safari in Africa. Ya see, I was always a dreamer – dreaming about going places and seeing things and doing stuff. I told my parents that I wanted to go and see the elephants and the lions and the rhinos in their natural environment. Waall . . . Mom thought the whole idea was *ridiculous* . . . which *I* didn't think it was at all. And she just laughed at the whole prospect of this ten-year-old trekking off to the plains and jungles of Africa. But Dad didn't laugh. I guess you could say that he . . . *humoured* me.

'He immediately started to gather books about Africa, schedules for ships and trains . . . and he even got a stack of iron bars for me to make cages with when I caught all those wild animals. I had made up my mind, but all *this* kinda took me by surprise because it was one thing having a dream, but another finding it becoming a reality . . . and at such *speed*.

'Before I knew it, Dad had set my date for departure and had it all planned out . . . catching a train to Baltimore, getting another for New York, and getting on a ship bound for Africa. I really thought

I was going. And then the day came, and I packed all my things and was thinking that I really didn't want to go after all. Like I say, it was one thing to *dream* about these things. That's what kids do.

'At the last minute Dad said, "Sorry, Jimbo" – that's what he often called me, Jimbo – he said, "Sorry, Jimbo, but there's been a derailment on the line to Baltimore so you're gonna hafta put off your safari for a bit. But I'll tell ya what. Why don't we go off to Atlantic City for a short trip?"

'And so we went off to Atlantic City, and while we were there, Dad said to me, "You know, son, I think it would be a good idea if you waited a couple of years before going off on safari." And I said, "I think that's a great idea, Dad."

'Of course, Dad had no intention of letting me go off to Africa at ten years of age . . . but he had great fun making all the arrangements and watching me get more anxious but never having the nerve to say "I've changed my mind". I guess what he taught me that time was not to make hasty decisions without thinking them through. Well, I'm not sure I learned *that* lesson.'

While Jim was growing up and becoming ever more curious about the world, Europe erupted in war. It never occurred to Jim that the war would have any direct effect on him, except to instil in him what became the greatest passion of his life – aeroplanes. 'I got real interested in planes during the Great War. I was about nine . . . and we used to receive a magazine called the *Literary Digest*, and most issues seemed to have photos of the war on the cover. And every time there was a picture that showed an aeroplane, I carefully cut the cover off and stuck it on my bedroom wall until the wall was covered in pictures of planes. For a dreamer, there was no better dream than the ability to fly. And I began to dream about flying . . . to be free like a bird . . . to be able to look down on the world from a height and see it perhaps the way God sees it.

'When I went to bed at night I saw those pictures of aeroplanes, and so planes were the last thing I thought of when I went to sleep, and I'd dream about flying my own plane. And when I woke up I'd see all those pictures, so planes were the first things I thought of.'

The war also inspired him to create plays, although he insisted he still had no ambitions to be an actor: 'Doing plays was just me having fun. I started to put on shows for others . . . in the basement of our house. I think a lot of kids do that kind of thing without having theatrical aspirations of any kind. For no other reason than the fact that it was fun I put on a show in the basement of our house called *Beat the Kaiser* . . . and I wrote it, produced it, directed it, and played all the male roles. My sisters played the females. And I made Mom and Dad sit there and watch. I remember thinking that Dad looked kind of swollen and red in the face, and I thought he was just getting sick. It was only years later that I realised he always looked that way when he was trying not to laugh.'

In 1917, the Great War in Europe brought a sudden and shocking interruption to the lives of the Stewart family. America entered the war, and Alex followed in the tradition of Stewarts before him by enlisting in October. Early in 1918, he was sent overseas:

'My dad went off to fight in the war in Europe when I was about ten. The whole family went off to New York to see him off. We went up the Statue of Liberty. Just to prove how fearless I was, I tried to climb out on to the giant lady's nose . . . but I was stopped. I wasn't so much trying to show I was unafraid of heights but that I was not going to show how afraid I was for my father . . . and how desperately I was going to miss him.

'I had decided a good way of keeping myself occupied while he was away was to have my own theatre. So before he went I told him I wanted to build a theatre in our basement and asked if I could have some wooden boards from the store to build a stage. So he told Mom to let me have what I needed.

'And off he went to war . . . and I felt alone . . . not in a good way . . . not in the way I liked . . . I was *lonely* without him. The house felt empty. So I got to work building my theatre, and with help from my friends, we built a proscenium and we had lights and curtains . . . it was something I got really into. My first production was a sort of remake of *Beat the Kaiser*, which I called *To Hell with the Kaiser*. It was a more elaborate production than the first. Cost a cent to see it. Even Mom had to pay.

'My next production was *The Slacker*. Thinking back on it, I was already becoming something of a conservative, I guess . . . or just a young patriot. Anyway, it was about a man who refuses to fight in the war. Finally he realises it's his duty to fight . . . and he wins the war all by himself. I played the lead . . . it was *my* theatre, so I felt I could do that. But I also felt the play had something *important* to say. What really fascinated me and my friends was the challenge to make it look like a battle was going on. It was crude stuff perhaps, but we had the footlights flicker to create the illusion of shells exploding, and we had red lights to create the illusion of fires. I was so *interested* in the technical things that I could just as easily have become a special-effects designer or art director in movies as an actor. But the biggest thing with me was that I got so *into* anything I did. I believe in the credo, "If a thing's worth doing, it's worth doing well", so it still wasn't a matter of me discovering I wanted to be an actor. I just wanted to make sure I did it well . . . or as well as I could.

'Dad was in Ordnance, and I knew that kept him a lot safer than the men who had to fight in the trenches. I somehow never believed he would get killed . . . maybe because I felt that sort of thing only happened to other boys' dads . . . or because I felt Dad was such a good churchgoing man God wouldn't let anything happen to him. So I never was afraid for him.

'It's incredible just how strong a simple faith in God can be. It isn't that God is actually going to protect your father because you have faith. It's simply that having faith takes away your fear. I know that's true from the terrible experience of losing my son [Ronald] in Vietnam. God just can't be there to protect every good soldier. It just doesn't work that way. You can only hope to do the best you can in this life . . . and trust there's something better waiting for all of us. And I guess that's what true faith is.'

When his father came home, the theatre closed down.

3

Inventions and Education

The child who started off 'a good round shape' as a baby grew at what might be generally accepted as a normal rate. But once adolescence set in, the changes were quite dramatic:

'I was just a normal-looking kid until I was thirteen. Then suddenly I *shot up* . . . and at the same time I got *thinner*. My folks were a little concerned if only because they had to keep buying me new suits to fit me. I had three new suits before I was fourteen. And I still grew a few more inches after that, but they never bought me a fourth suit. I had to make do with the third suit with sleeves that didn't cover my wrists and pants that stopped just short of my ankles.

'Both my dad and grandfather were tall, so my height was no great surprise. But no one in our family was so *thin*. Mom got very worried about that and she made me eat huge portions of oatmeal every morning. It didn't make me put on any weight . . . but it did make me hate oatmeal so much I haven't eaten it since.

'Being thin has been a problem for me in life from time to time. I guess all adolescent boys become self-conscious but I really *had* something to be self-conscious about. I decided no one was *ever* going to look at my legs, so I just avoided putting on a bathing suit. People got to thinking I had a phobia about water. My only phobia was about showing my skinny legs. Oh boy, *that* was a problem I had most of my life.'

Spending so much time in his father's merchandise store, Jim was allowed to have a go at using whatever tools, materials and gadgets were available, and before long he was creating quite sophisticated technical appliances. Henry Fonda, probably Jim's best friend in adulthood, said, 'Jim was no slouch. He had a talent for technical things. Never was much good academically, but he could make things. He told me that when he was twelve, he made a crystal radio. He said he did it with oatmeal boxes and wires. I didn't believe him, so he made one – and the damn thing *worked*.'

Gloria said, 'He was always finding things around the store and making things out of them. He had the imagination to visualise how things might work, and the wherewithal to actually *make* those things work. He and a couple of friends even began a small business. They'd make crystal radios and sell them, and Alex provided many of the parts they needed. Alex figured his son had what it took to be an engineer and wanted to do everything to encourage him.

'Jim was always making things as a boy – radios, little steam engines, little cars . . . and little planes that never actually flew but they moved across the floor, driven by a propeller. He never gave up, though, trying to figure out how to make the planes fly, and eventually he did it. Years later, he and Hank Fonda spent endless hours making model aeroplanes.'

However, he was not, as Henry Fonda noted, academically accomplished, and his school marks were poor. 'I just had a real hard time at school,' said Jim. 'I didn't know if I was just dumb or what. I missed a lot of stuff at school when I came down with scarlet fever [which developed into a kidney infection] when I was around fourteen. I was off school for three or four months, and that certainly put me behind. My folks hoped that my bad marks were down to those months away from school . . . but I never did do well.'

The chance finally came for Jim to fly in an aeroplane, and having been imbued with his father's sense of adventure, he literally took off to discover a whole new dimension to his life:

'I took my first flight when I was, oh, I guess fourteen or fifteen. It was in a plane flown by a fella called Jack Law, who'd been a pilot in the war. And like a lot of pilots who had no other way of making a living after they were discharged, they began what was called barnstorming. You'd see these amazing aerobatics performed in the air by these pilots in those old biplanes. And they'd come to town every so often, and people could pay for a ride. Fifteen dollars for fifteen minutes up in the air.

'Waall, I'd been working around the store for a bit and saving every nickel I earned, just waiting for the day when I could afford a ride in a plane. And then we heard that Jack Law was heading our way.

'My folks were mortified 'cos they thought planes were about the unsafest way to get anywhere, and they tried to persuade me not go up . . . they *forbade* me to go up. Some barnstormers had been killed . . . but that was when they were doing stunts. But I had made up my mind, and Dad could see that and he asked just about every customer if they'd ever flown in a plane, and some of them had, and none of them had been in a crash and no one knew of anyone who'd died while going up in a plane, and that kind of reassured him . . . a bit.

'The plane was in a nearby field, and I couldn't run there fast enough. Dad drove out to the field . . . but on the way he stopped off to pick up the doctor just in case I was in need of medical treatment.

'So I took my first flight . . . and I was *hooked*. I'd never experienced anything like it. I never did find anything to beat the feeling I'd been dreaming about. It was more than liberation. It was the ultimate experience of being in control . . . and being alone. I've always been a loner. I don't enjoy being *lonely*, but I enjoy being on my own. It's a feeling of freedom to be alone. And being up there was the most alone I ever got. I was soaring. It was sheer exhilaration. I just . . . it's so hard to describe . . . but it's like knowing a bit what it must be like to be God.

'I had no fear of being off the ground, and I have never had the fear some folks have. Driving a car scares me to death, but not flying. Dad, though, wasn't taking any chances. He stayed in his car with the engine running the whole time . . . just in case he had to step on it and get the doctor to the crash site!'

Obviously, the plane didn't crash, and Jim was hooked. But he didn't dare dream that he might actually learn to fly a plane himself one day. He did, however, continue to build and even invent all kinds of contraptions:

'When you're just a kid in his early teens and you don't have television or any of the things kids have today, you either made mischief or you made useful things. A friend of mine called Hall Blair made something we thought at the time was a pretty useful contraption. It was called the Whizzbang . . . a carnival ride of our own design. It was nothing more than a seat attached to a rope or a clothesline that we ran from the top of a tree down to the garage.

'We had to try it out . . . but when nobody volunteered, we made Hall's little sister sit in it and we flew her down this thing. And she screamed her head off . . . which I can't blame her for since the thing was so steep. But the thing was it *worked*. So Hall and I got to thinking we could do better if we made a chair driven by electricity. So we built the electric Whizzbang, and our first customer was a cat. Waall, the cat didn't think too much of it judging by its howls and the way it scrambled out of the chair in the biggest hurry ever. It was all claws and teeth and hissing and fur standing on end . . . and the cat was our first and last customer. I guess Hall and I figured we'd explored the ultimate possibility with the electric Whizzbang and we decided it was time to move on to other inventions.

'We started our own carnival attractions. In those days you'd go to a carnival and you'd be intrigued by some special attraction . . . like "See the invisible mermaid" . . . and you'd pay your money, go into a darkened room where a single light shone on a casket. You'd open the casket and . . . there was nothing inside. Waall, the mermaid was invisible! Then another door would open and you'd step outside . . . and that was that.

'I wanted people to get value for their money, so I put on a show in which I *guaranteed* people would see the invisible mermaid. I billed it something like "She's a mermaid and she's invisible, but you will be able to see her as if she were any other woman." And that's exactly what they got . . . only it was a young girl I talked into lying in a big box. No fish tail or anything. Just a girl . . . with the explanation that she's only a mermaid when she's invisible. People were paying just to see what the gag was. They knew it was a carnival gag.

'My friends Blair and Bill Neff and I came up with a thing we called "Men Only". It sounded very risqué . . . and it was advertised as being literally "for men only". We invited men to pay to take a look inside a closet and see what only a man would appreciate. Waall, we had the boys from the neighbourhood queuing up to take a look inside this closet. And when they opened the door they found a pair of men's pants hanging inside.

'We also came up with something that was more of a thrill ride . . . or that's what we sold it as. It was called 'A Trip to Mars'. For five cents or a dollar or whatever it was, our customers had the thrill of sitting on a board which was heavily waxed on the underside, and sent flying down the stairs into Blair's cellar. I thought it should be called 'Descent into Hell' since it was a short but hair-raising trip down . . . but I figured that wasn't a trip anyone wanted to take.'

Alex encouraged Jim to enjoy such frivolities in life, but he also made sure that his son underwent more meaningful and sobering experiences – even if Bessie disapproved. Jim recalled:

'When President [Warren] Harding died [in August, 1923], I went with my father to the Blairsville Intersection – about twenty miles away – where the funeral train would pass. We had to go in the dark of the morning because the train was due to pass at 3.30 a.m. Mom had told me I couldn't go, but at about 2.30 a.m. Dad woke me up and whispered, "Come on, Jim. We're going to see the President's funeral train." I don't remember any other time both Dad *and* I disobeyed Mom.

'It was a solemn time, but there was something kinda mystical about the whole experience. The moonlight was shining off the silver tracks. There were only about a dozen other people with us on the platform. And then the rails began to hum. Dad gave me two pennies and said, "Put them on the rails." So I jumped down and put the coins on the rails, climbed back up, and held my father's hand as the train thundered by. And for a few brief moments I saw the car, which had a huge glass window and inside was the casket with the President's body. Flags were draped over the casket, and two marines stood to attention, and I saw their bayonets glisten. It was such an amazing experience, I felt like I could hardly breathe.

'When the train had gone, I jumped down and found the two coins. There used to be the face of an Indian on the coins, and on one the feathers on his head had been spread into a great plume. I kept that one. On the other side of the coin were engraved stalks of wheat. On the coin I gave to Dad, it looked like the wheat had grown and burst, like the seed had ripened and scattered. Dad and I kept those coins.'

Now that Jim was growing, and despite his struggle to do well at school, it had become obvious to him that his father expected certain things, namely going to the schools Alex had gone to, and eventually running the store. While Jim would have little – or no – choice in what schools he would attend, he did find a voice to express to his father that his interest did not lie in running a store.

'As I got a little older, Dad obviously expected me to take an interest in the store. It seemed natural to him that I should kind of inherit the store from him. But I just wasn't interested. When I was thirteen, and the summer holidays had come around, Dad wanted me to work at the store to earn my own spending money. But I told him I didn't want to spend my vacation in the store. That kind of took him aback, and he said, "You gotta do something. What do you *want* to do?" And I said, "I'd like to run the movies in a movie theatre." I liked the idea of spending the summer watching pictures, so Dad had a word with the local theatre owner, and I got the job.'

What Alex was able to make Jim do was go to Mercersburg Academy. Jim recalled, 'My father was not prepared that I should go to any high school other than Mercersburg Academy, where Dad had gone, and it was an object lesson in "it's not what you know, it's *who* you know." I got such lousy grades at school that Mercersburg had no intention of admitting me. So Dad went to work on his connections in the Presbyterian Church, and Mom went to work on her connections through her side of the family . . . and before I knew it, I was pacing the halls of Mercersburg. Waall, I didn't do any better there than I had previously, and my grades were just shameful . . . *shameful.*'

There was a strong emphasis on religion at the school, although it was open only to white Christian males. The same was true of Princeton University, which Jim later attended; Princeton was definitely one of the more upper class of American universities, with many of its students coming from some of the richest families in the East.

Woody Strode, the black American actor who worked with Jim in *The Man Who Shot Liberty Valance,* said that he recognised racist traits in Stewart, and he accredited these to Jim's education. He told me, 'Jimmy Stewart went to schools that were exclusive only to white people. They were taught to love God and look down on anyone with skin darker than theirs. I don't think those schools actively encouraged hatred of the black man, but they instilled racism, and I'm sure many a Ku Klux Klansman came from those places. Jimmy's whole early life – his schools, his hometown of Indiana – created racism in him and all his peers. It's to Jimmy's credit that he didn't turn out to be a hard-case racist because he's too decent a person to be like that. But he never was comfortable around coloureds.'

Stewart denied he was a racist: 'It's true that Negroes were excluded from the school, but so were women, and I wasn't brought up to dislike women. Jews were also excluded and for the most part so were the Indians, although some of our Native Americans were admitted . . . although it has to be confessed, not that many got in.

'I would agree that my background had some effect on my view of the world because for so much of my younger life I was in a town where only white people lived . . . and at school I didn't have the chance to mix with people of other races. I didn't make those rules. And I sure never was a racist.'

Woody Strode, however, maintained that most white people never really understood what it was to be a racist. He said in 1976:

'Racism is inherent in most white people. They may not feel they're racist, but they can't help it. They can't help but notice the first thing about you is that you're black. That's understandable. It's when they continue to think of you as being "black" that it's a problem. People say, "I don't hate black people, so I'm not a racist." You don't *have* to hate black people. To be a racist you only have to be the kind of person who says, "I have no problem with coloureds – just so long as they don't live next door to me." You don't have to be violent either. There are coloured people who are racist against white people. It goes both ways. But blacks didn't enslave whites, and that's the problem. The black man was always inferior, and that's the institutionalised kind of racism that is inherent in white people. That's what you find in good sincere white Christian types like Jimmy Stewart. I felt that he tried hard not to be like that, but you have to be black to recognise it.

'John Ford, who obviously wasn't black, recognised it when we were filming [*The Man Who Shot Liberty Valance*]. He would goad actors, and he could be really cruel about it. He'd try to find their weak spot and aim at that. With Wayne it was his absence from active duty in the Second World War, and Ford would delight in reminding him of that. With Stewart, it was his prejudice about race. Even Ford saw it in him; that he didn't really believe the black man was equal to the white man. The civil rights issue was something that he – and Wayne – were just not interested in.

'Stewart was never rude to me – he was never rude to *anyone*. But I could tell that he preferred to be around Lee Marvin or Wayne than me. It was a matter of feeling comfortable, and I knew I made him feel *uncomfortable*. That was just his background, and I didn't resent it. I was used to it. I was used to people in the business being just so downright hateful to me because I'm black. Stewart wasn't hateful – just uncomfortable.

'And Ford knew this. So one day he asked Stewart what he thought of my costume. I was dressed in some old overalls and a really bad hat because in the film I was just a servant – or really a paid *slave*. It was a stereotypical role. So anyway, Ford says to Stewart, "What do you think of Woody's costume?" and Stewart said, "I think it makes him a bit too much like Uncle Remus." The thing is, he was *right*. But Ford jumped on this and said, "And what's wrong with Uncle Remus?" Stewart stammered that there was nothing wrong with Uncle Remus and before he could explain himself, Ford was calling to Wayne and the whole cast to come on over and said, "One of the actors here doesn't like Uncle Remus. In fact, I don't think he even likes Negroes."

'I was too young at the time to realise Ford was using me to get at Stewart. All I heard was Ford saying that Stewart didn't like Negroes, and that made me mad at Stewart, and Stewart was just even more uncomfortable around me. I'm grateful to Ford for giving me a career, but I don't feel I had to be grateful for the rest of my life – the way Wayne was, and Ford treated Wayne worse than he ever treated me.'

If a certain intolerance towards the black American was encouraged at the schools Jim attended, there was also a dedicated discouragement of sex. Jim recalled:

'It was forbidden to bring girls on to campus. Ya see . . . sex was a sin. That's what they told us. I never could quite believe that . . . but that was the rule. The only sex education we got was from church ministers. One of them pretty much summed things up when he said, "If you find yourself getting *urges*, put a portrait of Theodore Roosevelt on the wall, look into his eyes and say, 'Help me out here, Teddy.' You see, boys, I can't think of Theodore Roosevelt in connection with sexual sin, can you?" Waall, I had to agree with him. Now, if it was a picture of Clara Bow . . . !

'There were occasions when girls were formally invited to a college ball. Us fellas all had to wear tuxedos. But it gave us the chance to dance with a girl. By God, when you're eighteen and you get to dance with a girl, you start thinking, "Help me out here, Teddy." You couldn't get too close.

'I was actually a pretty good dancer. I'd learned some pretty fancy moves, and the girls liked that. I don't mind admitting that I had girls queuing up to dance with me . . . and the other fellas . . . they just hated that. But the more girls I danced with, the more I asked Teddy for inspiration.'

When inspiration didn't materialise, Jim had a way of getting round the rules: 'Waall . . . it was a little like trying to escape from Colditz, but you would go to the men's room and the girl would go

to the girls' room – or the staff room because we had no facilities
for women. You'd then sneak out for some fresh air, and a minute
later the girl would step out for some fresh air . . . and you'd meet
in a quiet place and you'd spend several minutes getting no help
from Teddy Roosevelt at all. I hafta tell you, I had fun. I was a
young man . . . a regular Joe . . . and a regular Joe likes to smooch
with a girl.'

Despite the risk of committing carnal sin, Jim reasoned that the
school's religious rules on sex were just a little too strict. He said,
'As I recall it, the Bible didn't say anything about "Thou shalt not
kiss a girl." I once said to one of those ministers who gave us so-
called sex education, "Isn't the first commandment in the Bible to
be fruitful and multiply?" And he got all steamed up and said,
"When you've got a wife, you can multiply all you want. But not
before." So I learned that the loophole in the Bible was that you just
had to make sure you didn't *multiply*.'

Despite romantic success, Jim continued to struggle to find
academic success:

'I just didn't do well at college. I certainly wasn't the worst student
there, but I was far from being the best. I was far from being *any
good at all*. I just found all the subjects so . . . *tough*. The best thing
I did was play my accordion. They were happy to have me in their
orchestra. I could also draw. Specialised in cartoons of people . . .
caricatures . . . so I became the art editor on the yearbook for a few
years. In fact, I *knew* I was good at drawing, and it was around that
time I made up my mind that I was going to have a career either in
architecture . . . or in the Navy.

'I certainly decided I *wasn't* going to be an actor. I joined the
college drama group. It was called the Stony Batter Drama Club. In
my first play . . . it was called *The Wolves* . . . I played a French
revolutionary. I had to wear baggy trousers that came down below
my knees. Everyone else wore tight pants and stockings. The
director thought I looked kinda silly in tight pants because of my
thin legs . . . which I had to agree with . . . so I got the part that
didn't need tight pants.

'I didn't think I did *too* bad. But the director thought I was just
the clumsiest actor he'd ever had the tragedy to work with. I wasn't

really clumsy. I just looked clumsy because I was so much *taller* than everyone else on the stage. I was already over six feet tall. And being so thin made me look even *taller*. So I felt uncomfortable on the stage. If you don't want people looking at you, you don't go on stage.

'Life wasn't so bad at college. Apart from struggling with my studies, my only real problem was the ribbing I took because of my height. And I hadn't stopped growing! I was also terribly under-weight. But because I was tall someone decided I'd be perfect for the campus [American] football team. For three years I somehow managed not to get my ribs broken as a centre player. I found the trick was simple: as soon as you get the ball, get *rid* of it. I happened to have a talent for throwing it accurately enough that they kept me in the same position for three years.

'Although I was thin and underweight . . . and despite concerns from the campus nurse . . . I was pretty darn fit. I could run. Not fast. But I could keep going. So I did well on the track events. I always thought it was important to stay fit and to have stamina. I gave up trying to develop muscle. Muscle doesn't make you live longer.'

Gloria would later hear all the stories of Jim's life at school, and the picture he painted to her was one that was a lot darker than the one he shared for the benefit of the public. She told me, 'He won't let you know it, but he really had a hard time at school because of his height and because he spoke slowly. They took to calling him Elmer. Jimmy would tell you it was all gentle ribbing, but as I'm sure you know, all schools – no matter how high class they may be – have bullies. And there were a few who gave Jimmy a hard time. They'd call him Elmer and imitate his speech. Jim says that people have always imitated him, but there were some fellas back then who were doing it to be cruel. What they didn't know was, Jim has the capacity to get really mad. He's had to learn to rein in his temper. Back then those bullies tested him too much, and they stepped over the mark – and he just started punching them, and they were all on the floor. He always kept quiet about that. He didn't like people knowing he could become violent at all. In many ways he's care-fully crafted his gentle, easy-going image. He didn't ever want to disappoint the people who knew him. He's learned to deal with his rage in other ways. Occasionally, though, it comes out.'

While Jim was learning to try and hold on to his temper, he was having much greater success in learning how to hold on to his money. Gloria told me, 'I heard all sorts of stories about how tight Jim was with money. When he was eighteen or nineteen and home for the holidays, he took a local girl to the cinema. Jim had plenty of spending money. He always worked during the summer hiatus, either in his father's store or sometimes loading bricks for a construction company, and he'd pay for the girl to go to the cinema with him. I always figured he felt the cost was worth it so he could make out with the girl in the back row. But after they left the theatre, they went to a shop for a soda, and when they sat down, Jim took out a single dime and put it on the table and said, "This is what we have to spend, so what'll it be?" Jim would call it "being frugal". He's still frugal, bless him.'

He defended himself by saying, 'I have always been frugal. I don't believe being frugal is a vice. I earned my money working in the school holidays at the store, and I just felt I needed to make my earnings go as far as they could.'

One of the great historical events during Jim's teenage years was not something he was actively involved with in any way, but it was an emotional experience for him. It was when pioneer aviator Charles Lindbergh flew solo from Long Island to Paris. Jim said:

'It happened on May 20, 1927 . . . on my nineteenth birthday. There was great excitement at the school because the builder of Lindbergh's plane – *The Spirit of St. Louis* – was Benjamin Franklin Mahoney, who had graduated from Mercersburg in 1918.

'I was back home in Indiana on holiday when Lindbergh flew the Atlantic. I made my own little model of *The Spirit of St. Louis*, and I got a large piece of beaverboard and cut out a large circular shape. At one end of the round board I marked out the Woolworth Building in Long Island, and I marked out the Eiffel Tower at the other end. And I strung a wire across from one point to the other and hung my model plane on it. Dad put it in his store window, and I'd keep running across the road to the *Indiana Evening Gazette* and ask "Where is he now?" They'd tell me, and I'd run back to the store and move the plane along the wire a bit. A crowd of people gathered outside the store and watched all night as the plane moved across the board.

'It was such an exciting event in my life. I was with Charles Lindbergh in spirit. Much later, it became important to me to be the one to play Lindbergh in the picture of *The Spirit of St. Louis.*'

As graduation from Mercersburg approached, Jim began to feel the stress of imminent failure. It would certainly disappoint himself, but more importantly, it would disappoint his parents:

'I just about scraped by in most of my subjects, but I had really bombed in Latin. I was able to take an extra exam which would allow me to graduate, so the night before graduation, I had to sit and take this other examination in Latin. My parents had already arrived for graduation the next day, and I knew that if I failed this exam . . . it would have just been too embarrassing to go on living. But I got through the exam, and the next day I graduated with my class.

'Then I had a shock for my father. I told him I wanted to go to the Naval Academy at Annapolis. I expected him to be disappointed because my father was a Princeton man, and he'd always wanted me to go to Princeton. It had always seemed important to him that I follow in his footsteps. And I think he genuinely felt that at Princeton I would get the very best education. So part of it was his pride, and another part of it was his desire for me to have the best. So I was real surprised when he said, "Well, son, let's go take a look at Annapolis," and we got in the car and went to the Naval Academy. We had a look around and I really liked what I saw there. Then Dad said, "Let's take a look at some other places."

'So we ended up driving to the University of Pennsylvania . . . and to Harvard . . . and to Yale and Dartmouth. And our last stop was Princeton. It was evening when we arrived, so we stopped in a hotel the night, and then in the morning we went through the main gate of the university . . . and there was Nassau Hall looming up ahead of us with the morning sun just rising behind it. It was really an impressive sight. And so I went to Princeton.'

Said Gloria, 'Alex had no intention of having Jim go anywhere but Princeton. Bessie was also always adamant that Jim should go there because it was steeped in the tradition of the Presbyterian Church. For years Alex had held class reunions at the Stewart house, and Jim was always introduced to his father's former classmates. These reunions often lasted all weekend, and Alex wanted Jim to drink in the atmosphere and to dream about being at Princeton. But Jim dreamed of being in the Navy.'

Once there, and with the prospects of going into the Navy all but dispelled, Stewart pursued an engineering degree and began dreaming of a career in aviation. But by the end of his first year at Princeton, in 1929, he was so far behind in his grades that he had to attend summer school. It was there that his ambitions were again thwarted. He said: 'My math teacher told me that I was barely adequate in algebra and calculus, both of which I needed to excel in if I wanted to become an engineer. He told me, "If I were you, I'd think about some other career or else you're going to find yourself in deep trouble and no career."

'What I was good at, however, was descriptive geometry and drawing, and my teacher said that I might just make it as an architect. So right there I decided I was going to be an architect. After that, I found my university days a little less traumatic because I did very well in my chosen courses. But I still had trouble with every other lesson.'

Gloria told me, 'Jim produced plans for a whole airport as his thesis, and did so well in his architecture studies that he received a scholarship for graduate work.' The work Jim produced in his architectural studies was, by all accounts, excellent.

4

The Lady's Man

In 1929 the stock market crashed and America began its terrible Depression. Said Jim, 'It seemed to me that was both the end of my days at Princeton and my dreams of becoming an architect. I just couldn't see any way Dad was going to be able to pay for me to stay on. But Dad was just so resolute . . . he took out loans . . . he had to let some of his employees go and he worked longer hours himself . . . just to keep me in college.'

Gloria knew that Alex also pulled all the strings that hung in his favour to keep Jim at Princeton. She said, 'Alex called upon his former classmates and they rallied round. There was a real bond between Alex and his friends from Princeton. Somehow, he was able to keep himself in work and Jim at Princeton, and that was because of the fellowship Alex had with his Princeton friends.'

Jim played his part in earning money by joining his friend Bill Neff in a touring magic show. Neff had become a professional magician and continually trouped from one Pennsylvanian town to another. Jim recalled:

'I took my accordion along, and whenever we arrived in town, Bill hung himself upside down by a rope around his ankle from a street light or a tree, and I stood and announced details of the night's show, playing my accordion for added effect.

'Bill did most of the tricks and I tried to cover up any mistakes with my playing. We had a lot of fun. Sometimes we were a big hit when everything went perfectly. Sometimes when things went wrong, we panicked . . . but later we'd laugh hysterically at ourselves. Like the time we were supposed to levitate a woman. Bill had devised an apparatus that our female assistant lay down on but which looked invisible to the audience, so when the apparatus was raised, she seemed to levitate into the air. Unfortunately, one night the stagehand behind the curtain fell asleep, and as much as Bill and I uttered our magical incantations, the woman would not rise up. Bill explained to the audience that some souls were more earth-bound, such as this woman, while I stood at the back coughing and hissing behind my hand in an attempt to wake up the stagehand.

'Well, he woke up all right . . . and realising his mistake, he pulled hard on the lever and the woman shot up into the air. Then he pulled the lever straight back down, and the woman came down to earth with a sickening thud. She was okay though . . . and the audience thought it was hilarious. I think they liked it best when things went wrong, so we couldn't fail really.'

One of Princeton's students was Joshua Logan. He played football, boxed and was active in school dramatics, where he honed skills that would enable him to carve out a successful career on Broadway and in Hollywood as a director. He would also help to shape the careers of both James Stewart and Henry Fonda. Logan told me:

'I met Jim through the Triangle Club, which put on various plays and shows at the university. Jim got involved because he was really good on the accordion. *That* was his greatest talent. He also happened to be a nice fella, but we really admired him for his accordion playing. We didn't know anybody else who could play the accordion, and it was such a useful instrument because you could just carry it on and off stage. So when we did a production called *The Golden Dog* and we needed a bit of a musical interlude, we asked Jim to do it. He was such a success and such a nice fella to have around that he featured in a number of other productions, always just coming on to play his accordion to rapturous applause.

'In our senior year, we joined the Theatre Intime, and while I performed as an actor and directed plays, Jim just had a good time walking on with his accordion and playing some tunes. There was no indication this tall skinny guy who everybody liked was going to become a movie actor one day. All he talked about was becoming an architect.'

Another student who knew Stewart well was Jose Ferrer who, like Jim, was set on a career as an architect until he discovered acting at Princeton. And, like Jim, he was a budding musician. He told me:

'James Stewart stood out from the crowd because of his accordion. We were both in the Charter Club. Universities have all these different clubs. There were the more impressive and prestigious clubs – and then there was the Charter Club. Our main preoccupation in Charter was music. I had a dance band, and Stewart had his accordion. Also, we both wanted to be architects, so we had something in common. But it was mainly music that made us friends.

'We put on these grand jazz weekends, which Charter paid for. Stewart and I took part in organising them. We had some of the best musicians come and play, like Jimmy Dorsey and Bix Beiderbecke. We also liked to drink. Those were the days of Prohibition. We used to catch a bus to Kingston where we could get bootleg beer. Stewart usually took along his accordion and led us all in a sing-song on the bus. I wasn't so keen on the accordion myself; I found it an irritating sound. But Stewart played really well.'

Another thing Jim did well was get the girls – even if they were with some other young man. And, according to Joshua Logan, he did it all so effortlessly:

'When it came to girls, Jim was never the shy guy people might like to think he was. Even then you could easily believe he was shy with girls and innocent. That was his *style* in getting women. Any Princeton student had to watch out for him at parties. Didn't matter how handsome you were, if your girl fell for that Jimmy Stewart way of looking like – of *being* – a backwoods hick, you'd find your girl dancing with Jimmy or disappearing into the moonlight on his arm. The girl couldn't resist him. And I think he pretty soon learned that he didn't have to make much of an effort to pick up girls. They latched on to him.

'One night a guy tried to punch Jimmy because his girl had dumped him for Jim. The guy was squaring up to him, and Jimmy just stood there, all innocent, saying, "Look, I didn't mean to steal your girl. Look, here she is. If she wants to go with you, that's fine. But if she decides she wants to stay with me, what can *I* do about it?" And this guy tried to land a right punch, but Jimmy just side-stepped to the left, kept his right foot where it was, and tripped the guy up. Then Jimmy helped him up with, "Golly, are you all right? Didn't hurt yourself, did ya?" And he seemed like he hadn't done a thing, and everyone felt it was the other guy who deserved what he got. And Jimmy got the girl. It was an *art* the way Jimmy got his girls.'

The Triangle Club ran an annual Christmas tour of several cities, and Jim and Logan often teamed up to perform musical numbers on these tours. 'It was kinda fun,' said Jim, 'because it was a way of getting down to New York and other big cities and all at no expense. There were seventy-five of us, all being transported, and it was a really genial experience.'

Joshua Logan remembered, 'What Jimmy won't tell you is that the tour was always a good way of meeting women. Girls just thought we were some kind of celebrities, and that's an easy way to get girls interested in you. Jimmy was a little less predatory on these tours because if you stole another fella's girl, you had to live with the consequences for the rest of the tour. But the girls just fell for Jimmy. I couldn't begin to guess how many girls he had to leave behind. Not that we were all innocent. It's just that when you think of Jimmy Stewart, you tend not to think of him as a ladies' man. But the girls loved him.'

Things wouldn't be any different when he got to Hollywood, where he would become the object of desire for some of Hollywood's most glamorous female stars. But the girl who stole

Jim's heart for years – some say all his life, or at least until Gloria came along – was actress Margaret Sullavan.

Jim recalled, 'I first met Margaret Sullavan when she was in a touring production of *The Artist and the Lady*, and the play came to Princeton . . . and I had the job of stage manager. I thought she was a really nice girl . . . and we had a friendship that lasted till she . . . ' (Jim paused as some far distant memory was reflected in his eyes, which began to brim. And then he finished his sentence.) ' . . . till she passed away.'

Joshua Logan, like many who knew Jim and Margaret Sullavan well, maintained that Jim and Sullavan loved each other from the start: 'There was much more to the friendship. It was there right from the beginning when she came to Princeton with a play. He was smitten with her. So smitten that he invited her to a Charter Club reception. Sullavan told me it was the longest, slowest, shyest but most sincere invitation she'd ever received from a man, and she fell for him too. There was love between them from the very start.'

Gloria was not unaware of the romance that lingered long into the Hollywood careers of both Jim and Sullavan: 'I always knew he was madly in love with Margaret Sullavan, and she was with him. But she was more in love with her career.'

Logan agreed with Gloria's assessment: 'Margaret was a career girl, and nothing meant more to her than that – not even her four husbands. But I think she loved Jim so much that she never wanted to risk what friendship they had by making herself available to him. I think she knew she would have been destructive for him. And although in many ways she was, as Henry Fonda [her first husband] said, a ball-breaker, I think she showed great consideration for Jim by not ruining his life.

'When they first met, they did have an affair. And it was a passionate one. But their love affair was short-lived because a Broadway producer came to see the show at Princeton, and a few weeks later, Margaret was making her debut on Broadway. Jimmy said to me, "I'll never find another girl like her." I said, "Cheer up, Jim. Why don't you become an actor and you'll be bound to run into her again?" I got the impression that he didn't shrug off that idea.'

Whether he was setting his sights on a career on stage, or whether he just liked playing his accordion to an audience, Jim accepted every offer to appear with his trusty instrument in Triangle productions. Said Logan, 'Jim got asked to appear in all those Triangle plays just because they liked the idea of having someone on stage who could play an instrument that could be carried. There was a spoof about Don Juan and Don Quixote called *Spanish Blades*, and Jim had the part of a troubadour who travelled all of Spain playing . . . his *accordion*.'

But before long, he was accepting roles in plays that didn't require his accordion. In *The Play's the Thing* he was a butler, and in *Nerissa* he was a 'contemporary proletarian', as Jim described it. 'The campus critics all agreed they thought I made a better butler than I did a proletarian, but they preferred my musicianship in *Spanish Blade* to my acting in either of the plays. So there really was no inspiration to become an actor.'

Logan went on to kick-start his own career as a stage director and in doing so, helped Jim make a career out of being an actor. Said Logan, 'I left Princeton a year before Jim did, and was involved in starting up the University Players at the Old Silver Beach Theatre in West Falmouth on Cape Cod. It was one of only a few summer theatres. I came back to Princeton, found Jim and said, "You're going to need to earn some money in the summer. Why not bring your accordion to West Falmouth and play your music in the tea rooms next door to the theatre? I'll give you some small parts in our plays." He said, "I don't know. I'm really not an actor." Actually, Jim has always liked to play down his acting ability at university. He wasn't at all bad really, or I wouldn't have asked him. But he didn't seem too interested. And then I dropped my bomb-shell. I said, "Margaret Sullavan is one of our company." That did it. He graduated [in 1932] and came out to Cape Cod.'

Jim maintained he had no real interest in becoming a professional actor, and in explaining how he found himself getting involved in the theatre, he neglected to mention that Margaret Sullavan had a great deal to do with his decision to join Logan's company:

'I never intended on doing another play after *Nerissa*. It was a dark time. The Depression made work prospects poor. I was lucky because I had a scholarship for my Masters studies, so I had some-thing to go on with. But I was really beginning to wonder where my future lay. And then I heard the news that Charles Lindbergh's baby boy had been kidnapped. It was something that happened not far from Princeton, so everybody was talking about it. And Lindbergh was kind of my hero, and I felt so *desperate* . . . so *bad* for him. I could only wonder how Lindbergh must have felt when they discovered the dead body of his son. That tragedy really coloured my life at that time.

'Then, shortly before graduating [Jim graduated in the summer of 1932], Josh Logan turned up and told me about the theatre company he had started up in partnership with Bretaigne Windust and Charles Crane Leatherbee. He said, "Come out to Cape Cod and join us." Waall . . . we talked it back and forth for about three hours . . . and finally I said, "Look, I'd like to come out, but my father may not like it because he expects me to go home for the summer. *You* clear it with him." And Josh got on the phone and talked it over with Dad, and I don't know how he sold Dad on the idea, but Dad gave me his blessing.'

If Jim was joining the University Players just to be with Margaret Sullavan, he was in for a huge disappointment, as Logan explained:

'The problem for Jim was, by the time he arrived in West Falmouth, Margaret Sullavan had left us to return to Broadway where she was a rising star. She was actually a pretty well-established star before joining the University Players. All our players were really in the company for the fun of it. We had another rising star of the theatre in our group – Henry Fonda. And he and Sullavan fell in love and on Christmas Day, 1931, they got married.

'Fonda and Sullavan had known each other for a few years and had performed in plays together. At first he hated her. When they arrived at Cape Cod, Fonda had no kind words for her at all. But like a lot of men, he fell under her spell. She could be a real bitch. But she was also a great deal of fun and very passionate. The fun and the passion won over Fonda and he married her.

'All this devastated Jim. He knew before he arrived that Sullavan

had left us, and that was a big disappointment. Then he learned she
had married Fonda, and that, I think, broke his heart. Yet he wasn't
the kind of guy who could resent Fonda for marrying the girl he
loved, and [when they met that summer] he and Fonda became the
greatest of friends. Besides, just a few months after the marriage,
Sullavan and Fonda separated and she began cavorting with other
men – important Broadway men. In the summer, Fonda was back
with us. Jim knew about all this before he came out to join us. And
yet he *still* came.'

5

Taking to the Stage

Jim recalled his first day at Cape Cod: 'I arrived at the Falmouth Theatre on Old Silver Beach with my accordion, and I began playing in the tearoom. I was supposed to entertain the audiences before and after each show. Maybe I was playing the wrong tunes, because I got fired after people complained that my playing gave them indigestion.'

That story, it seems, was one of Jim's slightly-taller-than-average tales. Logan said, 'The way Jim tells it, he got fired after the first evening. Actually, he didn't get fired at all. He played his accordion all through the summer. And he worked as an usher in the theatre. I was in touch a fair deal with Sullavan, and Jim always wanted news of her. I sometimes wondered if that's what kept him at Cape Cod through the summer of 1932.'

Jim said that it was the architect in him that ironically gave him the idea he might want to act for a living after all: 'I took one look at the Falmouth Theatre on Old Silver Beach . . . and I think I had my first thought that I might just want to be an actor after all. It was such a *beautiful* building. I think a beautiful building can have the same effect as a beautiful woman. You see it – or her – and you want to stay. Maybe with me it was my architect's eye

Divided by Three, a play about a youth stunned by the adultery of his mother, to be staged in the autumn and starring Judith Anderson.

Jim saw out the summer doing stock theatre on Long Island, and he even landed a small part in a two-reel comedy, *Art Troubles*, starring Shemp Howard of The Three Stooges. 'I wasn't thinking I could break into pictures,' said Stewart. 'I was offered the job at fifty dollars a day, and that was a lot of money to me at the time, so I just accepted it as a job.'

In the autumn of 1934, Jim returned to New York where he and Fonda moved into the Madison Square Hotel. Fonda was doing well on Broadway in *The Farmer Takes a Wife*, and Jim was anticipating success in *Divided by Three*. The activity in their Madison Square Hotel apartment was less exciting, and less dangerous, than it had been in the two-room apartment on the third floor at West 64th Street. Said Fonda, 'Jim was always in love with aeroplanes and the idea of flying, and his enthusiasm was kind of infectious. So we started building model planes. We were particularly keen on a Martin Bomber we were building. Our place was just full of balsa wood and wood shavings, and the whole place stank of glue. But before we could finish it, I got the call to Hollywood to make my first picture there, *The Farmer Takes a Wife*, which I'd done on Broadway.'

Jim went to work on rehearsals for *Divided by Three*. Hedda Hopper, then a B-movie actress, was also in the cast; she later quit acting to become an influential gossip columnist in Hollywood. She and Stewart immediately hit it off, but nobody got on with leading lady Judith Anderson. She complained about everything to do with the play – including the choice of James Stewart, who was supposed to be playing her son but was only ten years younger than she.

Henry Fonda remembered going to see the play: 'Anderson was a scary actress – as formidable as hell. But there was Jim, standing eye-to-eye with her on stage . . . and he was just so good. I went to his dressing room at the end of the performance, and I just sat there looking at him, shaking my head and saying to myself, "Where the hell did this come from? How in hell did he get to be so good?" I was busting my balls trying to make it as an actor, and here was this guy from Indiana who'd thought acting might be a lark, and he that kind of fell for that place. But I knew I wanted to *be* there.'

It was there his friendship with Henry Fonda began. In 1979, Jim said, 'My friendship with Fonda goes back forty-seven years. Started in 1932. I'd just gotten out of college. He had a couple of years before me as an actor. I started in a stock company that he had been in for several years.

'I was *never* the struggling actor. Fonda was the young struggling actor. He said I just *lucked* into it. But Fonda always knew exactly what he wanted to do, and there was no question about it. I just got out of college . . . I was going to be an architect . . . but the acting thing bites you like a mosquito . . . because you *really* get bit. It becomes an all-out thing.'

Fonda recalled the early days of his friendship with Jim: 'I just liked him. There was nothing not to like about him. He had this wonderful but quiet sense of humour that appealed to me. He made me laugh – and I guess I made him laugh. You can never quite put your finger on what makes two people click like that. But we clicked – kept on clicking all these years. We're quite different kinds of people – still are. Our views on politics are almost opposite. Jim's had a different kind of private life to me. Mine's been kind of turbulent, you might say, while Jim's has been very stable since he married Gloria. But he's never criticised me for my mistakes, and he never lectures me. He's just there for me when I need him. What more can you want from a friend? And he got me into building model aeroplanes. That's a passion we share. We sit for hours putting these model aircraft together. Like a couple of kids. That's a friendship I couldn't live without.'

Yet a time did come, during the Communist witch-hunts of 1947, when their friendship was unable to survive their opposing political views – and Fonda's distaste for the position Jim would put himself in by agreeing to work for J Edgar Hoover, Director of the FBI, in the right-wing quest to fish out Hollywood's Communists, caused a long-term rift. But the one thing that never came between them was Jim's love for Margaret Sullavan.

When I met Fonda in 1976, he made no mention of the fact that Jim was ever in love with Sullavan, even though, according to Joshua Logan and others, Fonda knew it. What impressed people about Jim was that he didn't bother everyone with his woes over losing Sullavan, while Fonda would let everyone know exactly how miserable he was. Logan told me, 'Hank complained about Margaret all the time, but Jim kept his thoughts to himself. I made sure Jim kept busy so he wouldn't waste his time mooning over his lost chance [with Sullavan]. He played in the tearooms, he was an usher, he helped in getting the sets built. And he played small roles on stage. I could see that he took acting seriously. He saw it as a craft which he had to learn – and which he *could* learn. He began developing techniques. I could see he enjoyed the process.'

When talking about acting, there were two things that annoyed Jim more than anything else. One was to call acting an art, and the second was to say that Jim's style of acting was just a natural extension of his own personality. He said:

'You hafta approach acting . . . not as an art . . . it's a *craft*. And the only way to learn it is to *do* it. I know that a lot of people go to acting schools and a few of them become successful . . . but you don't *hafta* go to acting school. The people who are good actors when they come out of those schools are good when they go in. They already have the talent. All they need is the *skill* . . . and you only get the skill by working as an actor. You don't get it in any acting school. You learn it on the stage . . . working with other actors . . . and directors . . . and in front of an audience. You *discover* what works and what doesn't. You find out what you're doing wrong and what you're doing right. It's a *craft*, not some strange religion. You don't hafta meditate to be an actor. It's like any craft . . . like carpentry or architecture . . . you may have the talent to do those things but you have to *do* those things to get it *right*.

'I always get kind of annoyed when people say to me, "You're a natural actor." If my acting looks natural it's because I've learned to make it *look* that way. I work hard at it. People talk about "The Method" . . . as if nobody but Brando or a lot of younger actors can really act unless they have "The Method". Those actors are good actors because they have *technique*. I use technique all the time. I couldn't get by without it. Talent you may already have. Technique is what you learn. *That's* the craft. If you want to call it an art, that's up to you. But to me, it's a craft.'

Acting was something Jim spent years learning to do, even though he had some acting ability to begin with. And he had something else that seemed, initially, to be his biggest drawback, one that might prevent him from ever becoming a successful actor – his looks.

Said Logan, 'There was never an idea that we could give Jim a leading role because he just didn't *look* like a leading man. But in the small parts he played in comedies, you always managed to get laughs in the right places. You began to realise that he had some indescribable quality – you couldn't put your finger on what it was – but he had *something* and myself and the other producers tried to figure out *how* best to use him. You tended to think that you could only cast him as a very tall and very thin man . . . which was, in hindsight, short-sighted of us. But Jim's come up against that problem all his life. When he got to Broadway producers only cast him as very tall, very thin men, and when he got to Hollywood, the studios went crazy trying to figure out what to do with him. What you learn in this business is that other qualities in a person can overcome all physicality. That's why Peter O'Toole, who's very tall, was able to play Lawrence of Arabia, who was very short. And why James Cagney, who's very short, could play big tough gangsters.'

Logan maintained that had Margaret Sullavan stayed, Jim would have found it difficult to enjoy a relationship with her because he had become so engrossed with developing his acting technique. 'Really, there was no time for women,' Logan said. 'We were all too busy for that kind of thing.' Henry Fonda didn't remember it that way at all: 'We all had our fun, if we wanted it. If you wanted to bury yourself in work and take cold showers, you could do that. I think Jim felt he'd gone to heaven, because at university he'd been mainly in the company of men. But here he was, in the company of men *and* women. There was a cottage where all the men lived and another cottage where the women lived. I guess a lot of the company just wanted to get to sleep after a long day's work. But we were just kids, for Christ's sake, and you only had to take off for an hour or so after work with some girl for some fun.

'Jim was no monk. Neither of us were. You hit it off with a girl during work hours, and after dark you did something about it. Jim had a thing going with an actress called Merna Pace for a while.

Next thing I know is, he's with another actress. And then another.'

Jim admitted he did recall spending time with several of the actresses: 'I liked a girl there called Cynthia Rogers. She was an actress. We were all young. Life was fun.'

Life continued being fun for Jim, but for Fonda there seemed little light at the end of the Cape Cod tunnel for an actor. So he quit the University Players and went to work for a small theatre company in Maine, working mostly as a backstage hand. He recalled, 'I carried on struggling as an actor, mainly because I *wasn't* acting, while Jim – *Lucky* Jim – stayed on and got a short cut to Broadway!'

There was good and bad news for Jim in 1932. James Maitland Stewart, Jim's grandfather, died at the age of ninety-one. Despite his rather sour attitude in old age, he had remained a respected pillar of the community in Indiana. When he died, the mayor and other important local civil and political figures were among the pallbearers.

The good news – and the short cut Hank Fonda missed out on – was that Joshua Logan, Bretaigne Windust and Charles Crane Leatherbee had made a deal with New York producer Arthur J Beckhard. He had agreed to try out a number of plays at Cape Cod in August, using the University Players, before producing them in New York.

Logan conceded that they were all lucky not to get 'completely screwed by Beckhard'. He explained, 'What we were totally uninformed about was that Beckhard was not one of the most successful of producers. In fact he was one of the most *un*successful producers. He had made a number of flops in New York, but he currently had a success on Broadway with Rose Franken's play *Another Language*. But despite its success, any money he was making on it was being lost by a badly managed tour of the play. We were so overwhelmed that a Broadway producer would agree to produce his plays at our theatre, using our actors, we totally overlooked the fact that he had got us to agree to footing all the bills of his plays at Cape Cod ourselves.

'We thought we were in the big time now, so we changed our name from the University Players to the Theatre Unit. But somehow we ended up with Beckhard's touring company for *Another Language* rehearsing in our theatre before going on to Chicago. Suddenly our company found itself locked out of our own theatre.'

Once the touring company had moved on, the first of Beckhard's plays began rehearsing with the Theatre Unit. But there were troubles from the onset. Said Logan, 'The first play was *Goodbye Again* [a comedy by Allan Scott and George Haight], but Beckhard gave the main part to Howard Lindsay, an actor who wasn't in our company. So that didn't go down well. Bretaigne Windust directed the play and made sure that some of our players got parts, including Jimmy Stewart.'

Jim's part wasn't much. He recalled, 'I played a chauffeur who came on – the set was the home of a famous author – and I carry a book which I give to the author's butler and I said, "Mrs Belle Irving would sure appreciate it if she could have this book autographed." The butler went off, came back and said that the author was too busy to sign the book. And I said, "Mrs Belle Irving is going to be sore as hell," and I got off. I was just fascinated by the whole idea of taking two simple lines and giving them *life*. That's what's so exciting about acting.'

Logan said, 'It wasn't much of a part for Jim, but he got the biggest laughs of each performance – just the way he delivered those lines. He got better at it each night, carefully working on every word, every syllable, until he felt he couldn't do it any better.'

The second production was Frank McGrath's *Carry Nation*, based on the life of the prohibitionist of the play's title. 'That's when it all went to hell,' said Logan. 'Beckhard installed his own director, Blanche Yurka, an actress who had less experience as a director than I had. I got the job of assistant director, which annoyed me *and* her. Then Beckhard cast his wife [Esther Dale] in the lead role of Carry Nation. She was just an *awful* actress. She progressed only into obscurity. Our own players were much better. She couldn't remember her lines.' Jim played a policeman called Gano; the role was slightly bigger than the part of the chauffeur in the previous play.

Despite the behind-the-scenes battles that raged, and which Jim stayed clear of, Beckhard decided to bring *Carry Nation* to Broadway in September 1932. The producer wanted to bring the cast and crew of the Cape Cod production to New York, but only to save on money and time. Jim was suddenly faced with a dilemma:

'I was supposed to be with the University Players for only the summer . . . and suddenly here was this chance to play on Broadway. But my parents expected me to return to my studies at Princeton. So I had to think carefully about the right thing to do.

'The fact was I just thought how awfully nice it would be to perform on a Broadway stage. This was something all the other actors craved, and I figured I was a lucky guy to have that opportunity handed to me on a plate. So I made every excuse I could think of not to go back to Princeton. Dad wasn't happy. I told him that he had enough expense with my sisters. Mary was going to take an art course at Carnegie Tech, and Virginia was going to Vassar. I told Dad I'd just be another expense he couldn't afford. He said, "Son, your tuition is *free*. You got a scholarship." I said, "But I need to be able to feed myself." Dad said, "Don't worry about it. We'll manage." Eventually I had to tell my folks that I was going to New York. They weren't happy. I never thought I'd actually make it as an actor. I just went along for the ride because opportunities just kept coming up.'

Arriving in New York, Stewart, Logan and another actor from the University Players, Myron McCormick, found a two-room apartment on the third floor at West 64th Street to share between the three of them.

James Stewart made his Broadway debut in *Carry Nation* in September 1932. He didn't expect to be there any longer than the run of the play. He recalled, 'We all went to New York and were there for four years, starting in 1932 . . . which always amazed me because it was right in the depth of the terrible Depression . . . and yet the theatre was absolutely more alive than it's ever been. There were usually thirty plays on Broadway all the time. Once you get bitten by the bug, you get trapped in the thing . . . it was very exciting for young people just getting started. I was in nine plays in four years, so you can see they weren't all successes.' Those nine plays gave Jim not only fairly regular employment, but also a grounding in professional theatre that some actors only dream of.

Just a few days after *Carry Nation* opened, Franklin Delano Roosevelt was elected president, and he announced that he was repealing Prohibition. 'Jim wasn't thinking too much like an actor in those days,' said Logan. 'He said, "That's it. We'll be able to drink *legal* liquor in a few months." I said, "Don't you realise what this means to the play? It's suddenly out of date. No one'll want to come and see a play about a zealous prohibitionist." And I was right. We played to half-empty houses and closed after four weeks.'

Jim's sister Virginia was in New York at the time. Virgina – or Ginnie – was, said Gloria, more like Jim than Dotie was. She was easy-going and even looked a lot like him. She was also a dreamer and easily distracted; she didn't get beyond her freshman year at Vassar. But she was Bessie's favourite of the three children and the one Mother spoiled the most.

Virginia had it in mind to become a writer, and in February 1940 she had an article published in the *Coronet* entitled 'My Brother Becomes a Star'. In it she wrote of the time she met up with Jim after the failure of *Carry Nation*, and they shared a Thanksgiving meal in a restaurant.

Almost as soon as *Carry Nation* closed, Beckhard announced he was putting on *Goodbye Again*. However, hardly anyone from the Cape Cod production was asked back; not even Howard Lindsay, who had played the lead role. Osgood Perkins, father of Anthony Perkins, got the lead. But Jim was offered his role of the chauffeur.

The play opened on 28 December at the Masque Theatre. It was a huge success, and ran for six months. Burgess Meredith saw the play, and he recalled just how Stewart was able to 'squeeze every drop of juice' from his two lines: 'Jim was simply brilliant in bringing out so much from two lines. You have to picture this tall, lanky guy, wearing this awful chauffeur's uniform, and he looks bemused and bewildered. Then when he says, "Mrs Irving would sure . . ." Jim stretched out the word "sure" so it became "*surrrrre* . . ." It was like he was just stuck on "*r*". And then he's left alone on stage. Any actor *loves* the stage to himself, except Jim's got nothing to say. So he just stands there looking awkward and baffled, and the audience is loving it. Then the butler comes back on, says "No", and Jim does another long drawn out "*r*" with the word "sore". And then he gets to the word "hell" . . . and his delivery of that word was just so brilliant that the audience roared with laughter every time. This was an actor who knew how to take two lines and make them into a highlight of the play in the way the playwright never foresaw.'

Around that time Henry Fonda arrived, out of work, in New York, and he promptly moved in with Jim, Logan and McCormick. As Henry Fonda recalled, 'I was out of work more often than Jim, and I'd been acting since 1925. He'd been doing it for a couple of months. That's why I called him Lucky Jim.'

Lucky Jim remembered it differently: 'Hank was the busiest of us all. He had parts in small theatres in New Jersey and in summer stock. He wanted to be on Broadway, but he had plenty of work off Broadway.' Joshua Logan agreed with Fonda, saying, 'I remember that everyone worked *except* Hank Fonda. Jim always seemed to be working, so was Myron and so was I, even if we were working as stage managers or even box-office managers – we did whatever jobs we could get. But Hank just always seemed to be out of work.'

They all managed to survive by spreading the cost as evenly as possible. Jim recalled, 'We had a general fund that we all put money into which was there for the leaner times . . . when we'd *all* be out of work. Otherwise, it was always the fella . . . or *fellas* who were working the most who bore the greatest financial burden.'

As well as complaining about the lack of work, Henry Fonda also complained about Margaret Sullavan, from whom he would soon be divorced. Logan recalled, 'Jimmy was having to listen to Hank complaining about Sullavan. And Jimmy patiently listened to it all. Maybe Hank wanted to make sure Jim was put off from attempting to try his luck with Sullavan because in 1933 Fonda and Sullavan's divorce came through.

'Hank knew how Jim felt about her. He'd say, "She's a ball-breaker from way back." I think he may have been *warning* Jim that this was a woman that would hurt him. But nothing Hank said stopped Jim feeling the way he did about her. He was in love with her for years . . . up until he met Gloria. And even after that he always had a soft spot for Sullavan. And so did Hank, despite his complaints about her.'

Despite the megrims, including lack of work and Fonda's misery over Margaret Sullavan, there were other things about life in New

York that brought back amusing memories for Henry Fonda when I interviewed him in 1976. Recalling their apartment, he said, 'It was an interesting kind of building; all the local whores worked from there. And there were always gangsters running in and out. We'd be in our apartment, minding our own business and having a beer, and the door would burst open and in would walk three or four characters in chesterfield coats with black velvet collars, and white Borsalino hats pulled low over their eyes. They'd keep their hands in their pockets, so you never knew if they were going to suddenly pull a gun. They'd check out the place, look in the bedroom, shrug and go, never saying a word. And a few nights later the same thing happened, only with different guys. They were always looking for their hookers. And when they didn't find them, they'd go to another apartment. You just sat there, said nothing, and let them do their business.'

Jim remembered, 'Gangsters ran the prostitution racket, and the prostitutes had a lot of clients in the block where we lived.' Which begs the question: did Stewart and Fonda take advantage of the services of the prostitutes? Logan, who had moved out of the apartment but still stayed over when he was in New York, said, 'There's no question. These were *guys*. These were *men*. These were young *fellas* and they had a bachelor pad, and there was little else to do in bachelor pads except drink and . . . fool around with girls. Hank would say, "Let's hire ourselves some hookers," and Jim would always be the more reluctant one. I think he always figured that some Presbyterian spy would find him out, and I think to some extent he felt guilty because he had a religious streak in him. But he only felt guilty *after* the . . . *event*. And over time, he felt less guilty. He told me, "We all need redeeming, Josh, and the more you fall, the better your redeeming." Jim spent years practising for his redemption.'

Jim denied they ever hired hookers: 'We couldn't *afford* 'em. We'd often come home to find our apartment locked because we couldn't pay the rent. So you'd scramble together enough to pay the landlord, and then you ate as cheaply as you could. If you had some money, you bought beer with it.'

Fonda, though, had another version of their poverty-stricken existence. 'With gangsters all over the place, it wasn't difficult to find a little tax-free work. Nothing serious. We didn't knock anybody off. But from time to time we kept an eye on the girls . . . the hookers. The trouble was, the hookers often wanted protecting from these hoodlums – they didn't want to hand over their hard-earned cash. So sometimes we'd let them hide out . . . and from time to time they showed their appreciation in more *personal* ways.'

When I asked him if that meant taking advantage of the girls' professional services, Fonda laughed and said:

'Yeah! Of course! When a reasonable-looking girl offers you a good time, and you've nothing else better to do, you don't say, "No thanks, not today." So we'd have some girls to ourselves. Usually Myron wouldn't want anything to do with it, and he'd go out. He'd say, "I don't want to be here if those gangsters come barging in and find their girls giving us freebies." Josh wasn't living with us all the time. So Jim had a girl in one room, and I was in another room with my girl.

'And yep, one night we got caught out. The gangsters came bursting in and caught me and Jim with the girls. It was either get beat up, or pay up. Jim decided he'd be a hero. He can get really mad, and when he gets mad he can be scary as hell. But part of it was also acting. He told them he wasn't afraid of them, and if they tried anything on him, he'd teach them what it meant to mess with . . . some kind of name he thought of for himself . . . something like "The Pennsylvanian Kid". I thought they'd just shoot him for sure. But they just kind of looked at each other, shrugged, said, "Have a good time," and left.

'Jim said to me, "Don't ever let me do that again." And because he acted so tough, they gave us a few other little jobs.'

Stewart did admit to having run some errands for the local gangsters:

'When you're struggling, you do crazy things . . . things you wouldn't do if you weren't so desperate. So me and Fonda made a few deliveries for the local gangsters. I think we were delivering parcels of money. Certainly not bombs. At least, nothing we ever delivered blew up! But I felt bad about it because . . . you never knew where the money came from or where it was going. But you had to figure that there was some . . . *immoral* background to all this cash. And finally I said, "I'm not doing this any more." And I told them this . . . and Hank thought they'd probably kill us . . . but they didn't.

'A lot of people seemed to have respect for these hoodlums. I never did. And the more I thought about it, the more I detested them and all that they did. I guess I was hearing a small still voice, telling me what they were doing was wrong . . . and if I helped them, *I* was wrong too. I'm no angel but . . . you hafta have principles in your life . . . and I guess I developed some principles at that time.

'There was one night . . . a dead body turned up in front of our building. He'd been shot by gangsters. Probably was a gangster himself. But none of it seemed real to us. We were living in our own world, trying to figure out how to make it in the theatre business.

'I often felt I wished I could have done more about helping to fight crime. I think I'd have liked being in the FBI. I always admired the work the FBI did . . . and I admired and liked J Edgar Hoover.'

In ensuing years, Stewart would not only play a role in fighting crime, but he came as close to being an FBI agent as anyone could be without wearing a badge or getting a salary from the Federal Government. He would also become a friend to J Edgar Hoover.

Fonda said, 'For years Jim almost idolised Hoover and he thought the FBI was the greatest law enforcement agency in the world. He never changed his mind about the FBI. He'd go on about how Hoover had cleaned up America by getting gangsters like Pretty Boy Floyd, John Dillinger and Baby Face Nelson.' Jim would, however, change his mind about Hoover. But that was only after Hoover's death in 1972.

According to Fonda, 'By 1933, we were able to afford to rent a speakeasy on West 40th Street every Thursday where we and other like-minded actors met. We called ourselves the Thursday Night Beer Club. We charged two dollars for a beer and a steak, which I usually cooked. Jim's job was to play the music and organise other musical guests. Then word reached the professional musicians playing on radio or in hotels and theatres, and they began coming around.'

Burgess Meredith was among the regular guests. At the time he was struggling to make a career as a musician before turning to acting. He said:

'We had some great nights. It kind of became the place to be. There were top musicians there like Benny Goodman, and actresses like Ruth Gordon, Helen Hayes and Margaret Sullavan.

'Sullavan loved Jim and Jim loved Sullavan. It should have been as simple as that. But they never did anything about it. Part of the reason, I would say, was because Jim didn't want to upset Fonda. But it was obvious to everyone that Sullavan thought the world of Jim.

'She really treated Jim different to the way she treated other men. She didn't really pay any attention to men unless she was interested in them sexually. You *knew* when Sullavan was interested in you, and there weren't many men who could resist her because she was so predatory about seduction. But with Jim she was simply affectionate without being predatory. She seemed to want to protect him, to nurture him, to help him become all he could be. I think Jim had made it clear to her at some point that while he may have loved her – and I mean that he was *in* love with her – they were never going to be lovers, and I think that had everything to do with his friendship with Henry Fonda. I don't know another man she would have taken that from, but she took it from Jimmy, and she never stopped being anything but loving and – well – almost maternal towards him. One night she suddenly announced that Jimmy was going to become a major movie star. She had just been signed to a contract at Universal Studios.'

Joshua Logan wasn't convinced at the time that Jim had what it took to be a movie star. He was sure that Sullavan was equally unconvinced and must have had an ulterior motive in predicting Jim's future success in films: 'I think it's likely that Margaret was proclaiming Jimmy Stewart as a future star simply to get at Fonda.'

Meredith disagreed: 'Margaret Sullavan never once said anything derogatory about Stewart, and she never stopped saying that he would become a star in Hollywood – and when he became a star, she always said, "I told you so." She *believed* in him. God knows, she could have said a hundred things just to stick in Fonda's throat – and she *did* say hundreds of things – but she never used Jimmy to do that. She really believed Jimmy would make it in Hollywood, and that was something even Jimmy didn't think he could do. But Sullavan truly believed in him.'

It was during his time at the rented speakeasy that Anthony Mann, the most influential director in Jim's career, came briefly into his life. Because of a rift in their friendship that occurred in 1957, Jim generally avoided questions about Mann, but he did tell me, 'The first time I met Anthony Mann was when he started turning up at what we called our Thursday Night Beer Club. Only his name wasn't Tony Mann then. It was Emil Bundsmann, and he wasn't a director. He was a stage manager. I believe he went on to direct some plays in New York.' Anthony Mann would become a strong influence in Jim's movie career – he was the man who made Jim famous as a star of Westerns.

Jim had become friendly with actress Jane Cowl, one of the American stage's greatest Juliets. Cowl was in her late forties, but still a figure of elegance and poise. Said Burgess Meredith, 'There was nothing romantic between Jim and Jane Cowl, but virtually every woman who met Jim seemed to love him, and I think Jane Cowl did.'

Cowl was to play the title role in *Camille* in Boston in the spring of 1933, and when she heard that *Goodbye Again* had closed, she demanded that Jim be hired as stage manager for *Camille*. This experience led to one of Jim's famous tales which, at various times, has had different endings. As Burgess Meredith remembered: 'Cowl was performing her climactic death scene, when Jim heard something hitting the stage door. He went to investigate and found a tramp throwing wood at the door. So Jim ran him off, but when he returned to his post, he had literally lost the plot. Noting the silence from the stage, he figured that Cowl had finished her death scene, and he brought down the curtain. There was a gasp from the audience, and Cowl rushed into the wings, proclaiming, "I hadn't finished dying. You have ruined my performance. I can never face an audience again."

'Well, Cowl did go back on the next night, and she eventually completed the run of the play. To hear Jim tell the story, he was fired. But he wasn't. He completed the run. The whole story sounds like one of Jimmy's yarns, but the incident was true, because it was a story that we all heard about back in New York. But Jimmy could tell the story like nobody else.'

Jim and Fonda finally got to work together again in the play *All Good Americans* in the autumn of 1933. Fonda said, 'We were hardly taking New York by storm. I was the understudy for the lead and all Jimmy had to do was play his accordion.' Jim recalled, 'They simply needed somebody who could play the accordion, and I was it. Only after I got the job did I realise that I had a scene where I had to throw the accordion out of a window. Waall . . . I was using my own accordion and I wasn't going to throw that anywhere. So I talked them into letting me play a banjo because banjos are a lot cheaper than accordions.'

According to Fonda, 'The play was a disaster. It ran about a month, and then we were out of work again. On our last night, we left the closing-down party and were making our way across Times Square at three in the morning, and the place was deserted. So I said to Jim, "I wonder if we'd get an audience if you played your accordion." So Jim started playing, and people came out of nowhere. So I started passing round the hat, and I collected around fifteen cents.'

Jim remembered it slightly differently, as a good storyteller might: 'I remember one night, Henry and I . . . we had played in a Broadway thing that folded after five days . . . took my accordion to the closing party. At about three in the morning we were heading back to our hotel across Times Square when Hank dared me to play my accordion to see if we could draw a crowd. It was *bitter* cold and there wasn't a soul in sight. So I began with "Ragtime Cowboy Joe" . . . and would you believe it! Half a dozen people appeared from *nowhere* . . . just to listen. Then twenty.

'Waall, this went on for about an hour until I felt something hit the back of my leg. I turned to find myself face to face with a *cop*. He said, "It takes me hours to get these drunks bedded down in doorways, and you come along making them awful noises. Now I gotta get 'em back to sleep." . . . I'd thought I'd really drawn a crowd of music lovers, but they were just hobos.'

Early in 1934, Jim sought the lead role in stage producer
Leonard Sillman's *New Faces of 1934*, a production about hopefuls
auditioning for a Broadway show. Jim discovered that Sillman was
staying at the Algonquin Hotel, and so he made sure he 'accidentally' ran into Sillman in the hotel lobby where he immediately
performed an improvised comic sketch. Sillman told Jim, 'I've
already signed another underweight young comedian.' The under-
weight comedian was Henry Fonda.

Around that time, Jim managed to get himself an audition for the
key role of Sergeant O'Hara in Sidney Howard's *Yellow Jack*, the
story of how soldiers were used as guinea pigs to test the origins of
yellow fever. Jim recalled:

'I gave a good audition, I thought. I'd read the play, studied it . . . I
think I impressed the producers. Then they said, "But can you play
the part with an Irish brogue?" Waall, I gave it my best shot, but I
just couldn't deliver a remotely believable Irish brogue. So I asked
a friend of mine, Frank Cullinan, who was a good actor and very
good at accents, to coach me to speak with an Irish brogue. I
persuaded the producers to give me another audition but . . . the part
had already been cast even though they were impressed with my
Irish brogue. So now I had a new skill to add to my CV – an Irish
brogue. But a few days later they called me and said the actor
they'd cast for O'Hara wasn't working out, and they gave me the
role.

'Our director was the great Guthrie McClintic, and the cast was
made up of all these serious-minded actors . . . all formally trained
and who lived and breathed theatre. And it was while we were
rehearsing that play . . . seeing these actors really caring about their
craft, really concentrating, trying to create something special on the
stage . . . that I began to think differently about acting. I began to
see that it was a *creative* process and that these people derived great
satisfaction from *working* at it . . . working real hard. And that's
when I started to think of acting as a serious craft.'

Yellow Jack opened at the Martin Beck Theatre on 6 March 1934
to critical acclaim, but the subject proved too depressing to attract
the public. After a short run, McClintic promised Jim a part in

was turning into a star and a damn good actor. I have to admit, it ruffled me.'

Fonda didn't really have too much to complain about. While appearing in *New Faces of 1934*, he was signed by an agent who landed him a contract with the Hollywood producer Walter Wanger, and so Fonda landed in Hollywood later in 1934.

6

Hollywood

Stewart was laconic about how he got to Hollywood. He simply said, 'One thing led to another and before I knew it I was in Hollywood under contract.'

In fact, during his time in New York, Stewart had several screen tests, but nothing ever came of them. However, during the run of *Divided by Three*, he was offered a screen test by Al Altman, a talent scout from Metro-Goldwyn-Mayer. Hedda Hopper would later insist that she had persuaded Altman to go and see Stewart in *Divided by Three*, but Josh Logan said that MGM had been alerted to Stewart's potential by the excellent reviews for the play.

Burgess Meredith said, 'Jim would never contradict Hopper's claims that she got him his screen test because after he became a star, she championed him in his career and in politics, and he was loyal to her for that. You can never get Jim to confirm or deny Hopper's claim. I think that says a lot about Jim's commitment to friendship. He's simply the kind of guy everyone should want as a friend.'

Further tests followed. Finally, Altman was able to offer Jim a standard beginner's contract for six months, giving the studio the option to sign him for seven years, starting at $350 a week. Jim signed, but was first committed to two more plays, *Page Miss Glory*, which ran for sixty-three performances at the Mansfield Theatre from 6 November 1934, and *A Journey by Night* at the Shubert from 15 April 1935. The second play was a disaster, running a mere seven performances and earning Jim, as a Viennese complete with a poor Viennese accent, his first bad notices. But it meant that, by the spring of 1935, James Stewart was ready to test the waters of Hollywood. Henry Fonda recalled:

'I was waiting for Jim at the station when he arrived in Los Angeles. I'd been there for hours, but Jim kept missing his trains from New York, so I never knew when he was going to arrive. Finally he pulled in. He said to me, "Where am I going to live?" I said, "Never mind that. Where's the Martin Bomber?" And there it was, in a special crate. I'd expected Jim to forget it, but he didn't. So I took him and his baggage over to the house in Brentwood that I was renting and he stayed with me.

'Jim was intrigued by our neighbour. Greta Garbo! Jim said, "Can we go and say hello to Garbo?"

'I said, "I haven't even spoken to her yet."

'Jim said, "Well, for crying out loud, Hank, she's your neighbour. Why don't you be neighbourly and say hello?"

'I said, "Because she's Greta Garbo, Jim."

'And Jim said, "Let's go and say hello right now."

'I said, "You just can't go and say hello to Greta Garbo."

'He said, "Why not?"

'I said, "Jim, for Chrissakes, she's *Greta Garbo*."

'She was at Metro where Jim was going to be working, and I said, "I reckon you'll meet her at the studio."'

Stewart never did get to meet Garbo, either at the studio or in the garden. Part of the problem, apparently, was that Garbo erected a particularly high fence between their properties. 'Garbo didn't like Hank's cats,' said Stewart. 'At least, Hank thought of them as *his* cats. They were just wild beasts that looked all cute and cuddly. And Hank kinda liked cats, so he was always putting out food for them. And, boy, did they multiply, so every month there were more of these wild cats. And this didn't impress Garbo too much, so she put up this high fence to keep the cats out. And it was there also, maybe, to keep *us* out.'

Fonda recalled, 'One night, Jim and I had had a few too many drinks, and I said to Jim, "You *must* have met Garbo by now. You work at the same studio, for Chrissakes." And he said he still hadn't met her. So we agreed we should meet her. But she had this high fence separating our properties, so we decided to dig a tunnel under the fence. It was thirsty work, so we made sure we had plenty of booze on hand, and we ended up consuming quite a bit of alcohol. And we didn't finish the damn tunnel because we hit a gas main several feet down.

'I said to Jim, "Let's keep going." He said, "Are you crazy? We'll have to dig down ever deeper and I'm just about all done in." So we gave up, and I was so disappointed not to meet Garbo that I just did all I could to beat Jim in finishing off our liquor.'

Jim recalled the story a little differently, agreeing to all events up to the point they hit the gas main. 'I wanted to keep on digging, but Hank wasn't used to too much hard labour and he gave up. And I wasn't going to keep digging on my own.'

Eventually Garbo moved. 'It wasn't so much us or the cats that drove Garbo away,' said Fonda. 'It was the fleas the cats left behind. The fence didn't stop them. They just hopped right over, and before we knew it Garbo was moving out to escape the plague of fleas she said we'd brought on her. I have to admit, those fleas were a helluva nuisance. For years, we were itching and scratching. We finally decided we'd also had enough of the fleas, and so we moved out of that house and into another one just down the road.'

The MGM executives were scratching their heads, having been presented with the long, lanky, thin guy from Indiana with the rather squeaky voice. 'They just didn't know what to do with me,' said Jim. 'I'm sure some executives were wondering why they'd ever signed me up. But they had a casting director . . . name of Bill Grady . . . and he really seemed to be the only one who thought I had something to offer . . . and *I* certainly didn't know what that was . . . and he just kept pushing me at producers while they tried to decide if I was a comedian or an oddball kind of leading man.

'Finally I got cast in *The Good Earth* . . . as a Chinaman! Bill Grady said I got the part because I was the only actor under contract who looked like I'd actually suffered a famine. It took all morning to put the make-up on. I was the tallest Chinaman ever. Paul Muni was the star, and to keep me from being taller than he was, they had to dig a trench for me to walk in. One day Muni fell in the trench, and three days after I started work on *The Good Earth*, I was fired . . . for being too tall.'

Jim was only 132 pounds when he arrived in Hollywood, so they tried fattening him up with supplements, and sent him to the gym every day to try and harden his muscles. 'I had this trainer . . . Don Loomis. He had enormous muscles. He looked like Mr Universe . . . and he was a taskmaster. I was being driven to exhaustion. I got to pressing 200 pounds fifty times, and I actually put on 20 pounds and I actually had some muscles. And he'd say, "More, give me more. One more. Two more." Until finally I said, "I can't do this anymore. I'm gonna *die* if you keep this pressure up on me . . . and then what will Mr Mayer think?" And Don said, "Mr Mayer doesn't even know who you are." I said, "Good point . . . but think how *you'll* feel when I drop dead." And he told the studio he couldn't do any more with me . . . and in just two weeks I was right back down to 132 pounds.'

It was decided that Jim would be introduced to the cinema-going public in a supporting role in *After the Thin Man*, the second in what would become a series of films based on Dashiell Hammett's Nick and Nora Charles mysteries. William Powell and Myrna Loy were cast, but, despite being major stars, they were only being paid B-feature salaries. Loy rebelled, and MGM found themselves locked in what looked like a long-running contract battle with the actress.

Bill Grady suggested to producer Harry Rapf that he cast Jim in *The Murder Man* – as a reporter called Shorty! 'I think it was the very bizarre notion that I play a character called Shorty that persuaded the producer it was just bizarre enough to work,' said Jim. Filmed in 1934, *The Murder Man* starred Spencer Tracy as a wisecracking newspaperman known for his scoops on major homicide cases who becomes embroiled in a personal situation when his father goes broke after being conned by two men. When one of the con men is found murdered, Tracy investigates, with the result that the surviving con man is arrested for fraud and murder.

When released in 1935, *The Murder Man* didn't make much of an impact, and Jim's supporting role was barely noticed. 'That was the way they worked you,' he said. 'You could do small parts in films, and if the films were no good, it didn't matter because you weren't the star. So you carry on working until they decide you either have what it takes, or you don't.'

He was quickly back at work, in *Rose Marie*, the second musical film that teamed Jeanette MacDonald and Nelson Eddy following their success with *Naughty Marietta*. Jim played the fugitive brother; 'Really the best kind of part for me at that time,' he said. 'I didn't have too many scenes, but everyone talks about this character, and at the end of the film I get my big scene. So my role was important, even if I didn't have a lot of screen time.

'I had some fun making the film. We had some location stuff to shoot. I shared a room with the film's director, Woody Van Dyke, and he liked me to put him to sleep at night by playing the accordion. It was just as well he liked me because he liked to do everything in one take to save time and money. But I fluffed some of my scenes, and we had to reshoot them. But he was patient with me and helped me do my best.

'And Jeanette MacDonald helped me a lot too. A wonderful lady. When we got to do our scenes together, she told Woody to make sure I had all the best coverage with the camera. Most actresses, I learned, liked to hog the best angles for themselves. But Jeanette knew the audience had to get to know my character in a short space of screen time. Woody was happy to do it.'

Jim went straight into another picture, *Next Time We Love*, this time on loan to Universal. 'Contract actors were like ballplayers,' he said. 'You were traded between studios. Universal wanted to use the MGM backlot for three weeks, so MGM said they could if they gave me a part in their film.'

There was actually a lot more to Universal's decision to cast Jim, according to Ray Milland, who was one of the film's two major stars. 'Margaret Sullavan was the star, and she was a *big* star at Universal, which was not a really major studio at the time, and they did anything she asked them to do. And one of the things she asked them to do was cast Jimmy Stewart in *Next Time We Love*. And what Sullavan asked for, she got.'

Jim was billed third, just below Sullavan and Milland. He played an international newspaper correspondent who is caught between his own career and that of his wife (played by Sullavan) as a Broadway actress. But the marriage is doomed and Sullavan loves another, played by Milland. Stewart's character, unhappily, dies of a disease in China, leaving Sullavan and Milland to marry.

Milland recalled to me how Sullavan, who had married the film director William Wyler in 1934, helped Jim develop his acting skills: 'Margaret went out of her way to make Jimmy look good in what I think was only his third film. Our director [Edward Griffith] raged at Jimmy because of his exaggerated stage techniques, and if he'd been a better director he could have helped Jimmy. But Margaret helped him, instead. Oh, they spent many hours into the night rehearsing . . . and I'm not saying they were having an affair. What was obvious was that Jimmy's performance improved with Margaret's coaching. But you just *knew* these two people loved each other.

'Whether they got up to anything . . . Well . . ! William Wyler certainly had his suspicions. He was married to Sullavan at the time, and when he saw some of the rushes, he said, "Well, she certainly got *something* special out of the lanky guy," and I don't think he was talking about Jimmy's acting.'

Apparently, when filming was over and Jim returned to MGM, he was 'a new man', as Gloria put it. She said, 'Margaret taught him a lot about screen technique. He had confidence that wasn't there before, and the studio executives were amazed. I think they had already decided he was going nowhere, but he showed in his next few pictures that he had a new sense of confidence. And Sullavan gave him that.'

Margaret Sullavan can therefore be credited with one of Jim's first good film reviews, from *Time* who said, when the film was released in 1936: 'James Stewart is natural, spontaneous, and altogether excellent.' The film itself was poorly received. 'A draggy, complex tale [which] will have to be sold on the star's past performances,' said *Variety*.

*

Recalling his arrival in Hollywood, Joshua Logan said:

'When I got to Hollywood in 1935, Stewart and Fonda invited me
to stay with them. I quickly realised they weren't the same two guys
I'd known before; they'd basically *gone Hollywood*. There was one
time we were on our way to a party at Ginger Rogers' house, and
we had an argument about Max Reinhardt's film of Shakespeare's
A Midsummer Night's Dream. It was a beautiful film, I thought. But
Jimmy said, "I saw the picture and it stinks."

'I said, "But it's a work of art; how can you say that?"

'And he said, "I'm telling ya, it won't make a nickel."

'I said, "You've only just arrived and already you sound like a
studio accountant."

'So Jimmy said, "Well, that's how films are judged. If they can't
make money, then they stink."

'I was still mad about this when we got to the party, and I got
more drunk and finally both Stewart and Fonda cornered me and
said, "We don't like the way you're behaving," and I said, "Well, I
don't like the way Mr James *Hollywood* Stewart was talking to
me." I said, "You know what I think?" They said, "What?" I said,
"I think you've both sold out for money. So I'm going to move out
of your money-tainted house and go my own way." And I did move
out. A few weeks later we all got together, put our differences aside
and were friends ever after.'

Stewart had his own spin on the story: "I'd have to say that while
Hank and I were . . . let's say, finding the Hollywood life a little
heady, Josh Logan just didn't have a clue what Hollywood was all
about when he came out there. Making movies is a business, and he
thought, at first, he could put Hollywood to rights and show them
that commercial success was just the icing on the cake. Integrity
and art were more important. And I guess we . . . that is, Hank and
I . . . we thought we knew more about making movies than he did,
although the truth was none of us knew that much back then. Of
course, the motion picture business is more complicated than all
that. You *strive* for something that may be thought by some as art,
or at the very least good craftsmanship. But you also know that
people have to go and *see* your work . . . a *lot* of people . . . because

the films have to make money for the studio, or pretty soon you're no longer working. That's just commerce. Well, Josh was a smart guy, but he hadn't figured that out when he came to Hollywood.'

What Jim had come to understand was that the commerce of film-making dictated that only the few prestige pictures, with major stars, had time and money lavished on them. 'The kind of film I was doing back then . . . they were just programmers for the most part.'

In 1936, Margaret Sullavan divorced William Wyler, her second husband, after only two years of marriage. Suddenly, it seemed, there was a chance for Jim to make Margaret his. But it was not to be.

According to Joshua Logan, 'Jim was not going to betray, as he saw it, his friend Henry Fonda. It just didn't make sense. Especially when Fonda remarried.' Henry Fonda married socialite Frances Seymour in 1936. With Fonda wed, Jim and another old friend from the University Players, Johnny Swope, were left to inhabit the Brentwood bachelor pad, and whenever Joshua Logan was in Hollywood, he stayed with Stewart and Swope.

Logan said, 'The other problem was that as soon as Sullavan divorced Wyler, she married her agent, Leland Hayward. Because of his friendship with Fonda, Jim was just too slow to act. I think that's when he knew he'd lost Sullavan for ever.'

Remaining firm friends with Sullavan, Stewart developed a good friendship with Leland Hayward, and with good reason – Hayward was a keen aviator. 'Margaret was also a pilot,' said Burgess Meredith. 'So the three of them would go on endlessly about aeroplanes. Jim spent a lot of his free time at their house. It was Leland who encouraged Jim to learn to fly.'

Stewart began flying lessons in 1936. He surprised himself by not learning to fly as quickly as he should have:

'I just didn't do well at first . . . flying solo. I should have been able to fly without an instructor after about eight hours, but it took me *twice* as long. I was too impatient and just wanted to do it on my own . . . but the more impatient I got, the longer it took.

'Then one day I was flying with my instructor, and he wanted me to do a simulated forced landing. This meant he had to suddenly pull back the throttle as though we had engine failure. I calmly picked a field to land in . . . it was a potato field . . . and I was gliding that baby in perfectly. What was supposed to happen next was the instructor . . . seeing that I was on target . . . would give the plane throttle so we would climb. But we just kept on gliding. I figured the instructor had forgotten or had passed out or died or something, so *I* pulled on the throttle . . . but it just wouldn't budge. By now we were virtually on the ground, so I didn't do a simulated false landing – I did it for *real*. I thought I'd done pretty good but the *instructor* . . . he was just plain mad at me. He said he'd tried to gun the plane, and when the throttle wouldn't budge he figured I was holding it on purpose. But I said that *I'd* tried to throttle the plane. That's when we discovered the throttle had jammed.

'He said, "You realise that we actually had a *real* emergency." I said, "Just as well I didn't know that or I might not have done such a perfect emergency landing." After that he thought I should do well enough on my own.'

After Jim received his licence, he got up before dawn every day, whether he was working or not, and drove out to the local airfield, Clover Field, to fly for an hour. Leland Hayward often accompanied him to the airfield, but they always flew their own separate planes.

Burgess Meredith wondered how much Hayward's desire to drive with Jim to Clover Field had to do with any suspicion he might have had about his wife and Jim: 'I'm sure Hayward knew that Jim held a candle for his wife, and I would suppose it's possible that he didn't want to take a chance that Jim would take Margaret up in his plane, so Hayward may have gone almost every day with Jim to the airfield . . . just to make sure. And yet Hayward never showed any sign of being jealous because Jim never really gave him cause to be suspicious. Jim was often over at their house, and they were just three good friends. But I'll tell you . . ! Jim loved that girl.'

7

Gangsters

During my 1979 interview with James Stewart, I asked him to name his favourite leading lady. He seemed to rifle through the files of his distant memory, saying, 'Oh, I don't know . . . there've been some good ones. Dietrich was one. Jean Arthur. Margaret Sullavan.' And then he seemed to make a decision based on one particular experience he never forgot. Much louder than usual, he proclaimed:

'Jean Harlow! I did a picture with her . . . *Wife vs. Secretary*. I had only a small part because in those days when you were a contract player you played small parts in big films and big parts in small films. This was just a short role . . . and this *beautiful* girl. My God . . . she was *beautiful*. I had this scene with her . . . and we sat in an automobile while I told her my plans in life . . . and we ended the scene with a kiss.

'The lines we had to say weren't much to worry us and when we did the first rehearsal we didn't give the lines much thought . . . And then we got to the kiss. Well . . . she was kind of in charge . . . and I knew immediately that I'd never been kissed . . . I mean *really* kissed . . . before that time. Well, we rehearsed that scene six times and each time she kissed me with more interest . . . and I got more enthusiastic each time. I have to say, that was a landmark in my career. In my *life*. I was just this skinny guy from Pennsylvania, and she had this platinum hair and this beautiful face like a little angel with attitude. And she kinda slouched because slouching was fashionable then, and she had this low cut dress on and . . . well, she had nothing on underneath. And *I* had to kiss Jean Harlow. Well, I was just . . ! That just has to be my most memorable screen kiss. And, as you can see, I haven't forgotten it after all these years!'

Jim had good reason to remember Jean Harlow; they enjoyed a brief fling together. What put Jim off dating Harlow was the discovery that her stepfather, Marino Bellow, was a gangster from Chicago. Jim had come to detest gangsters, although he never disliked Harlow; he just decided that an affair with her might be dangerous. Gloria told me that if he'd really loved Harlow, he wouldn't have allowed her gangster stepfather to stand in the way – but he liked her as a friend and preferred to keep it that way.

Wife vs. Secretary featured three of MGM's biggest stars: Clark Gable, Myrna Loy and Harlow. 'Being in a picture with those three made sure people went to see the picture,' recalled Jim. A comedy that reflected an increasing need for women to get jobs because of the Depression, it suggested that wives (Loy) should never trust their husbands (Gable) with their secretaries (Harlow) even if the secretary has a boyfriend (Stewart).

'I had a really nice scene,' said Jim, 'where I talk at length about the wonder of getting a twenty-dollar raise. It was a monologue. I guess people liked the way I did it, and I guess producers took note of that because, over time, I found the scripts being given to me often included a monologue.

'I talked about this with [Frank] Capra once. I said, "Why do I get these long monologues?" He said, "It's because there's something about you the ordinary guy identifies with, and when you basically deliver a sermon, people don't think you're sermonising. They believe you. If Clark Gable tried doing that . . . waall, who's going to believe the King of Hollywood could represent the ordinary guy." So I said, "So I'm just an ordinary guy," and he said, "Yes, but a very *special* ordinary guy." And I guess that's why I've been around so long . . . people think I'm *ordinary* but somehow *special*, and if I tried to analyse what that really meant, I would go crazy and never be able to work again.'

Wife vs. Secretary was a hit when released in 1936. *Film Weekly* recommended seeing it for the 'spectacle of three clever shining stars shining for all they are worth'. The London *Observer* said, 'What I liked best about this picture was the performance of Mr James Stewart as the secretary's fiancé . . . He acts Gable and Harlow off the screen . . .' Stewart, added the *Observer*, made you realise 'that good actors don't stop with your own generation – they keep right along coming'.

But before *Wife vs. Secretary* was a proven hit, MGM kept Jim in his place by giving him another supporting role, playing a bumpkin called Elmer who was the hapless love rival to Robert Taylor in *Small Town Girl*. Janet Gaynor was the object of their desire. It was the fourth film featuring Stewart released in 1936, with four more to follow in quick succession.

Next came *Speed*, a B-movie that gave Jim the leading role as a mechanic whose obsession to develop a high-speed carburettor is beset by a series of mishaps and the inevitable tug of love for the leading lady, played by Wendy Barrie.

Then came *The Gorgeous Hussy* with Joan Crawford as the mistress of President Andrew Jackson who is forced to leave Washington. Jim was almost lost in the small part of one of Crawford's suitors. Above him in the cast list were the likes of Lionel Barrymore, Franchot Tone (Crawford's then real-life husband), Melvyn Douglas and Robert Taylor.

'I was still pretty green, I guess,' said Jim. 'Joan Crawford certainly thought so. She kinda . . . played up a bit . . . complained to [Louis B] Mayer that her husband didn't have enough lines . . . and he told her to be more professional around the "newcomers", which I guess meant me. And she said, "Shall I change his diapers too?" I guess that was one Hollywood actress I didn't get on too well with.'

He moved straight to the set of *Born to Dance*, a musical that gave him second billing to the star, Eleanor Powell. Jim played a sailor who meets and falls for a Broadway understudy, played by Eleanor Powell. 'It was the composer Cole Porter who persuaded the studio to let me do the musical,' said Jim. 'I don't know if any of his reasons were a compliment or not. He said to me, "You don't sing too good, but I've heard far worse. The thing is, you're just the right 'type' for this part. Any guy watching the picture who sees you woo Eleanor Powell will believe *he* can be successful in love." Then the studio wanted to have a professional singer dub my songs, but Porter talked them out of that. He said, "Stewart's got a squeaky kind of singing voice, but it goes with his squeaky kind of speaking voice . . . and those long, lanky legs." As I said, I don't know if any of that was complimentary . . . but it sure gave me a good role in a successful picture.'

Finally, *After the Thin Man* emerged. It was the last of the films featuring Jim released in 1936. The image Jim had built up through his previous films gave this picture an unexpected surprise. Nick and Nora Charles, played by William Powell and Myrna Loy, investigate a murder, and the killer turns out to be a nightclub singer played by Jim. The film gave him the first chance to display some of the rage he had learned to keep a lid on. In the final scene, he waves a gun and rants at Elissa Landi, playing the girl who has jilted him, 'I want to see you go mad and madder and madder until you hang.'

Jim liked the irony that the film which should have been his first, turned out to be his ninth:

'If it'd been my first picture . . . waall . . . you would have guessed straight away I was the murderer. But because I'd played all these Elmer-types, you just couldn't *believe* I was the killer. The thing is, by this time, someone had decided that Jimmy Stewart did a pretty good monologue . . . so they wrote in a monologue for me. I guess I fooled 'em into thinking I knew what I was doing as an actor. The truth was, I *didn't* at that time.

'I was used to playing to a live audience. But all I had here was a camera, and I didn't know what to do for it. I was still learning and getting all the good advice I could. I was just so awkward . . . all hands and feet. I never knew what to do with them. Whenever I did a film [*The Murder Man*] with Spencer Tracy, I asked his advice. He said, "You've acted on the stage, haven't you?" I said I had and he said, "Just forget the camera is there. You're too aware of it. You're feeling threatened by it. Don't be. Let your hands and feet do what they do in life, not on the stage. If the camera likes you, it will like whatever you do."

'So I took his advice. Much later he said to me, "That advice I gave you. What I didn't tell you was, if the camera doesn't like you, you're finished. But I didn't think that would help your confidence. Lucky for you, the camera likes you, so it was good advice." And it was.

'I did a picture called *Speed* which gave me my first leading role . . . although it was a low-budget picture . . . and Ted Healy, who played my best friend, told me, "Think of the audience as partners . . . as collaborators . . . not just watchers. You want to *involve* them." So when I was acting, I was playing to this invisible audience. I *imagined* them. I didn't get all of this right straight away. I had to *work* at it. You learn your craft . . . and you only get better by working at it.'

Jim thought of his years at MGM as some of the best of his life. He often defended the studio star system. In 1975, he commented, 'When Metro-Goldwyn-Mayer took you on as a contract player, they treated you really well. They took you under their wing and you just worked the whole time. I know there were some who got to be big stars who later complained about the studio system, but I thought it was just wonderful because they took care of you.' In 1979 he said:

'I think the thing was . . . the big studio gave you a base of operation . . . and you were learning your craft by *working* at it. It was a full-time job. You didn't do a picture and then wait around and sort of look for another story. You had people looking for you. You had the publicity department which was a very important thing at the studio. You sort of got a following which they kept very close track on . . . and then they would start building you in newspapers and by advertising and so on.

'But I think the big thing with the big studios was . . . it was almost a family type thing. Today the big studios are completely different. Some of them have survived but they're . . . they're places where people can make pictures, they can rent the sound stages, they can rent the facilities, but there's this top office which in some cases is not really connected very closely with the picture business. It's just been amazing to me how so many fine young actors have developed but haven't had this wonderful experience . . . this chance to work at your job a lot and sort of develop and have people help you.

'In the old days the studios did business with each other with their contract players and also directors. You'd be loaned to other studios for money or in return for something else. I think that pretty much is what people mean when they talk about the "old Hollywood", the "golden years". I still think that's the ideal way to make a picture.'

Many of his peers criticised Jim for his defence of the star system. Stars like Joan Crawford, Bette Davis, Humphrey Bogart and Clark Gable often fought with their respective employers. So did Ava Gardner, an MGM star who said, 'The studios told you what to do, who to be seen with, who to sleep with. If you wanted to do good work, you refused to do the lousy films – but that meant you were put on suspension. If there was a project you liked, which you thought would be a quality picture, or even if you just thought it might make you a better actress, you asked to do it, and then you got told, "That picture is not for you." Some actors, I guess, never fought with their studios and just did as they were told.'

Van Johnson, also an MGM star, took a different view to Gardner. 'I was just so happy to be doing the job I loved. I was no prima donna. Mr Mayer put you in the films he felt you would be good in, and which the audience would like. It wasn't an exact science, so it didn't always work out that way. I get sick of hearing those stars who complain about the way studios treated them. If it wasn't for the studios, they would never have become stars.'

During the early months of 1937, Jim was loaned out to 20th Century-Fox for the starring role in a remake of that studio's 1927 multi-Oscar-winning silent classic, *Seventh Heaven*. He played a lowly Paris sewer worker in love with a prostitute, played by Simone Simon. They decide to marry, but before the wedding can take place, the First World War breaks out, and he goes off to fight. His fiancée remains faithful, and he returns from the war blind but to a better life.

Although it had been a huge success as a silent movie, as a 'talkie' it bombed. Fortunately for Jim, MGM were still keen to develop their contract player, and put him into a major supporting role in *The Last Gangster* starring Edward G Robinson as the titular gangster who winds up in Alcatraz. Jim was a newspaperman (one of many he was to play during his career) who marries the gangster's ex-wife, played by Rose Stradner. Jim's recollection of the film was, 'I didn't have much to do . . . and they made me wear an *awful* moustache . . . but it created a friendship with Eddie Robinson which I treasured.'

Legendary producer-director Cecil B DeMille hosted the prestigious *Lux* radio programme which featured radio versions of current movies, although not always featuring the actors from the original films. It was, however, common for up-and-coming film actors to appear in such radio plays, and in June 1937, Jim made his *Lux* debut in *Madame X*, based on MGM's current film version.

CBS also produced movie-based plays in their *Silver Theatre* programme which aired every Sunday afternoon, and Jim appeared in a number of those. But what MGM wanted was its own radio show to promote its own films as plays, and so it created *Good News* for NBC, sponsored by Maxwell House coffee. The programme was launched in November 1937, and James Stewart was chosen by MGM as its regular host. Metro snared its audience by promising that every one of its major stars would appear on the *Good News* programme – except for Garbo, who refused to have anything to do with it. 'I guess doing those radio shows was what made my voice recognisable in millions of homes across America,' said Jim. 'I realised this when everyone seemed to start doing imitations of me. Most of them were just *terrible* . . . but one or two were *better* than me.'

Jim's last film of 1937 was *Navy Blue and Gold*, a flag-waving light drama about the Annapolis Naval Academy. Jim, who had once dreamed of joining the Academy, now had the chance to pretend to be a naval recruit, along with Robert Young and Tom Brown. Young was the top-billed star but Jim had the central role of a cadet whose father had been dishonourably discharged from the Navy.

The *New York Tribune* noted that although Stewart 'has been denied Robert Young's beauty and has been endowed with none of the strong, silent intensity of Gary Cooper, he breathes life into his character. It is due to his expert rendition of a rather preposterous part that a rather preposterous show becomes generally exciting.' *Variety* thought it 'expertly made and sure box office', and it helped to secure Jim's place as an increasingly popular star at MGM.

Most people associate Hollywood with glamour, and it becomes difficult to accept that people like James Stewart were mere mortals trying to survive in an often destructive industry. Ask him, as I did, if it was a glamorous life, and he'd reply, 'I never knew exactly what glamour was. I think it was all developed by the publicity people and by the idea that the number of theatres in the country were growing all the time and the attendance was going up and the interest in movies . . . I think all that had to do with what they call glamour.'

While the studio publicity departments had the important task of getting good coverage in the newspapers for all their stars, they had another equally important job: to keep the trouble some stars got themselves into from ever getting into print. 'It's true,' Jim said, 'that they protected you if you were unlucky enough to get into any scrapes.' When I asked him if he got into any such scrapes, he thought for a while – a *long* while – and finally replied, very slowly:

'There was one time when . . . waall, I was seeing an actress who was . . . very amorous. And I was a hometown kinda guy and hadn't quite figured out how these people . . . my father always called them *bohemians* . . . got their kicks. And it turned out this gal who became a big star had a little habit. Waall, actually, it was a *big* habit. She liked to sniff a little something and then have a roll in the hay. You know what a roll in the hay is, I take it . . . [I assured him I did know.] Waall, we went out a couple of times and we had fun . . . and then she asked me to try some of this stuff . . . and I didn't want anything to do with that kind of thing, so I declined, and she got kinda mad and threatened to have me fired from the studio, and I thought that would be the end of my career.

'It turned out some photographer had pictures of the two of us together at some shindig, and he had discovered she was taking coke . . . I guess that's what it was. Don't know if they still have the stuff. Anyway . . . when she told Mayer to fire me, he showed her the photos and said he was either going to have to pay off the cameraman to keep the story out of print, or fire *her* . . . and he'd have to fire me too because the photo implicated me in her habit. So Mayer told her either Jimmy Stewart stays and he'll make the story go away or he'll just have to fire the *both* of us.

'Of course, she was looking out only for herself . . . but Mr Mayer knew what he was doing. He called me to his office . . . and I didn't know him very well because I was only a contract player and didn't have much reason to go before the boss of the studio . . . and he told me what had happened and that this actress no longer wanted me fired. He said he'd paid to have her particular problem go away and he made me understand how close I'd come to having my own scandal.

'Of course, the photos were just a tool used by an unscrupulous reporter to make money, and he could be sure that as well as being well paid, he could be sure of getting some kind of scoop from the studio in the future. It was the deal in those days. And so I wasn't exposed as a drug taker . . . and that was about the closest I ever came to a scandal.'

Jim did, however, enjoy a rather full social life during his early years in Hollywood. Joshua Logan said, 'Everyone gets this idea of Jim as this golly-gee guy who lived like a monk until he met Gloria. Well, I'm telling you, Jim was one of the most enthusiastic guys I ever met when it came to women and living life. I would say, though, that he was influenced a lot by Fonda. Every Saturday and Sunday they were on the town.'

Fonda conceded that he and Jim spent every weekend looking for 'a good time. We did the rounds of places like the Trocadero where Jim liked to hear the big bands – Glenn Miller, for instance, played there – and Ciro's and the Cocoanut Grove. And, oh yeah, there were a lot of young actresses who were also looking for a good time. When you were a contract player, which Jim and I were, there were a lot of contract actresses you got to know.'

Around the time Jim arrived in Hollywood in 1935, so did Benjamin 'Bugsy' Siegel. He was a killer from New York, where he worked for Mafia boss Charles 'Lucky' Luciano. Siegel was sent to Hollywood to set up various rackets, including prostitution, illegal gambling and taking over the film extras' union. Siegel had a good friend in the motion-picture business. Actor George Raft had worked for the Mob in New York during his pre-Hollywood days, and through Raft, Bugsy easily established himself. He liked to mix with the stars while extorting money from the big studios. Nobody dared to offend Siegel; he was known as 'Bugsy' because anyone who bugged him was likely to wind up dead. But Jimmy Stewart didn't share the cautious approach to Siegel that others – Cary Grant for instance – took. Gloria said, in 1979:

'Bugsy Siegel had a thing for Jean Harlow. Jim was very fond of Harlow. They had had a bit of a fling, and Siegel wanted his fling with Harlow. But Jean wasn't having any of it. One day Siegel came to Jim and said, "Jean's a good friend of yours. How about you tell her to go out with me." And Jim was furious and said – and you just don't say things like this to Bugsy Siegel – "Why don't you go to hell?" Jim told me he thought Siegel would pull a gun on him there and then. Jim was terrified but didn't show it. He towered over Siegel and just stood there glaring down at him.

'Siegel suddenly smiled and said, "Look, you've had your turn with Jean. What have you got to lose?" And Jim said, "My temper. And believe me, you don't want to see *that*." Well, he knew he wasn't frightening Bugsy Siegel, but Jim thought that Siegel respected him for standing up to him. At least, that's the only reason he can think of for not winding up dead. Jim had quite a run-in with the gangsters who were scamming Hollywood.

'The big difference between Jim and Siegel is that Siegel *liked* his violent side. It's what turned him on. Jim is the opposite. He *hates* the feeling of not being in control, and anger is very hard to control. He says, "Anger leads to dangerous situations." Jim doesn't enjoy danger. Flying his plane is not something that Jim finds dangerous. Driving a car, yes – flying, no! [Jim was, according to his own and Gloria's accounts, a terrible driver.]

'Jim had to get used to using guns as a cowboy star. But as a young man he *hated* guns because he hated the danger they posed. It wasn't something he was taught – it was something he discovered for himself when he nearly killed one of his friends with a gun. He had a hunting rifle, and had been out hunting with his friend Hall [Blair], and back at Hall's house, Jim cleaned his rifle and it somehow went off. Jim never quite understood how it happened, but the bullet only just missed Hall's head, and that shook Jim up as much as it did Hall. Jim put that gun away and didn't pick up another gun for years. He said that if he couldn't control such a dangerous thing as a rifle, he didn't want to have any contact with it.

'So, you see, while someone like Bugsy Siegel lived for danger and violence, Jim controlled his violence because he feared its consequences. But let me tell you, you don't ever want to make Jim mad because if he does get mad, it's a frightening thing to see. Duke Wayne used to josh him about it because Duke would get mad at people and bawl them out. He'd say, "Come on, Jim, embrace your anger. Get mad. It feels good to get it off your chest." You know what Duke was like: he'd try and provoke Jim, saying, "Come on, Jimbo, get mad at me." And Jim would back away, putting on a bit of an act, saying, "Waall, Dook, ya know . . . if I . . . er . . . get riled up at ya . . . waall, I'm afraid I won't be able to stop until I . . . uh . . . *kill ya!*" And Jim made it into a joke. But I'm not so sure it wasn't true. Thank God we've never had to find out if it was.'

As Bugsy Siegel integrated himself more into Hollywood social life, the more charming he became, and the more threatening he seemed. As Gloria told it, when Jim told Cary Grant to stop rubbing shoulders with Siegel, Grant said, 'Look, Jim, the guy's best pal is George Raft, and George says if Benny wants you to be his friend, you *be* his friend.' After a time, Grant felt he wasn't even in any danger as he got caught up in Siegel's circle of friends. One of those friends was Countess Dorothy di Frasso, the daughter of a New York millionaire who married Italy's Count Dentice di Frasso, a close acquaintance of Mussolini. Cary Grant had an affair with the Countess, as did Gary Cooper who was also rubbing shoulders with Siegel.

'Jim begged Coop and Grant to break off from Siegel, but they seemed to like his company,' said Gloria. 'For film stars, who were just about the most glamorous people in the world, the only people who could be remotely more glamorous were royalty and big-time gangsters.' The Countess was a part of Italian royalty, Siegel was the Mafia's top man in Hollywood, and the friendship of the Countess and Siegel and the associations that the likes of Gary Cooper and Cary Grant had with the both of them reinforced a rather unsavoury circle which Stewart wanted nothing to do with.

Men like Bugsy Siegel got their way in Hollywood using terror. There were violent acts performed by the Mafia, such as strike-busting or breaking legs, but the Mob's greatest tool was fear. Henry Fonda said that he summed up the Mafia's code of terror in the film *Once Upon a Time in the West* when he said the line, 'Men scare better when they're dying.' The Mafia would kill someone so that someone else would be scared enough to do what they were told. But James Stewart just refused to be terrorised, and that was a situation Bugsy Siegel didn't know how to handle. On more than one occasion, Bugsy got so psychotic that George Raft physically prevented him from going off to shoot Jim, and then had to use his wits to prevent *himself* from being killed by Siegel.

Gloria said, 'More than a few times Jim had a run-in with Siegel, who never gave up trying to make it with Jean Harlow. Siegel was jealous of Jim's friendship with Jean. I think he saw Jim as being one of the few men in Hollywood who'd had the love of Harlow, and it – well – bugged him.'

So why did Siegel never kill Stewart? Part of the answer, Gloria felt, is that Jim refused to be intimidated by Siegel, and Bugsy wasn't used to people standing up to him. 'It kind of sidelined him,' said Gloria. 'Siegel was successful because he terrorised people, but he just didn't get anywhere with Jim.' Cary Grant told Jim that he'd begged Siegel to leave Jim alone. Jim simply replied, 'You just better watch out for yourself, Cary. You're in so deep, you're in far greater danger than I am.' On at least one occasion, George Raft said to Jim, 'Let me talk to Benny. Try and calm him down.' Jim just said, 'If Siegel wants to try his luck with me, let him take his best shot.' Raft got frantic and said, 'If he takes his best shot, it'll be the last shot you hear.'

Gloria said, 'Even Hank [Fonda] told me that he'd told Jim to ease up on his criticism of Siegel. It's not that Jim was going around mouthing off to anyone and everyone. But he never stopped telling Coop and Cary to stop being in Siegel's company, because Cooper and Grant were two of Jim's best friends, and he was worried about them.

'So Siegel came to Jim – and Bugsy was really quite charming, the way Jim told it – and he said, "Look, Jim . . ." And Jim said, "It's *Mr Stewart* to you." And so Siegel said, "Look, *Jim*, if you don't stop bad mouthing me, I'll have to do something about it." And Jim like a fool said, "Then go right ahead, Mr Siegel." A lot of stars and producers and movie heads had been threatened by gangsters from New York and Chicago, but no one had actually been killed – except Thelma Todd.' (Todd was a popular comedy actress who married one of Lucky Luciano's Hollywood agents, had an affair with Luciano and wound up dead. Officially, her death remains unsolved, but it was an open secret in Hollywood that she was murdered by the Mafia.)

What really surprised Jim was when Siegel turned up for Jean Harlow's funeral, after she died of uraemic poisoning, aged twenty-six, in 1937. Jim saw Siegel weeping. Siegel told him, 'I really was fond of Jean.' Jim answered, 'I'm sorry for your loss. But it doesn't change my opinion of you. And if I ever get the chance, I'll see to it that you and your kind are driven out of this town.'

According to Gloria, when George Raft heard about this, 'he nearly had a heart attack. Raft went to Jim and said, "Jesus, Jim, cool it with Benny, will ya?" Jim just said, "His time is limited . . . and so is yours."'

Raft had considerable influence with the Mob. James Cagney and the Screen Actors Guild were doing what they could to drive the Mob out of Hollywood, but when Raft learned that some of Chicago's top mobsters were planning to kill Cagney, he was able to prevent it simply by having a word with Siegel. Cagney always credited Raft with having saved his life, but Jimmy Stewart wanted no such favours. Because Jim didn't like Bugsy Siegel, he avoided Raft, 'even though Jim actually thought Raft was a pretty nice fella,' said Gloria. 'I can only put Jim's survival down to sheer bloody-mindedness and knowing that he could be powerfully dangerous himself when aroused to anger. Jim told Cary Grant, "That so-and-so Siegel is in just as much danger from me." I'm relieved we never found out if that was true, but I think it's just possible that it was Jim's belligerence that kept him safe.

Maybe Bugsy Siegel never wanted to find out how dangerous Jim could be.'

This doesn't completely answer how it was that Siegel didn't have Jim killed, since it was usually the Mafia's method to send hitmen to do the job. But it seems likely that, following the murder of Thelma Todd, even Bugsy Siegel didn't really want another high profile Hollywood murder by the Mafia. In fact, the next such murder would be Siegel's own assassination by the Mob in 1947. There wouldn't be another such killing until the death of Marilyn Monroe in 1962.

All Jim ever said about Hollywood's gangsters was, 'To me, those men were cowards. When they made threats, you had to stand up to them because if you were weak . . . that was what they wanted – weakness. I wasn't taught to be weak in the face of any kind of evil.'

The feud between Jim and Bugsy Siegel continued for many years, leading to Jim's active involvement in crime-busting as a secret agent for the FBI.

8

What Shall We Do With Jimmy Stewart?

With regular work and a regular salary, Jim could afford to enjoy his social life. Along with Fonda, Joshua Logan and Johnny Swope, who was working as an assistant director, he was enjoying a hectic whirl of partying. 'We were like the Four Musketeers,' said Logan. 'But despite the fact we were all close friends, there was a bond between Stewart and Fonda which was stronger than anything the four of us ever had as a group.'

To the malicious gossipmongers of Hollywood, that bond between Stewart and Fonda was perceived as something more than mere male friendship. As Fonda recalled in 1976:

'We couldn't believe it when there were rumours that we were lovers, for God's sake! Anyone who knew us knew our sexual interests lay only in women – and plenty of them. I don't have a problem with homosexuals. A lot of guys in the business have hidden their homosexuality because it would damage their careers. You've heard the rumours about some of the men who were homosexual or bisexual. Well, there's some truth in some of those rumours. And frankly I couldn't care less – or not much, anyway – if people want to accuse me because I reckon I've got enough marriages behind me to make me secure enough not to let those accusations bother me. But Jim . . ! Those things really hurt him. He's a religious guy – and so conservative it almost offends my liberal soul. The very notion of Jim being a homosexual just embarrasses the hell out of him because it goes against his beliefs in every way.

'But he doesn't judge those who are homosexual. He's really a very non-judgemental kind of guy, and that's because he knows that he's not the perfect man. He doesn't pretend to be. When he was a young fella, he played the field . . . just like the rest of us did. I'd even say that he played the field even harder to dispel the rumours that we were a couple of homosexuals. I didn't try any harder – I was always doing the best I could! But Jim put that little bit more extra effort into it!'

It seemed to some, including Joshua Logan, that Jim was 'playing the field' with 'considerable enthusiasm' since arriving in Hollywood: 'It was my impression that Jim's womanising – which is what it was, however you try to tie it all up with a pretty ribbon – was due to the fact that he loved [Margaret] Sullavan and knew it was never going to lead to anything,' said Logan. 'So he saw just about every contract actress in town – like he was just doing everything he could to get over her. He never did, of course, but he gave it his best shot, with Fonda's help. People know about the sexual exploits of housemates Errol Flynn and David Niven, but I can assure you that Fonda and Stewart were just as dynamic. They just weren't the big stars Flynn and Niven were – not at that time. And Flynn and Niven made careers out of boasting about their sexual conquests. Fonda and Stewart never did, which is why it always comes as a surprise to people when they hear about it.'

Fonda was not shy in 1976 in admitting that he and Jim had 'a whole lotta fun with the girls. Jim was always such a nice guy, the girls couldn't help liking him. I always had to watch out because a girl might be with me one minute, and the next she's taken a liking to Jim. And he never seemed to do anything to encourage it. I said to him once, "For Christ's sake, will you stop stealing my girls." And he said, "Gee, Hank, I'm sorry, but I don't steal them. Ya see . . . they steal *me*." I never could get mad at him for it.'

At first, all of Jim's female companions were contract players, hoping, like him, to find greater success. During the first few months of 1937, Jim's social life shifted into a higher gear when Norma Shearer, the Queen of the MGM lot, decided he would be her lover. Although she had recently been widowed by the death of Metro's 'boy wonder' Irving Thalberg, she was, said Joshua Logan, 'wasting little time mourning when there were so many young men at the studio. Jimmy Stewart was six years her junior when he met her at a costume party at Marion Davies' house. Well, Jimmy had been knocking back a fair bit, and coming out of his Pennsylvanian shell through an alcohol-induced haze. When he saw Shearer, he went up to her and, with his eyes blazing, told her, "You are the most beautiful creature I have ever seen."

'In that single boozed-up moment, he had lit up her desire for him, and she regally took possession of him. By the time he had sobered up, it was too late. He was Norma Shearer's lover, and while the loving bit delighted him, what he didn't like was being shown around town in her yellow limousine like a prized possession. You'd see him slump down in his seat in the hope none of his friends would recognise him. She gave him a cigarette case studded with diamonds so that whenever she asked him for a cigarette in front of others, the gift demonstrated that he belonged to her.'

As Jim recalled:

'I did see a lot of Norma Shearer . . . for a while. I'm not sure L B [Mayer] was too happy because she was such a big star and I was still only a small-time actor. He'd rather she was seen on the arm of Clark Gable. Mayer never complained to me about this, but I heard there were . . . waall . . . certain grumblings.

'The way Josh Logan tells it, I was a subdued kind of possession of hers. Well, that's what she wanted me to be. She gave me a diamond cigarette case and she'd ask me for a cigarette, so when I got the case out, she'd say, "Just a little thing I bought for Jim." Which meant she'd bought Jim. Well, Jim wasn't playing her game and so when she asked me for a cigarette, I'd fumble around in all my pockets, saying "Now where'd I put those cigarettes?" and finally I'd pull out a crumpled packet of Lucky Strikes.

"Now I'm not saying I didn't have fun when I was with Norma . . . by golly, I sure had *some* fun! But I didn't want to settle into any serious relationship. I just couldn't be blunt about it, because I was not brought up to be impolite to ladies . . . so I just kept giving her crumpled Lucky Strikes and I did everything to *hint* that I was not her possession. I was also having a good time with pals like Hank Fonda and Johnny Swope, and a lot of those good times were spent in the company of . . . er . . . various ladies. Finally Norma got the message and very graciously released me. I say "graciously" because she made it seem she was bestowing some benign blessing upon me by giving me my freedom.'

Jim had a more enjoyable and less intense affair with Ginger Rogers. The union, according to Joshua Logan, was instigated by Ginger's mother, Lela. Said Logan:

'Lela Rogers worked in the RKO publicity office, and RKO was where Ginger was making all those fabulous musicals with Fred Astaire. RKO had a new starlet, Lucille Ball, and Lela was working hard to raise her profile. At the same time, Ginger had separated from her husband, Lew Ayres, and Lela wanted something – or someone – to take Ginger's mind off her problems. So Lela hit on the idea of having Fonda and Stewart accompany Ginger and Lucille about town, which would certainly get some space in the papers for Lucille. Jim liked to dance, so he became the obvious choice of companion for Ginger, so Hank was stuck with Lucille.

'It all went well for all four for a while. They went dancing at the Trocadero and the Cocoanut Grove, and Ginger thought Jim was a great dancer – which he was. He could move that long, lanky body really well. Hank just didn't have the same sense of rhythm.

'One night they had dinner out, and then the boys took the girls back to their place. Ginger told me she and Lucille thought they were in for a night of exuberant love-making when the boys turned the lights down low. Suddenly, the boys hustled the girls into the kitchen to wash up a week's worth of dirty dishes.'

Fonda had a different version of that event: 'After dinner at a place called Barney's Beanery, which was on Santa Monica Boulevard, we took the girls back to our apartment, and Jim and I were all set for a good time, but Jim and Ginger decided to dance in and out of every room. Before I could say, "Jim, for God's sake, don't take her into the kitchen . . ." they were *in* the kitchen. And we had piles of plates we hadn't washed up for a week. That was too much for Ginger. She started washing up, and Lucille joined her. And we were very grateful. When they'd finished, we showed them *how* grateful we were.'

The pairing of Fonda and Ball was not to last. 'Lucille always put on too much make-up,' he said. 'One night she came out of the bathroom after spending God knows how long in there putting on her paint, and when she came out, I couldn't help but go, "Yuk! Oh Christ!" And Lucille walked out, and that was that. But Jim and Ginger – they had a good thing going.'

Once asked by gossip columnist Sheilah Graham if she was in love with Stewart, Rogers replied, 'If I'm not, I ought to be. He's the nicest man in Hollywood.'

One of MGM's top directors, Clarence Brown, had wanted to film *Of Human Hearts* for a long time. Based on Honore Morrow's story 'Benefits Forgot', it was a study of rural life featuring a somewhat tyrannical minister and his rebellious son who wants to escape his narrow world to become a surgeon. The young man heads for Baltimore to study medicine, taking it for granted that his mother will gladly sell all her possessions to fund his schooling, even after his father dies and she is left alone and in hardship. The Civil War breaks out and he is sent to the front lines to work in a field hospital. He callously ignores the many letters his mother writes until Abraham Lincoln himself summons him to berate him for his lack of gratitude towards his mother. Finally, the young man sits down to write a letter to his mother, and he is back on the road to redemption.

Walter Huston was perfect casting for the father, and Brown was convinced James Stewart would be ideal as the grown-up son (the younger version of the son was played by Gene Reynolds). MGM executives were not convinced that Stewart had the depth that the role called for, but Brown was adamant, and he got his way. Beulah Bondi played Jim's mother (not for the last time on screen).

The reviews were not good. 'Long on narrative and short on romance,' was *Variety*'s verdict, adding, 'Chief cause for disappointment with the film is its slow pace, and the defeatist mood of the story.' The film was not a success, but Jim was acknowledged as giving one of his finest performances to date. 'I enjoyed making that picture,' he said. 'It was the challenge I needed. I thought I didn't do too bad. The problem was, the studio still didn't know what to do with me. I could just imagine them pacing up and down in some executive office asking, "What shall we do with Jimmy Stewart?"'

It wasn't too surprising that Jim next found himself at RKO, starring with Ginger Rogers in *Vivacious Lady*. Said Gloria, 'Oh, Ginger really liked Jim, and she wanted him to be in a picture with her. And she got her way because she was a big star at RKO.' Stewart played a small-town professor of botany who goes to New York to try and persuade his playboy brother (played by James Ellison) to change his ways, and ends up in a nightclub where he meets singer Ginger Rogers. They fall in love, get married, but when he takes her home, he can't find the courage to announce her as his wife. Instead, he introduces her as somebody he just met on a train. His life becomes increasingly complicated until he finally finds the courage to tell the truth to his parents as well as to his now former fiancée (Frances Mercer). For the second time, Beulah Bondi played his mother, while Charles Coburn played his father.

The film was actually an attempt to prove that Rogers could carry a picture without Fred Astaire. But in choosing James Stewart as her co-star, she was only half carrying the picture, with Jim proving to be 'a priceless bit of casting', according to the *New York Times* when the film was released in 1938. The *New Yorker* said the film was 'a good-natured, unpretentious entertaining comedy', and *Variety* thought it 'entertainment of the highest order and broadest appeal'. The public thought so too, and the film was a smash hit.

Making *Vivacious Lady* gave Jim and Ginger a good excuse to pursue their romantic fling, but, filming over, their romance was complicated when the real love of Jim's life at that time, Margaret Sullavan, stepped in. Sullavan's latest husband, agent Leland Hayward (who was also now Jim's agent), had landed her a lucrative contract at Metro-Goldwyn-Mayer. She won the starring role in *The Shopworn Angel* when Joan Crawford refused to do it. Producer Joseph L Mankiewicz had worked with Sullavan the year before, in *Three Comrades*, and thought her ideal to replace Crawford. When Sullavan insisted that Mankiewicz cast James Stewart opposite her, the producer agreed.

The Shopworn Angel was a remake of the 1928 part talkie, based on a play called *Private Pettigrew's Girl*, which in turn was inspired by a 1918 *Saturday Evening Post* story. Sullavan played a New York entertainer who receives minor injuries when she is knocked down by a car. The driver is a soldier (played by Stewart) who is about to go overseas to war. He, in turn, is smitten by her, pursues and woos her, and finally weds her. She convinces herself that by marrying him, he will somehow remain safe on the battlefields of Europe. He finally goes off to war, and while she is performing in a club one night, she gets word that he has been killed.

When released in 1938, critics were split over the film and the quality of Stewart's performance. *Variety* said, 'It is only occasional[ly] credible screen drama. Margaret Sullavan turns in a powerful performance [with] depth and eloquence. James Stewart is a natural enough rookie but there's little characterisation in his performance.'

However, the New York *Herald* thought the film 'boasts of two of the finest actors appearing on the screen today . . . [Sullavan] has invested scene after scene with eloquence and vigour. There is a quality to her voice and an authority in her every gesture. In much the same manner, James Stewart brings the Texas private to glowing life and keeps the characterisation solid and appealing, even when the script gives him little aid.'

Gloria, who was never jealous of Jim's relationship with Sullavan, said, 'Jim had two big plusses going for him in that [film]. And both were authentic. One was his lousy driving, and the second was his love for Margaret.

'Everyone knew that when Jim and Sullavan were going to appear on the screen, there'd be some kind of chemistry. I know, from what Jim told me, that she gave him more direction than the director [H C Potter] did, and he learned a little something more about screen acting every time he worked with her. But what really worked for him was that together they created chemistry – a lot like Tracy and Hepburn, only Tracy and Hepburn really did have a life-long love affair.'

Gloria believed that Stewart and Sullavan did consummate their love, but only at the beginning. 'Of course he loved the girl,' she said. '*All* the men fell in love with her. And she damn well knew it. She *used* men. But she never used Jim. Which is why I think she really loved him. When they fell in love, of course they had an affair. But when Jim knew that Fonda would be hurt by it, and when Sullavan kept getting married, he gave her up. Jim's no fool. He knew his friendship with Fonda was eternal, and if he married Sullavan, that would have been the end of his friendship with Hank. And he knew that if he and Sullavan got together and maybe got married, it would only end in acrimony, and that would be the end of his friendship with both Fonda *and* Sullavan. So he loved her from afar, and stayed friends with his two best pals . . . before he got me. Then I became his best pal.'

One of Jim's other great friends was film director Frank Capra – or, at least, he soon would be. He was one of Columbia's most important directors, making such successes for the studio as *It Happened One Night*, *Lost Horizon* and *Mr. Deeds Goes to Town*. Capra had seen a number of Jim's films and thought he would be perfect for a leading role in *You Can't Take It With You*, based on the Pulitzer Prize-winning play by George S Kaufman and Moss Hart. Columbia boss Harry Cohn agreed to Capra's demand that he borrow Stewart from MGM; Capra always got his way at Columbia because everything he did there during the 1930s resulted in big box office takings and thirteen Oscars in all.

Typical of Capra's work, the film was a wacky comedy with a somewhat serious philosophical message to it. It all centres around the Vanderhoff family, presided over by Lionel Barrymore as a former businessman who believes that the best things in life have nothing to do with what his money can buy. The screwy family under the one roof also consists of a daughter who wants to be a playwright and artist; a son-in-law trying to invent the perfect fire-cracker; a granddaughter who aspires to being a ballerina and her husband who plays the xylophone. There is another granddaughter, played by Jean Arthur, who is a secretary in love with her boss, played by Jimmy Stewart.

There is also an assortment of other oddball characters who are not related but all of whom have eccentric reasons to be in and out of the house. But the heart of the film, and the substance of much of its comedy, is the romance between Stewart and Jean Arthur.

Jim had fond memories of both Capra and Arthur. He said, 'Capra was not only a good director, but a fine fellow. We hit it off straight away and remained friends ever since.' In time, Capra would call on Stewart for help when he came under suspicion of being a Communist during the Hollywood witch-hunts of the McCarthy era.

As for Arthur, Jim said, 'Jean was an insecure kind of girl. She was just a marvellous actress . . . but she didn't seem to know it.' Capra was a little less gracious, though honest, when he recalled, 'Jean was always brilliant, first class – when she was on the set. The problem was trying to *get* her to the set. She wouldn't come out of the dressing room. She was convinced she could never somehow get out there and be any good. And yet she was good, day after day, scene after scene. I never saw her give a bad performance.'

Gloria recalled, 'I knew Jean a little. Because she was so insecure, some people have been unkind about her. But she suffered from anxiety – almost a phobia about acting. She was terrified she would mess it all up with one lousy performance and that would be her career over. Jim didn't see her anxiety as something to be criticised. He saw only her talent and did all he could to help her. He was still pretty green in movies, but he gave her encouragement and understanding. I don't think she ever got over her anxiety, but when they worked together he was so patient with her because once the cameras rolled, he knew she would be excellent. But it did tire him. There were days he came home from the studio and said, "I love Jean, and God knows I feel sorry that she's got this problem, but it sure wears you down dealing with it." I said, "Let Capra deal with it." He said, "But she's my screen partner. I want her to be comfortable with me. She has to know that I care." I still felt he should have let Capra do all the worrying, but that's Jim – he's just a decent guy from Indiana.'

Capra only ever had glowing things to say about Stewart, saying in 1980:

'On the one hand he was a regular guy. He liked to hang around and talk to the people on the set, but he never sought deep friendships.

If someone was to become his friend, then it just happened. He didn't seek friends. But he was friendly to everyone. And then often you'd see him go off on his own because he just wanted some quiet time to himself. I don't know what he was ever thinking about. I felt it would be an imposition to ask.

'The funny thing about Stewart is that he loves comic books. He'd sit there reading comics. I think his favourite was Flash Gordon. I thought it was so typical of Jim. He can be so serious about his work, he can lose himself in deep thought, but he can also be the kid he was in Indiana reading comic books.

'He's a good man, he is totally professional, and highly talented. People still think they know James Stewart because they think of a film like *It's a Wonderful Life*, and they say, "Yeah, that's what he's always like." I don't know why that is with Jim. With someone like John Wayne or Clark Gable you can say that and know it's pretty much true. But Jimmy Stewart played many kinds of characters. He *wasn't* always the same character, and I get mad every time someone says he was. It's true he has a certain charisma that is purely Jimmy Stewart – and I guess that's what people really mean when they say he's always the same – but he's a highly skilled actor with many layers.

'One of the best things about Jimmy Stewart, for me as a director, is that I don't have to argue with him or spend endless time trying to tell him what his motivation is. I simply say, "Look, Jim, it's like this . . . " and he'll say, "I got it," and then he does it. I only wish all actors were like that. So, after *You Can't Take It With You*, I always looked for another chance to work with him.'

Released in 1938, *You Can't Take It With You* was a big hit with audiences and most critics. It also won Oscars for Best Picture and Best Director, as well as nominations for Robert Riskin's screenplay, Joseph Walker's cinematography, and Spring Byington as Best Supporting Actress for her role as the daughter.

The films Stewart made through 1938 and into 1939 kept him constantly in work, and he was in such demand from other studios that he was often on loan-out. Straight after filming *You Can't Take It With You*, Stewart was again filming away from his home studio.

This time it was for David Selznick at United Artists, who co-starred him with Carole Lombard in the tearjerker *Made For Each Other*.

Stewart played a placid lawyer, meekly serving his demanding boss (played by Charles Coburn) and whose marriage (to Lombard) constantly bumps against the rocks. But when the couple's young son falls ill and serum has to be flown in at great cost, Stewart finds the courage to berate his boss and demand the money he needs. The story becomes a race against time as Stewart and Lombard anxiously wait while the pilot delivering the serum battles a terrible storm that threatens to crash his plane.

The film was a departure for Lombard from the wise-cracking comedies she usually made. On set, her legendary use of four-letter expletives remained vivid in Jim's memory. He said, 'Carole Lombard could swear like no other woman I ever knew. Other women swear . . . but Carole did it . . . like a *lady*. I don't much like to hear women swear . . . I find it kind of embarrassing. But with Lombard . . . she was the only girl I've known who can let out a stream of four-letter words and not embarrass you . . . because she did it in a *lady*like way.'

He was back at MGM for *The Ice Follies of 1939* (filmed in 1938 for release in 1939). Intended as a musical extravaganza on ice, the film top-billed Joan Crawford as a singing ice-skating star who lands a film contract, while her skater-choreographer husband, played by Stewart, attempts to produce a major ice show. Their work separates them until Crawford decides to put her marriage before her career. Happily, in the great Hollywood tradition, Stewart's ice show is turned into a film and Crawford is the star of it. The film flopped, partly because Crawford couldn't sing – four of her six songs were dropped from the film – and neither Crawford nor Stewart could ice dance well enough to be convincing. MGM, it seemed, were still asking, 'What shall we do with Jimmy Stewart?'

Next, he appeared in the screwball comedy *It's a Wonderful World*, as a novice private eye convicted of a murder he didn't commit and escaping custody. With help from a zany poetess played by Claudette Colbert, he sets out to solve the murder. It was filmed in just twelve days by director Woody 'One Take' Van Dyke, who had also directed Jim in *Rose Marie* and *After the Thin Man*.

In just four years, Stewart had co-starred with such leading ladies as Jean Harlow, Joan Crawford, Margaret Sullavan, Ginger Rogers, Jean Arthur, Eleanor Powell and Claudette Colbert. His popularity among audiences had grown, and although he was not in the same league as Clark Gable or Robert Taylor, by 1939 he had risen to become a popular star at the Metro-Goldwyn-Mayer studio. But he was always second-billed to the leading lady, and his own studio was still uncertain quite what to do with him to make him a top-league movie star.

It fell to Frank Capra at Columbia Studios to give him the role that would make him into one of the major players in Hollywood. The film was *Mr. Smith Goes to Washington*.

9

Star Status

'What I really wanted to do at the time was make a picture about Chopin,' Frank Capra told me in 1980. 'So I went to see Harry Cohn and told him, and he looked at me and said, "Forget it. Give me another *Mr. Deeds*!"

'I said, "I've already made *Mr. Deeds*."

'So I stormed out of the office, swearing I'd never make another film as long as I lived, and was in my office at the studio, preparing to move out when a writer called Sam Briskin came in and said, "I'd heard you had a row with Harry Cohn." He had a two-page outline in his hand, and he said, "Take a look at this."

'It was called *The Man From Montana*. I said, "This sounds like a goddamn Western." He said, "Just read it." I said, "Forget it. I'm leaving."

'Then I read it. It was about an honest young senator who exposes corruption in the senate and tries to prevent a bill going through by delivering a 24-hour speech – what we call a "filibuster".

'I told my secretary to stop packing my things, went to see Sam and said, "You're so goddamn right. This story is better than *Mr. Deeds Goes to Town*. We'll call it *Mr. Smith Goes to Washington*, and we'll cast Gary Cooper in the part.

'When I went back to Cohn with this, he was so relieved I'd forgotten about making the life of Chopin, he gave the green light on *Mr. Smith* there and then. I was all set for casting Cooper in the role when I started to think about Jimmy Stewart. There were a lot of film parts that were right for both Cooper *and* Stewart; they were both kind of folksy in their own ways. Both were perfect to play Mr Smith. But Stewart was younger, which made him better for the part than Cooper. He still looked like a country kid. He had strong principles of his own, and they would spill over on to the screen. I felt that in many ways, Mr Smith was James Stewart. I also felt that, considering the filibuster scene, Stewart was better equipped technically as an actor.'

In October 1938, Capra and his screenwriter, Sidney Buchman, went to Washington in preparation for the writing of *Mr. Smith Goes to Washington*. While he was there Capra was surprised to receive an invitation from J Edgar Hoover to visit the FBI. Among other things, Capra was taken to the FBI pistol range and had a go at firing a Thompson sub-machine gun. A photograph of this event was personally sent to Capra by Hoover. Capra had no idea that Hoover was virtually spying on him – Capra would find that out in due course, and seek help from Jimmy Stewart.

Jim talked about Frank Capra as being 'his favourite director'. (He also used to refer to Anthony Mann as one of his two favourite directors, but the rift that would come in 1957 put an end to that.) Said Jim:

'Capra always did a lot of coverage on any scene. He'd do take after take, from just about every conceivable angle. He always wanted to get the very best he could on film.

'One day he offered me a lift home in his car, and on the way asked me if I'd like to take a look at the day's rushes. He had his own screening room at his house. Waall, I never went to see any rushes because I hated to see this young, gangling guy on the screen and I was always convinced that one day the public might feel the same way . . . so I thought that if I avoided seeing me, somehow no one else would notice what *I* always saw. But I didn't want to offend Capra, so I agreed. Waall, I was there watching rushes for about two hours. There was every single shot from that day – take after take, from every angle.

'The next day he asked me again to come and see the day's rushes and I couldn't say no. I was sitting there watching the rushes for three hours, and still they hadn't ended. And then I noticed Capra had fallen asleep. I didn't dare leave without telling him, and I didn't dare wake him. So I had to sit through the rushes, which was just *painful* for me. At the end, he woke up, and I said, "Frank, I got to be honest with you. I *hate* watching these things. I appreciate you inviting me to watch them with you, but I just don't want to see any more."

'I thought he would get mad and give me a hard time about it, but he said, "Why didn't you say something before? Of course you don't have to watch the rushes." So I never watched them again.'

Capra had cast Jean Arthur to star opposite Jim, but according to Capra, Jim was so absorbed in his work that he didn't have as much time to devote to the actress as she would have liked. 'He was working hard to get everything right, and Jean felt that he should have paid more attention to her neuroses. She spent a lot of time in her dressing room throwing up because she was more insecure than ever. Or maybe she just wanted Jimmy's attention. She never really spoke kindly about him for a long time after that.' After *Mr. Smith*, Jean Arthur's career quickly wound down. She made seven more films up to 1944 when Columbia released her from her contract, then made only *A Foreign Affair* in 1948 and her last, *Shane*, in 1953.

Portraying Mr Smith presented Jim with some of his biggest challenges:

'The biggest problem I had was getting the right quality in my voice for the filibuster. Mr Smith talks for twenty-four hours, and after a while he gets a sore throat and his voice becomes hoarse. I practised a kind of coarse rasp, and when Capra heard it, he said, "Jim, that's just awful. You're supposed to have a sore throat, but you sound just like an actor trying to put on a voice with a rasp." I said, "That's exactly the position I find myself in." He said, "Well, keep trying. You've got to do the scene better than that."

'This really had me worried. So I went to see an ear, nose and throat doctor, and asked him if there was anything that would give me a sore throat. He looked kinda surprised, since folk usually want him to help them get *rid* of a sore throat and there I was asking him to *give* me a sore throat. He said, "Do you realise it's taken me twenty-five years of hard study and practice to cure sore throats?" I said, "Doc, I really need to have a sore throat. I'm in a movie and I have to *have* a sore throat, and I need to *sound* like I have a sore throat." He said, "All Hollywood folk are kinda crazy, but *you* take the cake. Okay, I'll give you the sorest throat you've ever had, but don't complain when it hurts like hell." I assured him I wouldn't, so he put some dichloride of mercury into my throat – just a drop – and he had to put it near my vocal cords without putting it on my vocal cords. He said, "How's that?" I could hardly speak and when I said, "How does it sound?" it came out like a really bad rasp – a *real* rasp. And he said, "You got it, all right."

'The doctor was quite glad of my business in the end because I hired him to come on to the set and supervise me and keep my throat sore. And so when you see the filibuster scene, you'll know I've really got a sore throat.'

When released in 1939, *Mr. Smith Goes to Washington* received rave reviews and won Jim his best personal notices to date. *Newsweek* wrote, 'With the exception of a few sorties into the extra-callow, James Stewart gives the most persuasive characterisation of his career as a home-made crusader against political corruption.' The *Nation* was so impressed with Stewart, it said, 'Now he is mature and gives a difficult part, with many nuances, moments of tragicomic impact. And he is able to do more than play isolated scenes effectively. He shows the strength of his character through experience. In the end he is so forceful that his victory is thoroughly credible.' The *New York Times* thought Stewart's Mr Smith was 'a joy for this season, if not forever'.

Jim was rewarded for his pains in delivering his finest performance so far with the New York Film Critics Award. He was also nominated for an Oscar but lost to Robert Donat for *Goodbye, Mr. Chips.*

The film's good reviews may well have saved it from getting

shelved amid a torrent of political backlash. Jim told me, 'I never really thought of it at the time we were making it, but it was a touchy subject. It was premiered in Washington and all the Senate were there, and Congressmen . . . and half of them walked out. Even in those days they didn't like the idea that there could be corruption in high places.'

Democrat James Byrnes accused Capra of betraying everything that was sacred to America. Joseph Kennedy, US ambassador to Great Britain, warned Harry Cohn and Columbia that the film would be viewed by Europeans as Nazi propaganda. Such was the concern in Hollywood that they would suffer a severe backlash from the Senate that the big studios put around $2 million in a hat to pay Columbia to shelve the picture. But Cohn stood firm and refused to ban the picture. Besides all the political fuss, it was already on its way to becoming a hit, due to the good notices and excellent response from preview audiences. The politicians might not have liked *Mr. Smith Goes to Washington*, but the rest of America did, and it was a huge success. In consequence, James Stewart was now a major force in Hollywood. He had achieved star status.

At MGM, Jim had played just about every kind of part there is to play – except a cowboy. That radical idea came from Universal, who acquired him on loan-out for their Western *Destry Rides Again*. The picture was directed by George Marshall, a veteran of many cowboy sagas.

In 1939, when *Destry Rides Again* was filmed, most Westerns were B-features, aimed at unsophisticated audiences who wanted action but didn't care too much about quality. But that year a mere handful of Westerns gave the genre respectability, including two from John Ford – *Stagecoach* and *Drums Along the Mohawk* – Michael Curtiz's *Dodge City*, Henry King's *Jesse James* and Cecil B DeMille's *Union Pacific*.

What made *Destry Rides Again* different to the run-of-the-mill B-Westerns was that this was a lusty spoof, tailor-made for sultry Marlene Dietrich. Her career was actually in the doldrums, and she needed a picture to give her popularity a much-needed boost. Producer Joe Pasternak came up with the idea of starring Dietrich in a sexy Western romp; her salary was just $75,000, a sixth of her usual at her home studio, Paramount.

Jim recalled that Pasternak had his personal reasons for casting Dietrich in *Destry Rides Again*: 'Joe Pasternak had a . . . er . . . fantasy about Dietrich singing "The Boys in the Backroom" . . . and he wanted to make it come true. He saw her as this bar-room girl in black stockings . . . singing a sort of "Lili Marlene" song. And he didn't just want her for the *film* . . . he wanted *her* . . . which she knew. He didn't get her.'

What Jim didn't explain was that the man who did get Dietrich was *him*. Burgess Meredith recalled, 'Oh, Dietrich wanted Jim as soon as she saw him. And men couldn't resist Marlene. She was not – how shall I put this – an *average* love-maker. She knew all kinds of tricks. So once she seduced a man, he was hers until she got bored with him.

'She knew how to play to a guy's weakness. One day Jim was in his dressing room and she locked him in and told him she was coming back with a surprise. She had found out that Jim loved reading comic books and he liked Flash Gordon. Marlene had gone to the props department and got them to make a life-size doll of Flash Gordon. Then she locked him in his dressing room and had the guys bring the Flash Gordon doll over, so when she opened the door for him, he saw this life-size Flash Gordon she'd had made for him – and he was hers.'

Away from the set, Jim and Dietrich spent evenings having dinner and, according to Meredith, 'making love at night, with Dietrich teaching him things he'd never dreamed of.' Jim never publicly admitted to having an affair with Dietrich, but in 1981 he told me, 'That was such a long time ago – in another lifetime. But, yeah, we had some fun together . . . nothing too serious . . . just horsing around.' Gloria said that she knew Jim and Dietrich had been 'a red-hot item'.

Dietrich, however, never referred to their affair in her memoir *Marlene Dietrich: My Life*, but a rumour sprang up that Dietrich had become pregnant by him and that he had insisted she have the child aborted. Burgess Meredith said, 'If you ask me, the person who began those rumours was Dietrich. I think she considered it an unpardonable sin when Jim told her it was over.'

Gloria never believed Jim had made Dietrich have an abortion. 'Nobody makes Dietrich do *anything* she doesn't want to do. And the very idea of an abortion is abhorrent to Jim. It just isn't a part of his belief.'

Just why Stewart parted company with Dietrich is something Meredith felt he had the answer to. 'She was bisexual and she liked the ladies as well as the men. I think Jim enjoyed the somewhat extreme sexual skills Dietrich had – at least, they were extreme by his standards – but when she tried to persuade him to have a girl-friend of hers joining them, he drew the line. And he finished it, and she couldn't forgive him for that. So I believe she came up with that rumour, but nobody ever believed it. I mean, we're talking about Jimmy Stewart, for Christ's sake. Besides, what Jim didn't know at the time was that while she was seeing him, she was also having a relationship with Erich Maria Remarque [the author of *All Quiet on the Western Front*]. I know she was *The Blue Angel* and all that, but she was no angel.'

Jim was always very complimentary about Dietrich's professional relationship with him on the set: 'I thought by then I knew pretty much all there was to know about acting for film . . . but then she catches me doing something. She said, "When the camera is shooting over my shoulder and it's on you, you tend to look at me in one eye and then the other. The camera picks this up and magnifies it, so your eyes are flicking from left to right and left again." I said, "But that's what happens in real life. You can't look in both eyes at the same time. You switch your focus from one eye to the other." She said, "Yes, but when caught on camera, it's distracting. To hold the audience, look into just one eye – doesn't matter if it's the left or the right eye – just *one* eye." And she was right, and I've done that ever since.'

Jim was aware that he was not the producer's first choice to play Destry:

'Pasternak didn't actually want me for the film. He wanted Gary Cooper. I think I came cheaper than Coop . . . so . . . I got the part. Coop was to have played a man who rides into town looking to avenge the death of his father. When Pasternak got me, he didn't think I could play a part like that so he made my character someone who becomes a deputy in this wide-open town but who doesn't believe in wearing a gun. But finally he has to put on his gun . . . and that kind of paved the way for *Shane*, I always felt. And that idea kind of appealed to me. I thought that this made for a different kind of Western.

'The audience of course found it hard to remember me in the film because of the famous saloon brawl between Dietrich and Una Merkel. I remember when we shot the scene. Those gals really gave each other hell . . . and they seemed to . . . uh . . . enjoy it. They were slugging it out and kicking each other, and I just thought that someone was going to get hurt. But they had such fun, it was fun to watch. The fight ends when I have to pour water over them – a *whole* bucket of water. You'd be surprised just how much water there is in a bucket. The director George Marshall had me throw bucket after bucket over them, in long shot, in close-up. I just had the most fun pouring buckets of water over those two girls. And when *Life* magazine did a story on the film, they wanted a shot of me pouring water over Dietrich and Merkel for the cover, so I got to do it all over again. The critics didn't realise it back then, but it was really a satire on the kind of Western Tom Mix used to make.'

Destry Rides Again won Stewart critical acclaim when released in 1940, with Bosley Crowther of the *New York Times* calling his performance 'a masterpiece of underplaying in a deliberately sardonic vein – the freshest, most offbeat characterisation that this popular actor ever played. It was, in my mind, even better than the rampant young senator [in *Mr. Smith Goes to Washington*].' *Time* magazine thought Stewart 'turns in as good a performance or better [than *Mr. Smith*]'.

Despite the praise, and the success, Jim's own studio's executives seemed mystified that he should have been cast in a Western; it had certainly never occurred to them that he could be a cowboy-type. Jim said, 'They [MGM] felt justified in thinking I couldn't play a cowboy because after *Destry* was released, I got letters from Western fans saying that I got it all wrong as a Western sheriff. They said I wasn't tough enough. But hardly anybody at that time was making Westerns for . . . audiences with insight. They were all B-movies with the good guys chasing the bad guys, and they all looked the same and had the same actors and the same sets. *Destry Rides Again* appealed to a much broader audience.'

It was that broader audience that made James Stewart into one of the biggest stars MGM now had. However, it would take a little longer for fans of cowboy films to accept James Stewart as a major Western star alongside the likes of John Wayne and Gary Cooper.

MGM did, however, have the sense to cast him with Margaret Sullavan in *The Shop Around the Corner*. The idea to pair the two actually came from Ernst Lubitsch, who produced and directed the film. The story was set in a gift shop where the head clerk, played by Stewart, keeps the business running smoothly. In search of romance, he finds a female pen pal, played by Margaret Sullavan. Because of the Christmas rush, the shop advertises for a new salesperson, and Sullavan duly applies for the job. But when she is interviewed by Stewart, he rejects her application, although the shop's manager (played by Frank Morgan) overturns his decision and she is hired. Unaware that they are lovers by correspondence, Stewart and Sullavan dislike each other intensely. Much of the film's comedy thus centres around the pen pals' attempts to meet up, finding they only succeed in coming face to face and arguing. The film cleverly exploited the chemistry between Stewart and Sullavan as two people who seem to loathe each other yet find they are really in love.

Said Gloria, 'Margaret had recently had a child, and Jim was dating a lot of other women. Lubitsch knew that by casting Jim and Margaret, they would have the chemistry that was always there between them on the screen, but their private lives would provide a certain amount of detachment which the story required them to have. And he was right. Margaret was always very good at saying and doing things to make people mad, and she was even able to get Jim mad.' Stewart commented:

'I never could be angry with Margaret for long, even though she said and did a lot of things that riled a lot of other people. We had a scene in a restaurant, and I had a line, "I will go out on the street and I will roll my trousers up to my knees." Waall, I just couldn't say the line right, and she got really mad at me. I was standing there with my trousers rolled up to my knees, and I hated doing it because

I had skinny legs and I felt so awkward, so I couldn't say the line right. Margaret said, "This is just ridiculous. Say the line, for God's sake." I got mad back and said, "I don't want to do this scene today. They should have given the part to some other fellow who's got decent legs. I just don't want to do this scene any more today."

'She said, "Are you refusing to work?"

'I said, "Yes," and she said, "Then I refuse to do the picture." Waall, that stopped me in my tracks . . . I could feel her anger aimed directly at me. I said, "I changed my mind. Let's do the scene." So we got it done.

'You never quite knew what she might do when the cameras rolled, and that made the work so *interesting*. It wasn't that she did anything really *big*. It was always the little things. You'd do a scene and she might just say a word or two differently to before, or she'd do something with her eyes, like give you a look she never did in rehearsal. And although they were just small things, with her they were *major* because it made all the difference to a scene, and a camera would pick up those little nuances, and that's partly what made her so good.

'She also hated too much dialogue. Some days she'd say, "We're talking too much and we don't need all these words to show the audience what we mean. We can do it with a look." Getting the right look from me was important to her. She liked to do little things when the camera was only on me; like she'd stick her tongue out at me while I was trying to remember my lines and trying to get the emotion right . . . and I'd get really mad . . . which was exactly the right emotion. She made all the difference . . . like getting me to smile a certain way. Now I can smile with the best of them, but she would just look at me all kind of soft and gooey . . . and I'd give exactly the right smile. And if I gave her the wrong look, even though she might not be in the shot, she'd say, "Stop right there. What the hell are you doing? You're not making me feel the way I'm supposed to feel." And I'd say, "You're not even in the shot so how's anybody gonna know?" And she'd say, "*I'll* know." And then I'd just crack up with laughing.'

When released in 1940, the film garnered good reviews. *Variety* thought that the film generated 'humour and human interest from what might appear to be unimportant situations', and added that 'it carries further to impress via the outstanding characterisations by Margaret Sullavan and James Stewart.' The film continued to win over critics in ensuing years, and in 1978 the *New Yorker* called it 'one of the most beautifully acted and paced romantic comedies ever made in this country'.

Stewart and Sullavan were teamed again in *The Mortal Storm*, filmed in 1939 and released in 1940. With the Second World War now raging in Europe and America still keeping out of the conflict, Hollywood studios made a number of films that aimed to show its sympathy for the beleaguered Allied forces and disdain for the Nazi party. However, MGM tried to disguise its criticism of the Nazis by setting *The Mortal Storm* 'somewhere in Europe', even though the story is clearly set in Germany. The story centred on a family headed by a biology professor (played by Frank Morgan). The family is split between those who support Hitler and those who don't. When Stewart, as a suitor to the professor's daughter (Margaret Sullavan), helps a Jewish professor to escape over the Alps, he becomes an outlaw. When Sullavan becomes an enemy of the Nazis, Stewart tries to lead her to safety, but she is shot and killed.

Of the film, Stewart said, 'It was clearly anti-Nazi, and the director [Frank Borzage] only made a meagre effort to disguise the fact. In fact, it was so obvious that a representative from Germany told Metro that after the war was won by Germany, they would not forget our picture. Actually, at the time it looked like they *would* win the war because France was just about to fall. But Borzage, Margaret, myself and some others said we didn't give a damn about the threats. Robert Young had his concerns, though. He had a wife and kids to think about. Fortunately, nothing happened to Bob or his family, and it may be that I and some of the others who didn't take the threat seriously were just too naïve to realise that had Germany won the war, we would have been in *big* trouble . . . just for making a motion picture. I figure in the end, that was an example of the fight for freedom that the war was about.'

MGM exploited the casting of Stewart and Sullavan, declaring *The Mortal Storm* to be 'the love story of today with the popular sweethearts from *The Shop Around the Corner*'. But the chemistry that *The Shop Around the Corner* had relied on was swamped by the darker elements of this film's story, and critics and public alike were less enthusiastic about this film than they had been about the former. The New York *Herald Tribune* found it to be 'dated and romantically distorted', although of Stewart it said, 'he acts with such intense sincerity that the personal tragedy which is the core of the piece is the most satisfying note in the proceedings'.

Jim recalled, 'I guess not all the critics liked that picture . . . especially Josef Goebbels, who disliked what we had to say about the Nazis and banned all MGM films from being shown in Germany. And because we kinda upset Mr Goebbels, I guess the film was something of a success.'

10

An Oscar and a Commission

In 1939, most Americans did not consider that the war raging in Europe had anything to do with them. Jim was thinking differently. His first active involvement in the war was to invest in what would become a flying school set up by Leland Hayward, Jack Connelly (an engineering inspector for the Civil Aeronautics Authority) and Johnny Swope. It was in response to a move by General 'Hap' Arnold of the United States Army to prepare its Air Force in case of war. He encouraged civilian aviators to set up flying schools that could, if war came, be used as instruction centres for the Air Force.

Hayward, Connelly and Swope persuaded Jim, and a number of other stars including Henry Fonda and Cary Grant, to invest in their Southwest Airways corporation. They purchased the Sky Harbour Air Service in Phoenix, Arizona, transforming it into Thunderbird Field.

'I just felt that the war would inevitably involve America,' said Jim, 'and it was important to prepare places where the Air Force could train its pilots, because there simply weren't the facilities to train them. Our Air Force at that time was inferior to many other countries' air forces. So I made an investment, and it took a long time to make any profit from it, but that wasn't the idea in the first place. The profit was in what the facility achieved, which was the training of thousands of pilots. We set up two more facilities, Thunderbird Field II and Falcon Field. Pilots from the Allied countries came to those places to train. It was a valuable enterprise, and I was proud to be a part of it.'

Before 1939 came to a close, Stewart found himself being traded by MGM to Warner Brothers in exchange for Olivia de Havilland. MGM needed de Havilland for David Selznick's *Gone With the Wind*, and Warners, to whom Miss de Havilland was under contract, accepted Stewart as fair trade, casting him in the romantic comedy *No Time For Comedy*, based on S N Behrman's hit Broadway play.

Jim played a successful playwright who scribes a succession of comedies for his actress wife, played by Rosalind Russell. But he finds that his talent for comedy seems to be on the wane. He gets involved with a flirty socialite (Genevieve Tobin), coming to the conclusion he must write a socially significant drama. After a series of romantic confusions, his marriage survives and so does his talent for writing hit comedies.

The film was popular with the public when it was released in 1940, but many of the critics couldn't resist using its title to sum up their feelings about it. However, the film was successful enough to merit a reissue several years later, though with the title changed to *Guy With a Grin*.

Some time after Olivia de Havilland and James Stewart were traded by their respective studios, the two stars became a romantic item. Burgess Meredith, who was now sharing the Brentwood bachelor pad, recalled:

'For Jim, Olivia looked like being the real thing. I am sure they were in love, although both liked to pretend that they were only playing the game. Olivia played the game really well. Whenever a reporter asked if she would marry Jim, she said that she would, but in such a way that it sounded like she was being frivolous. Jim never refuted the claims, and I know that he did once ask her to marry him, but again he didn't seem too sincere about it, and they both laughed at the idea. But I am sure that behind the frivolity, there was a love that was growing.

'I think she was more enthusiastic about him than he was about her. I think he was afraid to fall in love with an actress because he knew such a relationship, if it developed into matrimony, wouldn't work. So he kept a kind of distance emotionally. He was the same, I would say, with all his girlfriends. He liked to show them a good time, but they were never the most important things in his life. His work was more important. I think that was his safety net. If he wouldn't give them a hundred per cent of his time and his interest, then things would never get too serious.

'But the biggest thing that prevented Jim from giving all his love to one woman at that time was Margaret Sullavan. He would never admit it, but he *still* loved her, even though he knew he would never have her.'

James Stewart had enjoyed one of his biggest successes with *Destry Rides Again*, which had only been made to halt the decline of Marlene Dietrich's career. In 1940 he was about to receive an even bigger success, thanks to the declining career of another great actress, Katharine Hepburn.

Hepburn was a shrewd businesswoman who decided to do something about her career doldrums by acquiring the rights to the highly successful play *The Philadelphia Story*, and then selling the rights to the highest bidder. This turned out to be MGM.

The story told of a society wedding between Tracy Lord and George Kittredge. Her ex-husband, C K Dexter Haven, still loves her, yet when he discovers that a magazine is going to publish a scandalous article about Tracy's estranged father, he gallantly steps in and makes a deal with the editor, arranging for a reporter and a photographer to cover the high-society wedding. Emotions get mixed and situations confused, and finally Tracy remarries Dexter.

Hepburn maintained a position of authority over the production by having casting approval, and the first piece of casting was herself, as Tracy Lord. She wanted Spencer Tracy and Clark Gable for the roles of the reporter and ex-husband, but she happily settled for James Stewart and Cary Grant.

Jim recalled, 'When I read the script, I took it for granted that I was being offered the part of the fella who's gonna marry Katharine Hepburn. I kept thinking, "The reporter is a much more interesting role. You know, if only I had that part." But I was okay about playing the other guy until I was told, "But you *are* playing the reporter." That for me was the best part. It was even better than the part Cary Grant had.' Grant knew his role was a lesser one, but he accepted it because he was promised top billing as well as the highest salary, $137,500. He donated his entire fee to the British War Relief Fund.

Jim dispelled the long-held notion that the film's director, George Cukor, was mainly 'an actresses' director': 'Cukor could direct *any* actor. He let you know what he wanted but he also allowed you to be free. Cary Grant and I had a little scene where we're talking, and somehow we got off the script but we carried right on . . . just ad-libbing but staying in character . . . and Cukor kept right on filming and he was so pleased with the results that he used that take in the finished film.' Of Hepburn, he said:

'I loved working with Katharine. She was fun . . . but she was very serious about the film. She was almost the producer, and when I had to do a scene in a bathing suit . . . waall, I just told Katharine that I looked ridiculous in a bathing suit because my legs were just so . . . *thin*. She said, "Show me your legs," and she said it with such authority that I hoisted my pants up until she could see my knees . . . and she took one look and said, "You're right. Those are just the *worst* legs I've ever seen." And so she talked Cukor into letting me do the scene in a bathrobe.

'She was pretty good at giving orders. One night . . . it was a Friday . . . just as we were finishing for the day, she said, "I want to come flying with you tomorrow. I'll meet you at Clover Field at eight o'clock." So I got there in the morning . . . and she was waiting. And from the time I started the engine, she was asking about everything . . . so I was trying to answer all her questions. I'd got the engine started and she hollered, "Wait! The oil gauge is below the red?" So I told her, "That's the way it always works." And she said, "But the oil shouldn't be below the red marker." And I said, "But Kate, it *always* works this way." And she kept on about it, so I just let the engine run a bit longer. As we were taxiing she started hollering, "The oil still isn't on red." I said, "Don't worry about it." Then she said, "Make sure you reach the right speed before you lift off," and I said, "Don't *worry*, Kate. *I'd* like to survive this takeoff too." She just kept hollering orders at me as we climbed higher.

'I decided to take her up to Saugus, and as I was about to turn, she said, "Don't turn!" So I climbed to five hundred feet, then eight hundred, and I got to a thousand feet, and was just starting to turn when she said, "No, don't turn!" And when I tried to turn again she still hollered, "Don't turn!" I said, "Kate, if we don't turn we'll be in China!" So she said, "All right, you can turn."

'I said, "I thought we'd go up to Saugus," and she said, "The oil gauge is still below the red. I want to go back." So I turned around and headed for Clover Field, and I circled as we lost altitude . . . and all the time she was telling me what to do and what not to do . . . and I knew she wasn't taking her eyes off the oil gauge. When we landed . . . waall, it wasn't really a landing – more like a controlled *crash* – she said, "Thank you," very curtly, and climbed out of the plane, went straight to her car and drove off . . . and she never mentioned flying to me ever again.'

In September 1940, Congress passed a bill calling for the annual drafting of 900,000 men between the ages of twenty and thirty-six. Two of MGM's biggest stars, James Stewart and Robert Montgomery, immediately announced to Louis B Mayer that they were enlisting.

'Mayer just couldn't understand it,' said Jim. 'He said, "You don't have to enlist. Wait until they draft you, and then we'll get you both exempt." He promised me that there would be a whole array of pictures that would be better than any I'd been in before. He promised me just about anything and everything to get me to change my mind. I told him that I had no intention of applying for exemption and that I would be volunteering. The fact was, by then any intelligent person knew that America would be pulled into the war. It was a global conflict. How could we not get involved?'

Henry Fonda recalled, 'Jim came from a family who never shirked their responsibilities when their country was at war, and he wasn't going to be the first Stewart to shirk. So he didn't want the studio to bail him out. That's just the way Jim is.'

Before Jim attempted to enlist, he and Olivia de Havilland went with Henry Fonda, Tyrone Power and several other celebrities to

Houston, in August 1940, to perform at a fundraiser in the Houston Coliseum on behalf of the British war effort. Fonda recalled, 'Jim and I had perfected a magic act to perform. I use the term "perfected" loosely, but it didn't matter when the tricks went wrong. We were just having a lot of fun and so was the audience. We came back for an encore and I played the cornet as well as I could and Jim had his trusty accordion. We raised more than $100,000, so it was worthwhile.'

In November 1940, Stewart had his Army physical, but he was turned down because he was ten pounds under the required weight for a man of his height, according to the War Department's standard.

'Jim was just devastated when they turned him down,' said Burgess Meredith. 'I told him that if all he needed was another ten pounds, then all he had to do was eat a high-fat diet. What made things worse was the fact that the press had discovered his rejection and they were splashing embarrassing headlines all over the place about being a movie hero who was too lightweight for Uncle Sam. That just really destroyed him.'

Jim recalled how his father telephoned him in response to reading one of those headlines. 'Dad called and said, "I'm coming out to Hollywood. I'll punch a few of those reporters' noses. We'll start law suits against them." I said, "Dad, that won't help at all. You can't treat the press that way. It'll only make things worse." He said, "Then we'll hire a public-relations man. I'll get the best in the business." I said, "No, Dad. Just leave well alone." Of course, my father was just letting me know in his way that he was on my side. It was his way of saying, "You've got nothing to be ashamed of, son." And I appreciated that.'

He took Meredith's advice and ate two pasta dishes a day, along with anything else he could manage. 'He stuck at this for four months,' said Meredith, 'and I could see that he looked heavier.' But Stewart maintained that his eating regime didn't put on an ounce.

The Philadelphia Story was premiered at the Radio City Music Hall in the autumn of 1940 to rave reviews. The New York *Herald Tribune* said, 'Stewart contributes most of the comedy. His reaction to a snobbish society built on wealth is a delight to watch. In addition, he contributes some of the most irresistible romantic moments to the proceedings.' The *Hollywood Reporter* announced, 'There are just not enough superlatives sufficiently to appreciate this show.' Released nationwide in December, *The Philadelphia Story* continued to rake in the profits wherever it was shown. Word began to trickle throughout Hollywood that the film would be heading for Oscar success.

Jim made three films in quick succession during the final weeks of 1940 and into January of 1941: *Come Live With Me* and *Ziegfeld Girl* for his home studio MGM, and *Pot o' Gold* for United Artists. All were released in quick succession in 1941.

In *Come Live With Me*, Stewart played a struggling writer who meets an attractive immigrant, played by Hedy Lamarr, who has fled from her Nazi-occupied country. So that she can become a US citizen, he agrees to marry her in exchange for a weekly payment. He also gets inspired to write a novel about his situation which he sends to a publisher, not knowing that his new wife is the publisher's mistress. By the end of the film, she has fallen out of love with the publisher and in love with her husband.

Ziegfeld Girl was an extravagant musical, with the drama being directed by Robert Z Leonard and the musical numbers by Busby Berkeley. It featured a trio of the studio's top female stars, Judy Garland, Lana Turner and Hedy Lamarr. Stewart had what was virtually a supporting role, as Lana Turner's boyfriend, but he received top billing because he had become such a major star. The film was one of MGM's biggest successes of 1941.

In *Pot o' Gold*, Jim played a music store manager who, with the assistance of Paulette Goddard, helps a struggling band to success on the radio. The film was, in Stewart's opinion, 'easily the worst film I ever made'. He said, 'I just couldn't bring myself to watch that picture until 1950 when I was staying at a hotel in New York. I turned on the television, and there was this *awful* film.'

Ziegfeld Girl and *Pot o' Gold* were filmed simultaneously. Jim recalled, 'That was a kind of mad time. I would be working on one film in the morning, and another in the afternoon. I never knew where I was. One day I turned up at MGM to find that Lana Turner's character had died. I said to the director, "You'll have to remind me. Did *I* kill Lana?"'

Jim was delighted when he learned that he had been nominated for an Oscar for *The Philadelphia Story*, but he didn't expect to win: 'The funny thing is I never thought my performance in that picture was all *that* good. I knew my performance in *Mr. Smith* was better. And I knew that Fonda's performance in *The Grapes of Wrath* was better than mine in *Philadelphia Story*. In fact, I voted for Hank, and I told him so a week or so before the awards.'

Fonda said to Jim, 'You're going to win it.'

Jim replied, 'No, can't see how. I guess people just think I'm good at playing newspapermen.'

'One thing's for sure,' said Fonda. 'I won't be there. You know how I feel about all that Oscar crap. It's not the losing that I mind. It's the "*Oh no, not him*" gasps when you win. So I'm leaving town until it's all over.'

'Where are you going?'

'Sailing off with John Ford. Down to Mexico. Get some fishing in.'

'I don't want to go to the awards either. I was kind of embarrassed last year. And I've got two pictures on the go at Metro so I'm awfully busy. I wish I wasn't working so I could come fishing with you. Waall, have a good trip, Hank.'

Jim told me, 'So I made up my mind not to go. Then, later, I got a call from some guy at the Motion Picture Academy, saying "Will you be coming to the ceremony?" I said, "Waall, I'm really busy at the studio and . . ." He said, "Look, I'm just checking on all the nominees, Mr. Stewart. But I do hope that you *can* make it. I really think you would find it in your *best interests* to *attend*."

'That kinda baffled me because that year was the year the Academy worked really hard to make sure all the results were kept a secret. That was the year they introduced sealed envelopes with the names of the winners inside. *Nobody* was supposed to know who had won which award. So I couldn't figure if this guy knew something and was making sure I'd be there, or whether he was just making sure all the nominees were there. But it seemed to me he was maybe trying to tell me something. I never did know. But I decided I'd better go to the awards . . . and just as well.'

It *was* just as well because at the Oscars ceremony, on 27 February 1941, he was named Best Actor. The only other Oscar the film won was for its screenplay by Donald Ogden Stewart. Katharine Hepburn lost to Jim's ex-girlfriend, Ginger Rogers, for *Kitty Foyle*, a part that Hepburn had turned down. However, ultimately, Hepburn in *The Philadelphia Story* is better remembered than Ginger Rogers in *Kitty Foyle*.

Fonda sent Jim a telegram to congratulate him. Back in Indiana, Alex had heard the news and telephoned his son. Jim recalled, 'My father said, "I hear you won some kind of prize. What kind of prize?" I said, "It's called a Best Actor Award. They give 'em out every year. I won it this year for *The Philadelphia Story*. Have you seen that yet?" He said, "Never mind about that. What does your prize look like?" I said, "It's a statuette of a man with a sword. It looks like gold, but isn't. It's called an Oscar." "Well," he said, "whatever they call it, send it over so I can put it on show in the store." And so I sent it to my father, and the Oscar was on show in the hardware store in a glass case.'

A few days after winning the Oscar, Stewart reported for a second physical. 'Bill Grady drove me from the studio. I just walked right up to the officer in charge and said, "Why don't you just run a whole test on me and forget to weigh me?" He said, "But that would be irregular." So I told him, "Wars are irregular, too. But there's a war coming, sure as hell." And the officer gave me the test and didn't weigh me. I walked – no, I *ran* – outside, saw Bill sitting in his car, and I just shouted, "I'm in! I'm in!"'

Louis B Mayer took another stab at trying to talk Stewart out of enlisting. Jim recalled:

'Mayer was just so desperate to say something that would keep me from enlisting. He even said that America would never be caught up in the war. He told me, "You're just giving up this wonderful screen career you've made for yourself, and all you'll be doing is sitting at some clerk's desk on a military base somewhere, and then you'll regret what you're doing." I said, "Mr Mayer, this country's conscience is bigger than all the studios in Hollywood put together, and the time will come when we'll *have* to fight." After some hour or so arguing the point with me, he threw up his hands and said, "You're just a bull-headed fella from Philadelphia." I didn't want to correct him and say I was from

Pennsylvania, so I just said, "Mr Mayer, you better believe it."

'The next thing he did was announce a big going-away party for me, and every star at the studio was summoned to be there. I knew it was a big publicity stunt – and I was right – because he had the publicity department put out the story that Metro-Goldwyn-Mayer was proud to have one of its biggest stars enlist in the Air Force.

'That was one *big* party. And most of the stars who were there came because they *wanted* to be there to say goodbye, not because they were told to. There were a lot of actors there, some of whom I only knew casually and had never worked with, but they all wanted to toast me with words of encouragement and even some with a certain amount of patriotic fervour. I could tell who were the actors who would also enlist when the time came.

'Clark Gable came up to me and said, "You know you're throwing away your career, don't you?" I said, "Yep, I know." He said, "You won't catch me doing that, but I wish you Godspeed." Waall . . . Gable may not have intended to enlist, but when his wife Carole [Lombard] was killed in a plane crash while touring to raise bonds for the war effort, he didn't waste a second enlisting in the Air Force . . . and he didn't put himself out of harm's way. He was right in the thick of it, on American bombers . . . getting shot at. He risked his life. So please don't tell me *I'm* the only one who risked everything.

'Rosalind Russell was there. She took out a handkerchief and wiped every bit of lipstick on my face that had been planted there by all the actresses. She gently rubbed off each little red stain, and under each one she wrote the name of the actress the stain belonged to. I carried that handkerchief with me for the rest of the war . . . as a good luck token.'

He realised he needed all the luck he could muster when, just a few days before reporting for duty, he ended up in hospital. Burgess Meredith recalled, 'Jim was flying in his little plane [a Stinson 105] when his engine started to stall. He made a forced landing, but came down with such a bump he was battered about and only just managed to stay conscious. I went to see him in hospital where he stayed for a day or two. He had a bump on his head the size of a baseball and there were cuts on his face, but he was sitting up and smiling. I said, "Jim, are you sure you can survive a war? You have trouble just surviving in your own plane." He said, "It isn't a matter of surviving. It's a matter of doing the right thing." I never could tell if he was frightened or not. He didn't wear his heart on his sleeve.'

James Stewart reported for duty on 22 March 1941. The pick-up point was the Pacific Electric Company. Burgess Meredith was there to see him off: 'There were all the guys who were to be inducted, and Jim was happy to lose himself in the crowd. There were fathers and mothers and brothers and sisters in their hundreds, crying and cheering, as well as hundreds of students from UCLA all wearing World War I German helmets and mocking the Nazis with songs and signs. It was like a carnival or the opening of a big Saturday college football game.'

Jim climbed aboard the bus along with the other recruits, and was transported to an induction centre in Los Angeles where he became Private James Stewart. News cameramen and photographers, sent by MGM's publicity department, captured every moment. Jim smiled for the cameras but was embarrassed to have his celebrity status exploited. 'I could tell that all the other guys felt they should kind of keep their distance from me,' he said. 'I was suddenly the loneliest private in the world. I wanted to be just one of the fellas.

'At least there were no photographers at Fort McArthur where we were posted. The first time we had a mail call, the sergeant lined us all up, and gave us our letters one by one, so if you had ten letters, you had to march up to him ten times. Most guys had four or five letters, but I had – oh, I dunno – a whole *lot* of letters from fans which the studio insisted on forwarding to me. So I was marching back and forth to the sergeant . . . and I just stuck out like a sore thumb. But I made a point of making jokes about it to whichever fella I found myself standing in line with . . . like "Another tax bill from Uncle Sam" or "Got a letter here from a cousin in Europe who says the Germans are peeing in their pants 'cos they heard us Yanks might be coming." And that helped the other guys to relax around me, and pretty soon we were all just enlisted men facing an uncertain future.'

After five days at Fort McArthur, Private Stewart was assigned to the Army Air Corps unit at Moffett Field. When news filtered through to the outside world about James Stewart's location, hordes of female fans and press photographers descended upon Moffett Field hoping for a chance to glimpse the film star in uniform. To avoid them, Jim decided to remain in camp for the first few weeks, declining every overnight pass. Meanwhile his fellow recruits took every opportunity offered to them to get away out of camp, often leaving Jim very much on his own.

'It was a kind of mass hysteria,' he said. 'I guess it had to do with someone famous being in uniform. One fella there said to me, "You can't give up your overnight pass with all those girls out there waiting for you. You can have any one of them." I said, "One girl would be okay. But there are a hundred of 'em . . . and I wouldn't give good odds on my getting out *alive*." So I just stayed on post for weeks until the fuss had died down and everyone forgot about me.' Or so he had thought.

Within weeks, Stewart was promoted to corporal and given the task of drill instruction. Within just a few months he was listed as an aviation officer candidate. However, neither the public nor MGM had forgotten about James Stewart, and a barrage of requests for interviews with Jim landed on the desk of the commanding officer. When Jim insisted he didn't want to be interviewed, his commanding officer declared a ban to all members of the media.

Jim was not convinced he would be left alone, but he was – but only because the MGM publicity department began working over-time that summer of 1941, sending articles supposedly written by Stewart to magazines and newspapers. 'It was just embarrassing to have my name on articles writing about what it was like being a movie star having to live off a meagre salary and training for war,' he said. 'I tried to have it stopped, but it was in my contract that the publicity department could write anything they liked and put my name to it. It made me realise that when I came out of the Air Force, if I went back to being an actor, there would be some changes in my contract.

'There was one article I was supposed to have written in which I said that the topic of discussion in my barracks was whether Deanna Durbin's new husband was right for her or not. Of course, Deanna was a major star at MGM and the article was publicity for *her* . . . not that *she* had anything to do with it. Apparently I told my army pals that we can all be sure her husband was certainly worthy of her.'

Not everyone was fooled by the MGM press fodder. Ed Sullavan, writing in the New York *Daily Times* in August 1941, noted, 'If the Metro press department doesn't stop these floods of imbecilic, ghost-written letters from Jimmy Stewart, the war department will court martial him on the grounds of sabotage.'

The temptation to stray from the discipline of army life soon became too much for Jim, according to Burgess Meredith: 'Even a dedicated guy like Jim couldn't stay faithful to the military all the time. He started seeing an actress from MGM – Frances Robinson – and on his day and night passes, he spent his time *out* of uniform with the girl . . . by which I mean that he was wearing civilian clothes while off base. Mind you, "out of uniform" also meant out of *any* kind of clothing. He was a guy, for God's sake.

'The shit really hit the fan when his father came up from Indiana and found that his boy was wearing civilian clothes and running around with an actress. Alex wanted to know why Jim hadn't got a commission yet, and Jim made some lame excuse. The trouble was, he'd become somewhat unfocused. Alex shook Jim up quite a bit, and before too long, Jim stopped seeing Frances Robinson.'

Not that Stewart gave up girls altogether. He frequented the home of Leland Hayward and Margaret Sullavan whenever he had passes, and there he met singer Dinah Shore. Before long, Jim and Dinah were a couple, and it became clear to those who knew them best that the two were in love.

Despite giving his heart to Dinah, he still managed to refocus his energies on the Air Force. He fulfilled the academic requirements and passed a test flight, which earned him his wings and a promotion to second lieutenant. While he was waiting for his commission, due in January, the Japanese bombed Pearl Harbour on 7 December 1941, and America entered the war.

Now the War Department itself brought pressure to bear on James Stewart to use his celebrity status for the war effort. On 15 December, Jim joined Edward G Robinson, Walter Brennan, Orson Welles, Walter Huston, Lionel Barrymore and a host of other Hollywood stars in a radio programme. Broadcast on all networks, it was called *We Hold These Truths*, and celebrated the 150th anniversary of the Bill of Rights.

In January 1942, Jim received his commission. Expecting to concentrate all his efforts and energies into the Air Force, he was confounded when the War Department ordered him to make regular appearances over three months on a radio show with ventriloquist Edgar Bergen in which the dummy Charlie McCarthy displayed overt patriotism by signing up to all the branches of the American armed forces. 'That was just a total embarrassment for Jim,' said Burgess Meredith. 'All he wanted to do was his job in the Air Force, but he couldn't get away from being an actor. He began to wonder if the Air Force would actually allow him into combat. That really bothered him.'

It was his celebrity status that won him an invitation to the White House in January 1942, in honour of President Roosevelt's birthday. In February, he carried out one particular duty as a film star which he was honoured to do: he presented his friend Gary Cooper with an Oscar as Best Actor for his role in *Sergeant York*.

In March he was pressed into dramatic service again, for a radio play called *Letter at Midnight*. He played a soldier writing a letter to explain to the folks back home why it had been so important for him to enlist. A month later, he narrated a recruitment picture, *Winning Your Wings*, in which he had to tell the young men in the audience, 'Consider the effects these shining wings have on the gals.'

'I had to do a fair amount of morale-boosting stuff in documentaries and on radio,' said Jim, 'and while I knew it was necessary, I really was beginning to feel I'd never get off the ground as a pilot.'

In July, he was reunited with Cary Grant and Katharine Hepburn for a Lux Radio Theatre production of *The Philadelphia Story*, which had the ultimate goal of urging people to buy war bonds. Said Burgess Meredith, 'Jim was concerned that he really wouldn't get into the war, and he complained to me and to everyone, including Leland Hayward. So Hayward contacted General Kenneth McNaughton, who was involved in the Thunderbird Field project Hayward had going, and told him about Jim's complaint, and the General immediately had Jim reassigned.'

Seventeen months after his induction, Lieutenant James Stewart was relocated to Kirkland Field near Albuquerque in New Mexico to train bombardier pilots. 'I found, for the first time since I had put on my uniform, that I finally felt free of that part of me that was an actor,' said Jim. 'Most everyone still *knew* I was James Stewart of the movies . . . but they *had* to forget that, especially if I outranked them.

'The big problem I had for a long time was that I was older than most of my superiors . . . as well as a lot of the guys who had the same rank as me. That made me feel kind of old . . . and I was only thirty-four! Then I got to the point where I felt I was doing nothing but training pilots, while all I wanted to do was the job I was trained for . . . fly the bombers and . . . waall, just do the *job*. So I asked for a transfer.'

In December 1942, his transfer was accepted and he found himself in Hobbs Field, also in New Mexico, where he began training in earnest to pilot a Flying Fortress. 'Flying the bomber wasn't the problem for me,' he said. 'It was learning all the specifics of navigation I had trouble with because I never was any good at math. So I had to work harder than most everyone else. The young fellas . . . they could work out a navigational problem in just a few minutes . . . while it took me more than an *hour*.'

Despite his struggles, he passed all the required tests, and in February 1943 he was transferred to Salt Lake City with thirty other newly qualified pilots to receive their assignments to various air groups. 'When I graduated as a B-17 commander, I found myself being stranded in Salt Lake City while everyone I'd arrived with got their assignments.' He confronted his commanding officer and asked, 'What's the hold-up?'

When he was told to be patient, Jim delivered what could have been a passionate and angry monologue from one of his movies. 'I *know* what's going on. Someone is stopping me from getting into the war because they're afraid I might get killed and then someone's gonna hafta explain how they got James Stewart the *movie star* killed. Waall, I'm no better nor no worse than any other pilot you got. No, scratch that. I'm *better* than most any pilot you've got, and I want to do the job Uncle Sam's paying me to do. Everyone knows that the war in the Pacific is taking every pilot as soon as he can fly, and it's the same in Europe. And if anyone in the Air Force thinks the Japanese or the German air forces are gonna attack Idaho, they're crazy!'

His monologue had little effect other than to incur his commanding officer's wrath. 'If you talk that way to me again, I'll have you *demoted*,' the CO told him.

Jim recalled, 'Waall, I thought I'd made quite a speech but . . . I didn't seem to make much of an impression 'cos I found myself sitting around for a couple more weeks. I never knew if I would have been moved a little sooner if I hadn't blown my top at my commanding officer. Then I got assigned to the 29th Group at Gowen Field in Boise [in Idaho] and I just *knew* that the war wasn't being fought from Idaho.

'I was there for a week, and I got itchy again and complained to my commanding officer. He said, "All I know is, I got orders to classify you as 'static personnel'." That meant just how it sounded. I was *stuck* there. He said to me, "From now on, you're an instructor in first-phase training." I wanted to blow my top, but I knew that wasn't a good idea, so I kept my mouth shut and got on with my job.'

But, according to Burgess Meredith, he didn't keep his mouth completely shut: 'Jim told Leland Hayward to find out what or who was holding him back, and Hayward used his contacts and found that the Air Force simply had a problem about sending one of America's favourite movie actors off to war.'

With a squadron to train, Stewart soon discovered that his job in Idaho was not as cushy as he had expected. The winter snow made for hazardous conditions. He was devastated when his room-mate, who was also an instructor, was killed during a takeoff with a trainee pilot at the controls. 'You expect to lose friends and comrades in action,' he told me, 'but to lose someone in *training* . . . that kind of thing brought you up sharp and made you realise that things were gonna get a whole lot worse in combat . . . *if* I ever got into combat.'

While there was a certain amount of instruction Stewart could give on the ground, most of it could only be done in the air. 'To teach a pilot how to avoid crashing if any of the engines were knocked out, you had to be flying,' he told me. 'That's when I realised that giving instruction was not free of danger. I had a few near misses of my own.'

During one night's flight, Jim took the co-pilot's seat while a new flight commander took the controls. When the navigator asked to see how everything functioned in the cockpit, Jim allowed the navigator to take his co-pilot's seat. Suddenly, the No. 1 engine on the co-pilot's side exploded and the navigator was temporarily blinded by the flash. With the engine on fire, Jim fought in the cramped conditions to haul the navigator out of the co-pilot's seat so he could reach the No. 1 fire extinguisher selector valve. Putting out the fire and taking control of the bomber, Jim landed the craft safely.

But not every incident turned out so well. In one single week, Jim lost three members of his squadron. Barely able to talk about it, he said, 'We were fighting time and the snow, and you know that you've done your best . . . but there's always the nagging feeling you could've done *more*. You didn't have time to dwell on things that went badly.'

Jim would never boast about saving lives, but he confided to Gloria about how he averted a death on occasions. She told me:

'Jim saved himself and his men plenty of times. When talking about the war to me, he'd say "I was really saving my own skin," but I knew that he felt that the lives of the men he was instructing were his responsibility. When he lost men, he felt the weight of that responsibility heavier than ever. But a whole lot more of his men survived because Jim, who usually seems to go through life in slow motion, was as slick as oil when he flew. He'd take over the controls at the last second to avoid collisions that would have killed everyone on board. He always allowed the pilots he was training to try and get themselves out of trouble, and only when he knew, at the very last moment, that the pilot wasn't going to do the trick, Jim took the controls and made an almost instinctive manoeuvre to avoid tragedy. There might have been other instructors who would never have allowed their trainee pilots to get so close to the point of no return, but Jim said to me, "You *had* to give them every chance if they were going to have the best chance to survive in actual combat." And a lot of his boys *did* get themselves out of trouble at the last minute. I asked Jim, "Didn't you just want to take over the controls?" And he said, "I *wanted* to, but I knew I *couldn't*." He said, "I hope that some of the boys who got them-selves out of trouble lived longer in combat because of it."

'He knew he was sending these young men off to risk their lives, and he knew there was a high mortality rate among pilots and crew. But he had to put that out of his mind. His job was to try and give them a better chance to survive. When he had to allow his squadron to fly without him, he never left the field tower until every one of his planes had come home. There were some officers who watched the first few planes of their squadrons come back, and then those officers would leave the tower. But Jim stayed until every last man had returned.'

Although he concentrated his efforts on his job, Jim still had time for his romance with Dinah Shore, who managed to keep up with his various transfers. Sometimes she would stay at nearby hotels, or if Jim had more than just a few days leave, he would return to Los Angeles and stay with Leland Hayward and Margaret Sullavan and pursue his romance with Dinah Shore from there.

Just how serious his relationship with Shore became is some-thing Jim always remained teasingly mysterious about. Joshua Logan said, 'I heard that he [Jim] wanted to marry Dinah, but he always shrugged it off and said, "I was just kidding people 'cos they kept saying, 'When you gonna get married?'" I never did know what the truth was.'

Burgess Meredith felt he knew. 'Jim wanted to marry Dinah, and she seemed just as enthusiastic.' Gloria told me, 'If it wasn't for the war keeping Jim and Dinah Shore apart, I would never have become Jim's wife, so I'm glad the war kept him available for me.'

In fact, Jim felt that if he was never going to be sent into combat, he *would* marry Dinah. But if there was a chance he would be sent overseas, he had decided that the last thing he wanted was a wife worrying about whether her husband would ever come home alive. Said Gloria, 'Most people in love got married because the man wanted to make his girl his wife before the war separated them. But Jim had what he thought was a more pragmatic approach.'

Gloria said that years later, in his raconteur days, Jim told an obviously exaggerated story about how he and Dinah made up their mind to drive from Los Angeles to Las Vegas to tie the knot. 'But on route, Dinah started saying that at nine o'clock they would do such-and-such, and at eleven they would do so-and-so, and that the following morning they would go to some such place, and Jim decided that she had worked out their whole future in such minute detail that he just turned the car around and headed back to Los Angeles.' What Jim didn't know was that Dinah had been seeing actor George Montgomery. It seems she didn't know how to break the news to Jim.

In June 1943, he was allowed time back in Indiana for the wedding of his sister Virginia to a Russian designer, Alexis Alexander Tiranoff. Alexis was an outsider in many ways and, according to Gloria, he didn't stand a chance of being integrated into the Stewart clan. 'Jim, his father, the uncles, all called Alexis a lightweight. He was just a happy-go-lucky kind of fella who never knew where his next job was coming from, and Jim said that it was just typical of Ginnie to marry someone like that because of her dreamlike ways. Jim never considered that she was much like him in that respect.'

Alexis managed to distance himself further from the Stewarts when he and Ginnie had their first child, a daughter, who was promptly baptised into Alexis' Russian Orthodox religion and not into the Presbyterian faith. A second daughter also failed to make it on to the Presbyterian membership records. 'That was a cardinal sin to Jim's father,' said Gloria. 'Until the day Ginnie died, Alex always had a short fuse when it came to Alexis and Ginnie.'

Jim's other sister, Dotie, fared much better, in the eyes of her father. She was artistically gifted and admirably sensible; she was her father's idea of what a young lady should be like. 'She was also a very down-to-earth girl,' said Gloria. Keen to pursue art and illustration from an early age, she moved to New York during the Second World War and worked in the graphics department of *Mademoiselle* magazine. Some of her drawings were used as posters by the American Red Cross, and examples of such posters were to be found hanging all over Alex's hardware store.

In March 1944, she married one of Jim's former classmates from Princeton, Robert Moorehead Perry, who went on to teach at New York University and then became a Presbyterian minister. He was the perfect son-in-law as far as Alex was concerned. Their marriage produced four children.

11

Over There

By the summer of 1943, Jim had been promoted to captain. But, as Leland Hayward discovered, there was a feeling in the War Department that James Stewart should have felt satisfied with his rank and his achievements without ever having faced combat. However, his commanding officer at Gowen Field, Colonel 'Pop' Arnold, persuaded Colonel Robert Terrill of the 445th Bombardment Group (Heavy) in Sioux City, Iowa, to request that Captain Stewart be transferred to his group. So Jim next found himself in Sioux City, where he was appointed commander of the 703rd squadron, consisting of twenty B-24 Liberators. From Sioux City, there was only one place to go – Europe.

The night before he was to leave America, Jim met his father in Sioux City. 'I remember that parting well,' said Stewart.

'We were both afraid, but neither of us wanted to show it. So we talked about everything except the fact that I was leaving for Europe the next day. He always liked to feel that if I needed him, he'd be there, but from that morning until whenever, he wouldn't be able to be there. And I had always felt that I *needed* him whenever there was a crisis in my life . . . and there I was about to face the greatest danger . . . and I couldn't have him.

'When it was time to say goodbye, he just kind of stared at the ground and then up at the sky, and I knew he was struggling to find the right words . . . something that would be appropriate . . . to express how he felt about me and what advice he could give me. He seemed to start to say something because his mouth opened . . . and then it closed. Just snapped shut, almost in anger, because he didn't know what to say. So I just put my arms around him, and we embraced. Then . . . he didn't say a word but just turned around and walked away as quickly as he could.

[As Jim continued telling me this story, towards the end, his voice began to break.]

'As he disappeared from my sight, I discovered there was an envelope in my pocket. I waited until I got back to base before I opened it . . . and as I lay on my bunk, I opened the envelope and read it. I still remember it . . . word for word, because I kept that letter . . . Still have it. He said, "Dear Jim, after you have read this letter you'll be on your way to danger. I have enclosed a copy of the 91st Psalm and I am staking my faith in these words. I feel sure that God will lead you through danger. I don't know what else to say to you, son, but I continue to pray. God bless you and keep you. I love you more than . . . more than I can tell you. Goodbye, my dear. Dad." And . . . like I do now . . . I cried then.'

That was the first time Jim could remember Alex telling him that he loved him. Jim would read the 91st Psalm so many times, he eventually knew it by heart.

> *He that dwelleth in the secret place of the most High shall abide under the shadow of the Almighty. I will say of the Lord, he is my refuge and my fortress: my God; in him will I trust. Surely he shall deliver thee from the snare of the fowler, and from the noisome pestilence. He shall cover thee with his feathers, and under his wings shalt thou trust: his truth shall be thy shield and buckler. Thou shalt not be afraid for the terror by night; nor for the arrow that flieth by day.*

The next day, 11 November 1943, Stewart and his squadron of twenty B-24 Liberators took off for England.

'You can't just fly a B-24 to England from Iowa,' said Stewart. 'The B-24 just doesn't have the fuel capacity to make that trip in one go, so you go all over the place so you can refuel and hopefully not get caught by the enemy.' The route took Jim and his squadron via Florida, Puerto Rico, British Guyana, Brazil, Senegal and Morocco, stopping at each location to refuel.

The squadron finally reached its destination: the Allied air base at Tibenham, a village in Norfolk. 'On our arrival we were welcomed by Lord Haw-Haw [the Nazi propagandist] on the British radio. He knew we were there because he mentioned the 445th Bomber Group by name and said how the Luftwaffe would soon wipe us out.'

Jim was also greeted by a 'Dear John' letter from Dinah Shore. She told him she was going to marry George Montgomery. 'Jim didn't blame Dinah,' said Gloria. 'Even when he learned that she had been seeing Montgomery while she was seeing him, he seemed philosophical about it. He was upset about it, but he said, "I didn't marry her when I could have, and I guess Dinah wanted to be a wife." Typical Jim! Now and again you'd like him to get *mad*!' If Dinah Shore hoped for a husband who would stay home for the war, she was unlucky; George Montgomery also enlisted.

Jim's squadron had barely been allowed to settle into its new unit when it was sent to Northern Ireland to receive instruction from the RAF, which had the necessary experience in how to get hundreds of bombers into the air at the same time. 'Getting twenty bombers off the ground is no problem when you've practised it a hundred times,' said Jim. 'But there were times when we had a thousand bombers taking off from England and converging over the Atlantic, and you had to know *exactly* what you were doing, or you could bring a dozen of your own aircraft down.'

Back at Tibenham, Stewart's squadron didn't have long to wait for its first taste of real action. In December the 445th Group took off on its first mission. Its target was the naval base at Kiel, a harbour in north Germany. Jim recalled:

'A lot of the missions kind of blend into one, but I remember that first mission quite clearly. It was the first, and we were all terrified . . . although no one wanted to admit it or show it. I had a way of coping, which was to concentrate on all the technical stuff. You have to keep your mind occupied . . . to stop it from thinking of the fear. But the fear is always there . . . lurking in the mind . . . not in the back of your mind but at the front, like a curtain of fear which you have to keep pulling aside so you hope not to see it.

'My concern was to keep my squadron in one piece and to get the job done. Your first thought as squadron leader is for your own plane, but you also have to know what every other plane is doing. If just one of them gets out of formation, you're on to it, telling 'em to get back in formation.

'I tell ya, it was a peculiar sensation when we hit our target and got back to England in one piece. You want to feel kind of euphoric but you have to maintain some kind of control. I think a lot of my guys thought I was just plain aloof or brave . . . but I was no braver than the rest of 'em.'

Jim never liked to boast, but due largely to his leadership skills, his own crew didn't lose a single man on any of the twenty missions he led. Some of his airmen would be injured or wounded from enemy fire, but 'by some miracle', as Gloria put it, none of his crew lost their lives. In ensuing years, Gloria heard praise for her husband's leadership qualities from some of the men in his squadron. 'The men in Jim's squadron had such confidence in him that there was never a case of any man cracking up under the pressure. Hundreds of airmen suffered breakdowns, but none of Jim's men did. That says a lot about the kind of man Jim is.'

Jim recalled his plane's nickname. 'It was the Nine Yanks and a Jerk. You can try and figure out what connotations that may or may not have had! The name was already painted on when I got it, and I didn't bother changing it. I thought it might change our luck. We were kind of known as a *lucky* squadron, and I wanted it to stay that way.'

One of Jim's most vivid recollections was the British winter. Because Norfolk juts out into the sea and suffers from having both an east and a north coast, it is subject to the weather blowing down from the north and from the east. 'I'd never felt cold like it,' he said. 'It went right through you. It was a wet kind of cold. The fog was sometimes thick . . . and freezing . . . and wet. You just wanted the weather to clear and get back into the air . . . sometimes. Other times, you were glad when the fog was too thick to take off in. I wrote to my father about the weather, and he sent over boxes of vitamin pills. He also sent me several gunny sacks with plastic linings that I was able to fill with hot water and place around my bed.'

Gloria heard stories about how Jim would keep the spirits of his men up, sometimes by playing the piano in the officers' club. But Jim insisted that for the most part he purposely maintained a distance from the men under his command. 'When you're in command, you don't make friends of the men of lower ranks. That's not to be precious or anything about your rank. It's just the *practical* and *proper* way to run a command. You can't make the men you command into your friends. Comrades, yes, but not . . . not friends. You might have to chew a man out for some indiscretion, and you can't do that to a friend. The other men were friends to each other . . . but I wasn't one of 'em. I was their *commander*, and I think they understood that. So I was on my own a lot . . . which was fine with me because I like to be on my own at times. I have no problem being on my own.'

He had a place within himself he could go. Part of it came from his experience as an actor; he could mask his feelings. Some of it was just the way he was. Gloria heard from the veterans how Jim often seemed bereft of any emotion. She knew it was because he never wanted his men to know what he was thinking. And yet whatever may have occupied his mind at any one time, when there was a problem to deal with, he always seemed to find a way of easing any tension with humour. One of Stewart's gunner sergeants, John Robinson, revealed in his book, *A Reason to Live* (1988), this facet of Stewart which mystified yet sometimes delighted the men of his squadron.

One night Captain Stewart came into the Nissen hut that Robinson shared, asking about a keg of beer that had been stolen from the officers' club. While Stewart delivered a monologue – about how the beer had been stolen, how the base commander was treating the theft as a serious crime, how this hut was the suspected hiding place, but that Stewart himself thought this was unlikely – he calmly looked beneath the blankets, discovered the keg, poured himself a beer and drank it, and then said 'Goodnight' and left. Nothing more was heard of the matter.

Captain Stewart demonstrated that he was a commanding officer who, while unwilling to display friendship, had considerable understanding. Jim said he preferred to 'keep things loose with a little humour on the ground, because in the air, you never knew what life would throw at you'. What he didn't want to demonstrate was that he could be just as afraid as they were. He said:

'You wouldn't be human if you weren't afraid from time to time. I would think about it sometimes . . . I think we all did . . . but once you were in the air you put it out of your mind very quickly. You had too much else to think of. You were always glad to get back to base, and once back you'd think about it for just a few seconds, but before you had time to dwell on it, you were back up again.

'The only time I can honestly say I got really afraid was at a time when we were pushing really hard and morale was getting kinda low. We were flying one raid after another. One night I got really afraid of what the dawn might bring. Our group had suffered a number of casualties during that day. A lot of time when we flew, I'd lose men from other aircraft in my group. All I wanted to do was keep them alive and do our job. For some reason . . . I dunno why . . . I felt like I might not be able to do it this time. At dawn I was going to lead the men of my command deep into Germany, and I found myself imagining the worst. I'd seen men frozen by fear. Fear is deadly in those circumstances. It's insidious. Fear breeds bad judgement. It's like a disease . . . it's contagious. I knew I was putting my whole crew in danger just by being afraid.

'Whenever I got like that, I went to chapel. In fact, I went to chapel regularly. I was brought up to have faith, but in war when you know that life can be suddenly shortened, you get to thinking about religion more. You hope there really is a hereafter. Those were the times I recounted the 91st Psalm.

'Sometimes there'd be a moment during a raid that would suddenly scare you – that's what happens in dangerous situations. And I'd recite the 91st Psalm, and it somehow helped me to forget my fear. I didn't pray for my own life. I prayed that I wouldn't make a mistake. My biggest fear was making a mistake that got my men killed.'

Those were the moments the men of Captain Stewart's squadron never knew about. What they generally saw was a man of determination who simply got the job done – whatever it was. In his book, John Robinson recalled a time when the crew had not been paid for more than two weeks. When Captain Stewart was told that there would be a further delay, he walked into the finance office and asked the lieutenant there why the crew hadn't been paid. The lieutenant replied that the men would be paid, but it would take a few more days to get around to it.

Stewart rubbed his chin thoughtfully, and then said, 'Lieutenant, we just don't have a few days. I believe we ought to pay them right now. Not in a few days. I mean kinda like now – in the next thirty minutes. If the crew isn't paid by then, I believe that we will just have to find a new finance lieutenant because this one will be on his way out of here to the Infantry.' The men were paid within the next half-hour.

During one mission, the flight deck of the Nine Yanks and a Jerk was hit by flak. Jim and his co-pilot were badly shaken and received minor injuries. Jim fought to keep the Liberator airbound as they headed for home. He told me, 'That bugger shook like a . . .' and then he couldn't think of a suitable comparison. 'That was one time I wasn't convinced we'd get back in one piece.'

Eventually the runway at Tibenham came in sight. 'I virtually carried that thing in,' he recalled. It hit the runway hard, almost breaking the nose end from the rest of the craft. The plane dragged along the runway, finally coming to a halt, its neck broken with its tail sticking up at one end, and the nose pointing upwards at the other. That was the end of the Nine Yanks and a Jerk. But Stewart and his crew emerged alive. John Robinson witnessed the crash-landing, and he ran over to Jim who was standing by the tip of the left wing. Captain Stewart told him, 'Sergeant, somebody sure could get hurt in one of those damned things.'

Although Jim never lost his crew, there were many occasions when other crews never returned. At such times, he felt the loss as much as anyone. But he found the greatest consolation among the villagers of Tibenham. 'In those times when you lost some crews,' he said, 'the local people were always there with encouragement . . . always there to almost replace the family of so many of the men that were lost. And this was such an impressive thing to all the rest of us who kept on going because it was a tremendous help in so many ways . . . having to do with the feeling of [the job] and the dedication to the job we had to do.

'The local people really did treat us well. I know there was this saying about being oversexed, overpaid and over here, but I always found the English so kind. They sometimes brought us real eggs . . . you know, we only had powdered egg, which was sort of like eating rice. And the *taste*! After nearly fifty years I still can taste it. And there was this wonderful thing that every once in a while, after maybe a bad mission, the next morning they would send us real eggs . . . real wonderful tasting eggs.'

Some of the local people apparently provided other services. Gloria told me, 'When Jim said "oversexed" he wasn't wrong. A lot of the men used sex to help them through the fear, and there were prostitutes who did their bit for the war effort! They might not have all been professional call girls. Some, I think, were just local girls. But there weren't that many of them, and there were a lot of men, and Jim reckoned that the Tibenham base must have had the biggest outbreak of clap the Air Force had ever seen. He said his own squadron wasn't caught up in the epidemic although a few of his men had the clap. He didn't want to single those infected men out, so he had his entire squadron stand to attention while he gave them a speech about morality and chastity and how they'd better be careful if they couldn't maintain those two virtues. And then he had the whole squadron march to the infirmary to have their shots, whether they needed them or not.'

Gloria said that Jim was very honest about the relationships he had with women before he met her. 'You can't keep a man – even a man like Jim – away from women.' She was sure, however, that none of the women he would have 'fraternised' with during the war would have been prostitutes. 'He was still a film star, and a lot of women were eager to have a film star like Jim,' she said. 'So the opportunity would have been there whenever Jim went into the village. But he had to be very careful. He couldn't mess around with a lot of girls because it would have been a scandal. But there was a local lady he used to see. She was someone he spoke to a lot of times before he got involved. I think they had an *understanding*. It was just a wartime romance. It was not going to have a future. Besides, she had reasons why she couldn't commit to a man. She had been widowed by the war, and since she was a lady of some importance in the village and was expected not to play around with the Yanks, they had to be very discreet. She had needs. So did Jim. I know he had his faith to help him stay sane, but he also needed something a little more . . . earthly.'

Promoted to major, Stewart flew far more missions than a squadron commander was expected to do. Squadron commanders were not as expendable as other airmen, so the Air Force brass were getting worried that James Stewart might manage to get himself killed. This wouldn't be good for the Air Force and it certainly wouldn't go down well with the American public.

Part of the problem the brass had was Jim's tendency to put himself in what they considered to be unnecessary danger. In December 1943, he led a raid on a munitions plant in Bremen. After making his pass and managing to avoid being hit by anti-aircraft fire, he realised he hadn't been able to see the target properly. In this situation, it was normal to simply expect that the rest of the group would hit the target and head for home. But Jim felt he hadn't done his job properly, and doubling the risk of being hit by flak, he went in again. This time he saw the target, dropped more bombs, and turned for home. His motivation was that he had to hit the target 'no matter how long it took'. He said, 'If you're gonna do a job, you got to do it well.'

Some thought he was trying to do it *too* well. But the fact was, Jim always tried to balance the need for getting the job done and keeping his men alive, as he proved during a raid on Ludwigshafen on 7 January 1944. The mission seemed like any other, with an attack by enemy fighters on the forty-eight Liberators of 445th Group. That day the group's defences fought off the attack without loss. Ahead of Major Stewart's group were other squadrons, all being led by the 389th Group.

After 445th Group completed its job and were heading for England, Jim saw that the 389th had taken a wrong bearing across German fighter airfields in France. Radio contact had been lost so Jim decided to go after the wayward group. He found it under attack by German fighters. Like the cavalry arriving in the nick of time, Jim's Liberators appeared and gave covering fire. Eight Liberators of the 389th were lost, but Jim's group returned home intact.

There were some among the brass who felt that Jim had made a reckless decision that could have cost more lives. But cooler heads prevailed at the ensuing divisional inquiry and it was recorded that a lot more lives would have been lost if it had not been for the timely intervention of Major Stewart's group. Consequently, it was decided that he should receive a Distinguished Flying Cross.

By March 1944, Jim had flown twenty missions in just four months. This proved to be too much for the Air Force, and a decision was made to remove Major Stewart from danger by transferring him to the Second Wing Division headquarters at Old Buckingham, just a few miles from Tibenham. There he was given the post of operations officer for the 453rd Bombardment Group. 'I just wasn't comfortable with the whole thing,' said Jim. 'I really felt they were trying to stop me from getting killed . . . not that I wanted to get killed . . . but I didn't want to leave my men to face danger while I was somewhere a whole lot safer.'

Jim tried to talk his way out of it, but he was finally told, 'This is an order, Major Stewart,' and Major Stewart knew there was no point in arguing. He duly transferred to Old Buckingham.

There he discovered that the morale of the 453rd was low, with one of the worst success rates of all the English-based American Air Force groups. A new commanding officer had just taken over, Colonel Ramsey Potts. Major Stewart was promoted to lieutenant-colonel and became the group's operations officer, responsible for planning all duties on daily bombing raids, as well as overseeing the training of newly arrived pilots and crews, and holding media briefings. But his first task was to help Colonel Potts whip the group into shape.

'Colonel Potts was a good man,' said Jim. 'A fair man. He called several airmen in to see him who had managed to avoid getting into combat. They said that they just were not going to fly and there was nothing he or anybody could do about it. He listened to them, and, without issuing direct commands or shouting at them, he managed to persuade all but one to return to active duty. The one who wouldn't go, he had removed from the base and let the medics and the psychiatrists deal with him.'

The men of the 453rd seemed to respond to Jim's quiet, methodical and humorous style of leadership. 'I guess it also helped that some of the men liked my movies,' he said.

Within a few months, the group was flying raids every night, and its rate of success rose dramatically. Lieutenant-Colonel Stewart was still able to fly, but with much less frequency than before. He admitted that when he was on the ground while his men were in the air, he often had a feeling of hopelessness. On those occasions, he again turned to the 91st Psalm. He recalled, 'You could only stay on the ground and hope you'd done your best to keep your men from getting killed. You knew you couldn't do more than train them, but I felt somewhat guilty at times that I wasn't up there to . . . *help* them.' During April and May of 1944, the group lost almost sixty aircraft. Jim recalled, 'I had the peculiar notion that if I were flying more, I might have somehow saved some of those planes . . . but . . . who knows?'

During the spring of 1944, there was a concentration of raids on German airfields in occupied Europe. 'It was the big build-up to D-Day,' said Jim. 'Our planes managed to put around a thousand German pilots out of action . . . so that was a thousand or so enemy fighter planes that were not flying on D-Day . . . and that was a vital part of the invasion of Normandy. I may not have been flying much during those weeks before D-Day, but I was doing my job the best I could, and I felt I had . . . we *all* had done our work well.'

Lieutenant-Colonel Stewart felt he did his own personal best when leading a mission. But, confident as he was at the controls of a bomber and determined as he was to lead a successful raid, he never allowed himself any futile or irresponsible acts of derring-do. While he was leading a thousand planes on a mission to Germany, he decided to turn back. As he recalled:

'The weather was not what had been predicted and conditions were just awful . . . far too dangerous for the men. There was, in my judgement, no chance of success. We had a lot of brave pilots by then, and a lot of 'em were saying, "Come on, Colonel, let's keep going," but I made what I believed was the right decision. And those were the decisions you sometimes made. It wasn't about proving how brave you are. It's about doing your best to make the right decisions as a commander. We tried to make all our airmen realise that staying alive was just as important as winning the war, because if *nobody* stayed alive, the war couldn't be won. I don't care for people who say, "You have to sacrifice your life to win." You don't *give up* your life. You put it on the line. If you're good enough at what you do and you have the right amount of luck, you stay alive.

'I know a lot of men who didn't live to see the end of the war. I know we talk about the sacrifice such men made. I prefer to think that those men sacrificed *the right* to preserve their lives at the cost of others, rather than just giving up their lives.

'I remember seeing the film *Patton* and hearing the speech he gave. He said, "No man wins a war by dying for his country. He wins it by making the enemy die for *his* country." But in war, things are never that black and white.

'I've known men die because they were trying to save the lives of their comrades. I don't think those men who died thought to themselves, "I'll get myself killed so my buddies will live." They just saw their buddies were in trouble, they went in without a second thought for themselves . . . it was an impulse . . . because they were thinking only of their buddies in trouble, and they got killed while performing a courageous act. And, okay, maybe there were fellas who gave up their lives on purpose so a lot more other guys can live. Those things happen in war too. That's all about courage too. But what I wanted my men to know was that the most important thing they had was their *lives*. And I instilled in them . . . I hope . . . the desire to *keep* their lives.'

By the war's end, on 8 May 1945, Stewart, still based at the 453rd, had been promoted to a full colonel. As well as the Distinguished Flying Cross, he was also decorated with the *Croix de Guerre avec Palm* for individual valour. He was the recipient of a second *Croix de Guerre avec Palm* when it was presented to the whole of the 445th Group.

For many years after the war, Stewart refused to discuss his war record. 'It just wasn't something to *boast* about,' he explained. But with the passing of the years, and with his willingness – indeed, his *eagerness* – to attend remembrance events and anniversaries to commemorate the fallen, he began to open up more. At such an anniversary at Tibenham in the late 1980s, he told me, 'I think that whole military experience that I had was something I think about almost every day, and one of the greatest experiences of my life. Greater than being in movies.'

12

Trying For a Wonderful Life

On 25 August 1945, Colonel James Stewart boarded the *Queen Elizabeth* at Portsmouth, along with almost fifteen thousand other American service men and women bound for home, and sailed for New York.

Five days later, the *Queen Elizabeth* docked. Popular bands, as opposed to military bands, played swing music as the men and women began to disembark. Although his family and friends were waiting for him at the St Regis Hotel in Manhattan, Colonel Stewart refused to leave the ship first. He insisted on personally seeing every soldier, sailor, nurse and airman off.

'It was a wonderful day,' he recalled. 'Cab Calloway and Sammy Kaye [and their bands] were playing this great music. Someone said that Glenn Miller would have been there if he'd still been alive. I just wanted to savour every moment, so I decided to see everyone else off the ship first. I was hoarse when I finally came ashore, and my hand ached from saluting thousands of times. There's this expression of *living in the moment*. I didn't want the moment to end. Then I met my family and some friends who were waiting for me in a downtown hotel. That was . . . by golly . . . that was just something that was full of emotion

. . . and it was . . . it was just a private thing for me.

'My father was insisting that there be a parade in my honour in Indiana. My father usually got his way, but not this time. I didn't want to be treated as some kind of hero. There were plenty of other heroes – *real* heroes – that earned that honour. For me, going home was a private thing.'

Despite his desire for privacy, he couldn't avoid the public image of James Stewart, and whether he liked it or not, he was being regarded as a hero. Mostly, though, it was a matter of performing a public relations duty when he had to appear the following day at a press conference at the office of Major General Clarence Kells in Brooklyn.

He was asked about his plans to resume his film career. He responded by saying, 'I'm just not a young fella anymore.' (He was only thirty-seven.) 'I guess I'd only be suitable for playing grand-father to Mickey Rooney.'

When asked if he would be appearing in any war pictures, Jim told them he was unlikely to appear in any Second World War pictures. And he kept his word. His reasons for avoiding all attempts to get him to star in the countless war films made throughout the 1950s and 1960s were, he said, 'very personal'. During the late 1980s, he told me, 'I am proud of my war record and I have respect for every man who lived and died fighting for freedom. And every woman who died. If I had made a picture about the war, and it turned out to be a bad picture, I feel it would have been disrespectful to those men and women. No one sets out to make a bad movie . . . but sometimes they turn out bad just the same . . . so I wouldn't take the chance. And I decided, without a second thought, I would never exploit my own role in the war for the sake of a movie. That would just be distasteful.'

While discounting the likelihood of making war pictures, Jim knew he couldn't count on making *any* kind of picture. He was aware that, like many others in his situation, there might not be a movie career waiting for him. Henry Fonda recalled, 'There were a number of us [Hollywood actors] who had served in the war, and when we came back there was a whole new generation of leading actors who had kind of taken our places. Some of the fellas who'd been big stars before the war came back looking like hell. That happened to Clark Gable. He looked ten years older. Jim [Stewart] had also aged quite a bit. Now there were the young fellas like Gregory Peck and Van Johnson. But it wasn't too bad in the end. Those of us who were under contract to major studios were welcomed back. Louis B Mayer almost died of happiness when he got Clark Gable back. He thought he had Jim back too, but Jim had made other plans by then.'

When Jim enlisted back in 1941, he still had eighteen months of his MGM contract to run. Leland Hayward had given up being an agent to concentrate on producing plays on Broadway. He sold his entire client list to MCA, and that included Jim. But Hayward was still Jim's friend, and he pointed out to Jim that the time he had left with MGM had, in fact, continued to run after his enlistment. That was why Jim had to do all the publicity MGM forced upon him after he enlisted. And it meant that eighteen months after enlisting, his contract had legally run out.

Hayward's advice to Jim was to avoid any more exclusive contracts because the old star system was beginning to crumble. New stars were making non-exclusive deals with studios; in fact, Hayward had started the trend by signing one of his last clients, Gregory Peck, to several non-exclusive contracts. Peck was allowed to work at virtually every major studio, and that in turn meant no studio could 'loan' him out. When a studio paid Peck for his services, no other studio was able to profit by it. Peck received all the money a studio paid – minus agent's fees.

In September 1945, Jim met with Louis B Mayer, who welcomed him back to the studio like a long-lost son. Jim recalled, 'Mr Mayer was very good at being my father . . . until I told him I wasn't coming back to work at his studio. He then said I was the son of some *other* kind of parent. Then I recall he broke down in tears and . . . waall, that was just pitiful. When he saw that didn't work, he told me that they had already planned my first big comeback film . . . in which I would play an air ace. Waall . . . that did it for me. I could see he was going to exploit my war record, so I told him that there was nothing else to say. He had something more to say though . . . "You'll never work again." And I said, "You know what, Mr Mayer? I don't know that I even want to be an actor anymore." And for a few moments, I actually considered it.'

Johnny Swope and Burgess Meredith had vacated the Brentwood home to make new lives of their own with their new wives – Swope was now married to Dorothy McGuire and Meredith to Paulette Goddard. Which meant that Jim had nowhere to live.

Alex wanted Jim to come home to Indiana. Jim tried to make him understand that if he lived in Indiana, he wouldn't be able to make movies in Hollywood. So Alex said, 'Make them movie makers come out to Indiana and make their pictures here.'

Jim patiently tried to explain that none of the studios would be moving to Indiana any time soon. 'Why not?' asked Alex. 'You've got one of them Oscar awards. That makes you an important person in Hollywood. Talk to them. Tell them Indiana is a great place to make pictures. Tell them we've got your Oscar in the store window.'

Jim had a hard time persuading Alex that Hollywood was not going to follow him out to Indiana just because he had an Oscar. 'They give Oscars to people every year, Dad,' he said. 'There are hundreds of Oscars throughout Hollywood. There's only one in Indiana.'

Yes,' said Alex, 'but it's probably the most important Oscar in the world.'

Henry Fonda came to Jim's rescue. He invited Jim to move in with him and wife Frances, and their two children Jane and Peter. 'We had a beautiful house in the hills with a small outbuilding which I'd built for my kids,' said Fonda. 'It was their playhouse, and so Jim lived in the playhouse for three months.'

Jim remembered the playhouse: 'It had all I needed. It had a bed, a small kitchen and a bathroom. When Hank built it, he didn't just build a toy house. It was the real thing. Small, but real. I'm not sure how Peter and Jane took to me putting them out of their playhouse . . . Hank still loved cats. The playhouse was swarming with them.'

In the evenings, Hank and Jim would sit in the playhouse and build model aeroplanes and listen to their jazz records. Jim was there for Christmas, and he agreed to help Hank persuade Peter, who was then only six, that Santa Claus was real. Jim recalled, 'I think it was the first Christmas after I came home from England . . . and Peter didn't believe in Santa. So Hank said to me, "You've got to help me make him believe Santa is real." I said, "I suppose you expect me to dress up as Santa and climb on the roof." And he said, "That's *exactly* what you hafta do."

'Hank and Frances had been kind enough to let me live in their . . . cathouse or playhouse – it was kinda both. Anyway, I dressed up as Santa and climbed on the roof and I was stomping about, and Hank was inside trying to convince Peter that Santa was on the roof. I was getting into the part, going "Ho! Ho! Ho!" and walking up and down . . . and I slipped and nearly fell off the roof. Later Hank said to me, "You almost fell off." I said, "Lucky I didn't." And he said, "I'll say it's lucky. How would I have explained to my son that Santa fell off the roof?" I said, "Next year, *you* be Santa." He didn't think too much of that idea.'

For a while, Jim tried to recapture the fun of Hollywood he had known before the war, going to parties and dating young actresses. Kirk Douglas, in his autobiography *The Ragman's Son*, wrote of a party he attended shortly after arriving in Hollywood with a young German actress whom his agent had fixed him up with. Jimmy Stewart was also there, with Hank and Frances Fonda. According to Douglas, Frances called the young German actress aside and talked and giggled for a while. The actress told Douglas she had to go to the ladies' room. By then people were drifting away from the party as Douglas waited for his date to return. After waiting for half an hour, he discovered that she had left with Jim and the Fondas; Kirk presumed Frances had persuaded her to accompany Jim.

Gloria, who discovered the story in Kirk Douglas's book, told me during one of our transatlantic phone calls, 'I asked Jim about it, and he said he didn't remember Kirk Douglas, who was virtually unknown at the time, at any party. But he said that Frances Fonda was always finding him girls to date, and it's likely she liked the look of Kirk's girl and took it upon herself to persuade the actress to dump Kirk for Jim. But Jim didn't know he'd ever stolen one of Kirk's dates. And he didn't need Frances to find him girls because he was perfectly capable of doing that himself. But it may be that by then Jim was beginning to lose interest in partying and going out with lots of girls. He'd changed since the war – or he'd just begun to act his age. That's why Frances took it upon herself to find him girls, even though he kept telling her not to.'

By early 1946, Jim had virtually given up going to parties. He was tired of the Hollywood life, and preferred to stay at home, enjoy a barbecue with Henry Fonda and build model aeroplanes. Said Fonda:

'I think he had come back to Hollywood and tried to pick up where he had left off, but the war changed him – no doubt. I asked him once what he was feeling, and he said, "I'm feeling that so much is just so . . . superficial." I said, "Are you unhappy?" He said, "No, I'm very happy. But in a different way." He started going back to Indiana a lot more to see his family. He talked a lot more about his father. Alex would chide him for not going to church every week. Jim had never gone to church regularly in the time I'd known him . . . but he was the most – not *religious* fella – but the fella with the greatest faith I ever knew.

'Alex, of course, wanted him to give up acting and come home and run the store. But Jim hadn't given up yet. I think he'd simply seen the worst of humankind, like a lot of us did, and Jim took it to heart. He'd grown up. I wish I had too! But he was also still a boy when he was with me, making aeroplanes out of kits. We didn't have to talk – to make conversation. Mostly we sat on the floor with all these pieces of aeroplane and a plane, and it was, "I've got part C which fits into the slot in part F." And "I've got parts A, B and G, what parts have you got?" That's all Jim and I needed to make us forget about films. But I could see he was worried about his career; no one was offering him any work.

'He also kept on about how all his friends were married with families, and he was still single. He kept saying he was getting old, and I said, "You're not even forty, for Christ's sake." He said, "Yeah, but I *feel* old." The war did that to some fellas. So I kept making him build aeroplanes.'

Jim moved out of the playhouse and went back to Brentwood. But for the next three Christmases, until he married Gloria in 1949, he spent Christmas Eve with the Fondas, enjoying the experience of waking up on Christmas morning and watching the children open their presents. 'Jim loved to come over and help put up the tree,' said Fonda. 'We had a beautiful tall tree, and because Jimmy was the tallest, the children gave him the job of putting the star on the top. He still had to climb a ladder to reach it, but the ladder wobbled, Jim fell against the tree, and he just kind of rode the tree all the way to the bottom. It was like something out of a cartoon. Ruined the tree, but it was the funniest thing.'

As the new year of 1946 began to grow old, Jim started wondering if any film offers would come his way. It was looking like Mayer's prediction that he'd never work again might come true. Fonda had just landed a film, his first since *The Ox-Bow Incident* in 1943. John Ford was going to make *My Darling Clementine* at 20th Century-Fox, and Fonda (who was Ford's favourite actor – not John Wayne) was going to play Wyatt Earp. Then Jim heard that Darryl F Zanuck, production chief at 20th Century-Fox, wanted him to play the other key character, Doc Holliday.

Said Fonda, in 1976, 'I think Zanuck's idea to cast Jim as Doc Holliday was a piece of genius. Nobody else saw Jim in the part, least of all Ford, but Jim would've been great. He's a real craftsman when it comes to acting, and he would have made everyone forget about Mr Smith and Destry. But Ford just wouldn't believe Jim could do the part. So who did he get? Victor Mature – a nice guy and very professional. And he was even good in the part. But he was never the great actor Jim is. Mature even admits he's no actor. He's said often enough, "I'm no actor, and I've got all the films to prove it." John Ford made one of his biggest mistakes not casting Jim.'

Ford, said Fonda, could be 'short on vision, despite what everyone says'. Of course, Fonda was speaking with some bias; he and Ford fell out during the filming of *Mr Roberts* in 1955 and never spoke again. But had Jim played Doc Holliday, it would arguably have been a piece of screen history, teaming James Stewart and Henry Fonda for the first time in a film that remains undeniably one of the great Westerns. (Fonda maintained that Ford got his revenge on Fonda after their spat by casting Jim in three films: *Two Rode Together*, *The Man Who Shot Liberty Valance* and *Cheyenne Autumn*.)

As it was, a film did come Jim's way in 1946. It would emerge in the short term as one of Jim's biggest disasters – but in the long term it would become the film for which he would be best remembered. It was *It's a Wonderful Life*, directed by Frank Capra.

Jim recalled the afternoon Capra pitched his idea to Jim: 'Frank called me and said that he had an idea for a movie and asked if I'd come over. So I went over, and he began telling me about this film. He said, "You're a fella in a small town, you see, and you're not doing very well. You want to do something for your wife . . . you want to help people . . . but everything is going terribly wrong. And you try to commit suicide . . ." And at this point Frank is slowing down as he hears himself telling this story. "And you try to commit suicide by jumping off a bridge into a river and an angel named Clarence . . ." and I could see this look of horror coming over his face, but he continued. "Clarence hasn't won his wings yet so he jumps into the water to save you, but he can't swim and you save him." Waall . . . he finished . . . he thought for a while . . . and I didn't say anything because I was waiting for him to say something more . . . and he said, "It doesn't sound too good, does it?" Waall, I had faith in Frank and I said, "Frank, if you want to do a movie about an angel named Clarence who hasn't won his wings, I'm your man."'

Jim was, indeed, the man – George Bailey, a small-town citizen who feels he has reached the point of desperation after all his plans have gone wrong, leaving him financially ruined and facing disgrace. Fortunately, Heaven sends Clarence (played by Henry Travers), to show George how worthwhile his life has been. The film then recounts George's life, showing all the good he has done. His undoing comes at the hands of a mean banker, Mr Potter (played by Lionel Barrymore). The highlight of the film is the Christmas sequence, when George wishes he had never been born – and his wish is granted. He discovers that nobody in his home-town knows him – because he hasn't been born. The young brother whose life he saved is dead. All the people whose lives had been enriched by him are now living in some kind of misery. He decides he wants to live after all, and Clarence changes everything back to the way it was. And, with it being Christmas on the day George is saved emotionally and spiritually, a miracle is wrought when the townspeople turn up at his house, having collected enough money to save him financially, in return for all he has done for them.

It's a Wonderful Life started filming on 8 April 1946. It was Jim's first film in five years, and he felt a little insecure to start with, but he rejected the stories, rife for years, that suggested he floundered at the start of shooting. 'Acting is like riding a bike,' he said. 'You never forget how to do it, but if you don't do it for a long time, when you try again, you might be a little shaky to start with. I was a little shaky, I guess, but nothing like the bewildered actor that has been talked about over the years.

'Someone said that Lionel Barrymore took me aside and gave me a lecture. He never did any such thing. What he did do was notice a couple of times that I was just getting my sound-stage legs back, and he'd just say something that would be encouraging.'

Donna Reed, who played the wife of George Bailey, confirmed Jim's story. She told me:

'Jimmy isn't a man who lacked confidence, and he didn't lack confidence when we started filming *It's a Wonderful Life*. He sometimes asked Frank Capra if he could try a scene again, and Frank always let him, and pretty soon Jimmy was in full flow.

'I found him, like everyone I guess, to be a wonderful person. He was always polite, always considerate of others. The only thing that took me by surprise was that he liked to be on his own a lot. I thought he would be gregarious. But he seemed at peace being on his own. He'd sit on the set sometimes and read a comic book. Sometimes he just seemed lost in thought. I often wanted to go up to him and ask what he was thinking but I thought that would have been intrusive.

'One day I tried a little sneaky psychology on him and said, "George Bailey has known wonderful times and terrible times. When you play him at his lowest ebb, do you find something in your own life that helps you to feel that way?" And he said, "I've got nothing in my life that ever made me feel like George. I'm happy with my life. I've nothing to complain about."

'But what I did realise, because Frank Capra told me, was that he didn't like to talk about the war. But that was true of a lot of the men who came back from the war; they didn't want to talk about it. So I don't think it was the war that often sent him off into his quiet little space. Henry Fonda once told me, "Aw, Jim's a loner. He likes his own company. You don't have to worry about him. He's content." And I guess that's how you can sum Jimmy Stewart up; he's content.'

Capra believed that although Jim was a contented man, he had an underlying 'sense of being as close to the edge as anyone could ever be'. Capra explained, 'Jim likes to keep a lot of himself beneath the surface of his skin. And every now and then he gets a part that allows those hidden attributes to come to the surface. Many of the parts Jim has played, like George Bailey and Mr Smith, are men who seem to be on the edge of insanity at times. That's not to say Jim is insane; far from it. But when Jim plays those parts, you often see something quite frightening. He can play a man close to breaking point better than any actor I know. And the man himself has to be able to find that somewhere deep within himself to play it. You see it in a lot of Jim's performances, not just Bailey and Smith – but Bailey and Smith are good examples.'

It is certainly true that in many of the performances Jim presented throughout his career, he touched on something that had a dark side. Many think of a typical James Stewart role as being a man who is always calm, gentle, humorous, amiable – in fact, they tend to think of the kind of character he would come to play in *Harvey* (1950). But, if anything, his role in *Harvey* was that of a man who is anything but normal and sane. George Bailey and Mr Smith were normal men in extraordinary circumstances. What we see on screen is a James Stewart losing control of those circumstances, and when he does, he often seems like a man who is literally going mad. He even conceded that playing those men that way was the only way he knew:

'An actor uses the tools he was born with – his body and his mind. My mind is – *anyone's* mind is – far more complex than anyone would like to admit to. I have found that in many of my films, I have had the opportunity to release something that is kind of pent up inside of me. The thing is, when you're giving a performance, it's all under controlled conditions, so, of course, I am not *going* mad . . . though some might think different. I don't *lose* myself in a role. I live it only at the moment of *doing* it. But if I look out of control, as my characters often are – especially in the [Anthony Mann] Westerns – that's because something I keep under control is allowed to be seen . . . but yet it remains under my control.'

Gloria had as good a theory as anyone (since nobody knew him better): 'I think it's all about his rage and his triumph to control it virtually all of the time. When he plays someone who's just about had enough with the world or with life or with a particular individual, what you get is Jim's rage bursting through . . . sometimes like a volcano. I've seen him like that for real, but it's only occasionally. What it does for him as an actor – and I've often heard of him being compared with Gary Cooper, for instance – is play a part with a sense of losing all control, while Gary Cooper would play the same part as a man who seems, perhaps, more bewildered by it all. Take *High Noon* in which Coop played this town marshal who seemed bewildered in his anger at the town's lack of support. If Jim had played the part – and he could have even though it's Coop's best role – Jim would have shown his rage at the town through gritted teeth and blazing eyes while fighting to keep his temper. You'd feel he could lose the gunfight *and* his sanity in the build-up.'

Henry Fonda told me, 'If you want to see the *real* Jimmy Stewart, you can find him in *It's a Wonderful Life*. Everything is magnified, but that's the closest you can come to the real Jim.'

Maybe that's partly the reason why, today, *It's a Wonderful Life* is arguably the most popular of Jim's films among his fans – they *see* something of the real James Stewart. It was certainly Jim's own personal favourite, but for different reasons – although his reasons for liking the film are undoubtedly shared by many, whether they are Stewart fans or not: 'It's my favourite film. The whole thing was done, not from a book . . . not from a play . . . not from an actual happening or anything . . . but just an *idea*. An idea that nobody is born to be a failure. As simple as that. I liked that idea.'

If, indeed, that is the appeal of the film today, then it was totally lost on the audience of 1946. Despite it being considered such a classic almost sixty years later, few people found it appealing at the time. In fact, it was a disaster. When it opened in December 1946, its reception by the critics was mixed. Bosley Crowther wrote in the *New York Times* that the film had a weakness which lay 'in its illusory concept of life. Mr. Capra's nice people are charming, his small town is a quite beguiling place, and his pattern for solving problems is most optimistic and facile . . . they all resemble theatrical attitudes, rather than average realities.' *Newsweek* conceded that it was hardly like real life but found it 'so expertly written, directed, and acted that you want to believe it'. *Variety* found in the film both the good – 'The recounting of this life is just about flawless in its tender and natural element' – and the bad – 'the ending is slightly overlong and a shade too cloying for all tastes.'

Since its release, critics have argued over the film's virtues, or lack of them. A 1977 review in the *New Yorker* found that 'in its own icky, bittersweet way, it's terribly effective.'

What really takes people by surprise today is the fact that the film was a resounding flop. Despite being nominated for five Oscars, including Best Picture, Best Director and Best Actor, the public stayed away. Jim tried to rationalise its failure, telling me in 1979, 'I just don't think it was the type of story people wanted to see right after the war. They wanted a war-related story like *The Best Years of Our Lives*, or at the other extreme they wanted a pure piece of slapstick, like a Red Skelton film. It's only a classic now because of television. I always hated the idea of television, but it's the one thing that found an audience for *It's a Wonderful Life*. Now everyone thinks it was a smash hit. And if people love the film all these years later, then I and Capra and everyone else involved with the film have done something good in life. But at the time, it was a huge disappointment to all of us.'

Jimmy Stewart had made his first film since the war, and already his career looked in jeopardy. But something more serious was brewing, not only for Jim, but for the whole of Hollywood.

13

The Secret FBI Agent

James Stewart was not unaware of the political climate in Hollywood, even before America entered the war. At a time when many in America were isolationists, The Hollywood Anti-Nazi League openly spoke out against Hitler and the Nazi Party at organised mass rallies. To many, this was a good thing. But to those who were more inclined to the Republican right, as was Stewart, this was an attempt to indoctrinate the American people into Communism. The League's chairman, screenwriter Donald Ogden Stewart, was, after all, a leading Communist Party organiser, and many of its members were known to be liberals and leftists. To some extreme right-wingers, to be a liberal was just as bad as being to the far left.

Since the early 1930s, Communism had been accepted by some Americans as the solution to the ills of capitalist America. A good many Americans shifted to the far left and flirted with Communist ideals; some stayed left, others moved to the more liberal centre, and others shifted to the far right in an attempt to combat the spread of Communism in America. By 1934, some in Hollywood were embracing Communism, especially among screenwriters who were often the best-educated people in Hollywood and, according to John

Wayne, 'thought themselves intellectually superior to mere actors, producers, directors and studio executives'.

James Stewart shared Wayne's political beliefs, both being right-wing Republicans, but while Jim was as much opposed to Communism as Wayne was, Jim tended to be less outspoken about it. 'Communism *was* a threat to Hollywood – to *all* of America,' he said. 'I just didn't speak at rallies the way Duke did. I did my political speaking at the ballot box.'

What Jim wasn't admitting to, however, was that he was also doing his political speaking behind closed doors and in the utmost secrecy. By 1947, he was working undercover for the FBI, at the personal behest of FBI Director, J Edgar Hoover.

Gloria did not know Jim when he first began his secretive work. But once they started dating in the summer of 1948, and certainly when they were married in August 1949, Jim could not keep her in the dark, and he told her all about his undercover mission for the government. (Whether Jim revealed everything to Gloria before or after their wedding, Gloria never said. But I suspect it must have been before they were wed since Stewart was active long before the nuptials, and it is inconceivable that he would enter into holy matrimony without his bride knowing about his secret life.)

It was Army Intelligence who first called upon Jim's services early in 1947. Being both a respected Hollywood star *and* an officer in the American Army Air Force Reserve Corps, and having emerged from the war as a bona fide, highly decorated hero, he was the perfect choice to help root out subversives in Hollywood.

'Army Intelligence wanted to recruit Jim as one of their agents,' said Gloria. 'But Jim wasn't interested in being a spy. He had a lot of good friends in Hollywood and he wasn't happy about the idea of spying on them and writing up intelligence reports on them and reporting back to Army Intelligence. They didn't *order* him to do it, and when he gave them a firm no, they seemed to give in.'

Jim may have thought that that was the end of the matter, but Army Intelligence was soon in touch with the FBI, and before long Jim was invited to Washington to meet J Edgar Hoover, who was director of the FBI from 1935 (aged forty) until his death in 1972.

'Jim thought he was going just as someone Hoover wanted to shake hands with because of his war record,' said Gloria. 'The thing about Jim is that he is a real patriot, so when he got the invitation from Hoover, he felt very happy about it. He wanted to shake Hoover by the hand and tell *him* what a good job the FBI was doing for the country.'

Jim met with Hoover, and was given a grand tour of the FBI building. 'Jim was just so impressed and quite overwhelmed,' said Gloria. 'He saw the FBI as an almost sacred institution. Jim said that Hoover was completely informal, warm, friendly and generous. He took Jim to his house where they had dinner, and Jim was like a fascinated child as he listened to Hoover talking about his work and about the history of the FBI.'

Listening to Hoover's sense of self-satisfaction about his crime-busting exploits, Jim was hooked. Hoover had been building to the moment when he would ask Stewart for his help, and for Jim, being asked personally by the head of the FBI for his help was almost like a calling from God. As Gloria put it, 'Jim went barefoot up the mountain, and saw the burning bush – only God's name was J Edgar Hoover.'

Hoover knew that Jim was sensitive about the idea of spying on his friends and colleagues. He was very cunning in the way he recruited Stewart. He said to Jim, 'I know that you are a loyal American. A patriot to your country. I know that, not just because of your very impressive war record, but because I have been able to sense it today.'

Jim was not usually impressed by flattery. Said Gloria, 'He had learned that in Hollywood, flattery was what you got when you're on top, and what you don't get when you're on your way down.' But this time the words were coming from J Edgar Hoover himself. Before he knew it, Jim was promising to do all he could to help the FBI. What Hoover had not immediately confessed was that the help the FBI needed was in rooting out known and suspected Communists in Hollywood. Jim thought Hoover was asking him for help to run the Mafia out of Hollywood, something which Jim was only too happy to do.

'When Hoover realised Jim was willing to help fight crime, Hoover played on it,' said Gloria. Hoover told Jim that it was important to 'fight all the kinds of evil there are' in Hollywood and throughout America. Jim began talking about the likes of Bugsy

Siegel and Lucky Luciano who were running their rackets in Los Angeles and Las Vegas, and he enthusiastically offered ideas on how to bust them. Said Gloria, 'Jim would have done anything to get those gangsters out of town, but he was also concerned about how it would all turn out for friends like Cary Grant who'd developed friendships with some of those people. He wanted to protect his friends, and he told Hoover as much.'

Jim related to Hoover how, in February of 1947, he and Cary Grant had thrown a huge party at the Clover Club in New York. It was in honour of Howard Hughes, the pilot who had made his inaugural flight of the *Hercules*, a huge seaplane and the largest aircraft to date. Among the guests at the Clover Club was Bugsy Siegel. Hoover told Stewart that the FBI knew all about Siegel being at the party; the FBI had infiltrated it, partly because they were investigating Hughes. He had been given government funds to build the *Hercules* as part of the war effort, but the aircraft had taken five years to complete at a staggering cost of $18 million – and the war was over. The government also knew that Hughes had friends in the Mob.

However, Hoover reassured Jim that anyone who was not directly involved in crime had no need to worry. He went on to emphasise how important it was to crusade against everything that was un-American, and asked Jim if he agreed. Gloria said, 'When Hoover asked Jim that, he could only say that he did agree.'

Hoover expressed the government's concerns about 'subversives' in Hollywood. As he continued to outline the government's mission at great length, by the end of his speech he was no longer talking about 'subversives' but about 'Communists'. Jim had agreed with everything Hoover said, and by the time Hoover had got his point over, Jim was expressing his eagerness to be involved. 'But Jim was clear on one thing,' explained Gloria. 'He would not take any kind of an oath that made him an official agent for the FBI, and he would not act as a spy of any kind.' He would not, he said firmly, 'be an informer'.

Hoover said he understood Stewart's concerns, and agreed that there needed to be no formal agreement between 'two American patriots doing their duty'. He explained that he only wanted Stewart to 'talk to people, encourage any who might have Communist ideologies to give them up, to get those people to spread the word'. Jim replied, 'I think it will take more than a little encouragement to get people who may be Communists to give it up.'

Hoover agreed, saying that the country was 'in danger' and that all patriots may have 'to fight with whatever weapons are necessary'. Jim said he understood and that he hoped they could find a way to 'fight without drawing blood'. Said Gloria, 'Jim said he'd do all that was necessary. The trouble was, Hoover hadn't told him everything.'

For one thing, Hoover had no intention of rounding up the Mafia in Hollywood. In fact, the official policy of the FBI was that organised crime did not exist in America. For years the Mafia had been literally getting away with murder in the United States, and the reason was, many believe, as sinister as the Cosa Nostra itself. J Edgar Hoover, it was claimed, had become compromised by his own greatest secret: he was allegedly a homosexual, and one of the FBI's greatest commandments was that no agent should be a homosexual. Of course, the public didn't know about Hoover's suspected secret until after his death in 1972, but the Mafia knew, and they allegedly had photographs of Hoover in compromising positions to prove it. Ironically, because of the Mafia's links with Hollywood, a lot of Hollywood people also knew of the suspicions that Hoover was a homosexual and that the Mob were blackmailing him. But if anyone had suggested this to Jim, he would have shrugged it off as mere gossip mongering. After all, they had said the same about him and Fonda. (Among those who, in my presence, maintained that the homosexual and blackmailing allegations were true, and who were in various positions to have that kind of knowledge – see my book on Frank Sinatra – were the film stars Ava Gardner, Peter Lawford and Sammy Davis Jnr. I also heard it stated by James Cagney, George Raft and Henry Fonda, and a figure from Charles 'Lucky' Luciano's Mafia who must remain anonymous – see my book *The Hollywood Connection*.)

The purported deal between Hoover and the Mafia was simple; the FBI did not investigate organised crime, and the Mob didn't release the photos of Hoover – especially the ones that reputedly showed him wearing women's clothing. Only a few of the Mafia were ever put behind bars, including Al Capone for tax evasion and

Charles 'Lucky' Luciano for running a prostitution racket. During the Second World War Luciano co-operated with the OSS (the forerunner of the CIA) in planning the Allied invasion of Sicily, with Luciano's Mafia contacts in Sicily assisting the Allies. For his help, Luciano was released and deported back to Sicily. Once free, he set up home in Cuba, to be as close to his American operations as possible.

The FBI watched the Mafia, made reports, but no action was ever taken by the Bureau to smash organised crime because officially it didn't exist – Hoover simply denied its existence and refused to investigate it (which eventually led to Senator Robert Kennedy's aggressive investigation into the Mafia). So even as Hoover and Jim discussed how they would round up the Mafia dons in Los Angeles, Hoover knew he had no intention of doing any such thing.

Hoover also neglected to mention to Jim that the Motion Picture Alliance for the Preservation of American Ideals, which boasted a considerable membership of Hollywood right-wingers, had invited the House Un-American Activities Committee, or HUAC, to Hollywood. The HUAC had one purpose – to investigate known and suspected Communists. Lists had been drawn up of such people, and the HUAC would be calling them to special hearings to declare their membership of the Communist Party.

Hoover had already acquired the services of a number of Hollywood's right-wing conservatives, including Ronald Reagan, who were given code names. 'Jim refused to have any kind of code name, as a dozen or so others in Hollywood did,' said Gloria. Reagan was particularly active in drawing up lists of suspected and known Communists.

Hoover was so paranoid about the Red scare in America, he wanted to make sure that even those who were his 'Hollywood agents' were not double agents. He asked Jim to keep an eye on the code-named informers, and supplied Jim with a list, 'which is how we knew that Reagan was one of them,' said Gloria. 'But who could even begin to imagine that Ronald Reagan might be a double agent? It's ridiculous. But that's what Hoover wanted Jim to check out and Jim did it.'

Jim never discovered any double agents among the official

informers. Hoover then began insisting that Jim draw up lists of anyone he suspected of being a Communist. Jim loathed the idea, but he made what Gloria said were 'token efforts'. People in Hollywood were taking sides, and many, on both sides, were speaking out very loudly. It wasn't too difficult to draw conclusions, or so Jim thought. And he didn't realise that the HUAC intended dealing out the harshest penalties to some of Hollywood's finest talent.

The realisation that conclusions and assertions were inconsistent with the facts came when he was questioned by the Los Angeles department of the FBI about Frank Capra. Jim had had no idea that his friend Capra was a suspected Communist. He also discovered that *It's a Wonderful Life* had become a target of the HUAC. The Committee asserted that the film had been 'un-American' for having as its villain a mean banker who, the HUAC asserted, was a representation of capitalist America. The fact that the film had shown its hero, Stewart, as a banker who used money for good, seemed not to have impressed the witch-hunters. Capra's earlier films, *Mr. Deeds Goes to Town* and *You Can't Take It With You*, also came under scrutiny for suggesting that capitalism was an evil. And then there was *Mr. Smith Goes to Washington*, which dared to suggest that there was corruption in the American Senate.

When Jim learned this, he complained to HUAC that Capra was no more a Communist than he was. They told Jim that Army Intelligence had drawn up a considerable file on Capra, detailing the director's Communist exploits since 1932, and the HUAC allowed him to see it. It said that in 1932 Capra had signed his name to the Communist Party election petition. Capra admitted to me that he had signed the petition, explaining, 'I'd read some Karl Marx during the Depression, which got me thinking about capitalism and how it had brought us into the Depression. A lot of people thought that maybe Marx had the right idea at the time.'

The file revealed that Capra had begun work on a project at Metro-Goldwyn-Mayer in 1932 called *Soviet*. This was subsequently cancelled because the studio felt the subject, a sympathetic view of the Marxist social experiment, was Communist propaganda.

Capra and screenwriter Robert Riskin had spent three weeks in the Soviet Union in 1937 while undertaking a world tour to promote *Lost Horizon*. Capra was welcomed by Soviet film directors and treated to the impressive sight of the May Day parade. Said Capra, 'I had become jaundiced about the capitalistic system – working for Harry Cohn [at Columbia] will do that. I could see the virtues of the Communist system, but what stained it was the poor standard of living the Soviet people endured. Had Stalin also lived in the same poverty, it would certainly have been something to admire because everyone would have been equal.'

On 16 May 1937, an interview with Capra had appeared in the Soviet publication *Izvestia* in which he was quoted as saying, 'Your country is young and talented. It seems to me that the future of cinema art undoubtedly lies with you, and not in America, where the bosses of cinema think only of profits and not of art.' Capra's tour of the Soviet Union was duly noted by American Army Intelligence, as was his involvement in a picket line in support of a strike at the Los Angeles Newspaper Guild in 1938. The HUAC file included an item from the West Coast Communist Party newspaper *People's World*, dated 30 May 1938, which stated that the strike 'was Communist inspired', and that Capra was 'a member of the picket line'.

The file included a report that Capra and Sidney Buchman went to Washington in October 1938 and had visited the FBI at J Edgar Hoover's invitation. Gloria said, 'When Frank Capra went to Washington and met with Hoover, it was just a ploy by Hoover to take a look at this film director he and the HUAC were investigating. It didn't help Capra that he said some critical things about [President] Roosevelt. Hoover had spies following Capra everywhere.'

As for Sidney Buchman, he had become a Communist in 1938, and his wife, Beatrice, was an important member of the Hollywood Anti-Nazi League, which was considered by HUAC as a Communist front organisation. Capra had addressed the league at a mass meeting in November 1938. Meanwhile, on 14 October 1938 US Army Intelligence had opened its file on Capra, and that file had continued to grow until 1947 when it was shown to James Stewart. 'Jim told them that there was no question about Frank Capra's loyalty to America,' said Gloria.

Jim was nevertheless given the assignment of investigating Capra. Gloria said that Jim had no intention of investigating his friend, but gave the FBI the impression he would do so. What Jim felt he had to do was convince Capra to prove himself innocent. 'Jim felt he was doing what he had to do,' said Gloria. 'He believed, and I think rightly, that there was a threat to America and to the film industry from the Communists, and he wanted to do something about it. He was Hoover's secret weapon. He was like an under-cover *undercover* agent.'

No other event in Hollywood history has caused so much long-lasting pain as what became known as the Hollywood witch-hunts. The process began in May 1947, when J Parnell Thomas chaired the House Un-American Activities Committee in Los Angeles. Behind closed doors, a number of prominent Hollywood people, termed 'friendly' witnesses, met with Senator Richard Nixon, passing on names of suspected and known Communists. The 'friendly' witnesses included actors Robert Taylor, Adolphe Menjou, writers Rupert Hughes and Howard Emmett Rogers, and studio boss Jack L Warner. Stewart was not among the so-called 'friendly' witnesses, but he was secretly passing on information to the HUAC and the FBI.

Those who stood on the First Amendment and refused to answer the question, 'Are you now or have you ever been a member of the Communist Party?' were charged with contempt. Those who were willing to admit past membership were asked to name others.

Ten men, most of them screenwriters who became known as the Hollywood Ten, all cited the First Amendment when they appeared before the HUAC in the autumn of 1947 in Washington. They were subsequently charged with contempt, ordered to return to Wash-ington in 1951 to answer the charge, and ultimately sent to prison. A few of them, such as director Edward Dmytryk, agreed to name names and were released from prison to resume their work in Hollywood. Henry Fonda, who was a liberal, told me, 'The problem was, the HUAC didn't consider Communism to be a political threat. They saw it as a *criminal* organisation, and so the First Amendment didn't have any meaning at those hearings.'

Many who were not among the Ten found it difficult to get work because they appeared on unofficial blacklists and greylists as suspected or known Communists. Those who were Communists, especially those in the Hollywood Ten who refused to give in, were not allowed to work in America again (or at least, until Kirk Douglas broke the blacklist in 1960; as co-producer of *Spartacus*, he openly credited the screenwriter Dalton Trumbo, one of the Ten). Those who were under suspicion were put on the greylist. Some of those people repented before the HUAC and agreed to name others they knew to be Communists, and so they were allowed to resume work.

Stewart thought the hearings 'did a lot of good because it did what it set out to do, which was stop the spread of Communism. You can argue the rights and wrongs of it . . . and God knows I've not always felt totally comfortable with what happened . . . but you have to draw the line in the sand and ask people if they're going to cross that line. And some of them did.'

The strain of his undercover work took an immense toll on Jim. He constantly argued with himself over the rights and wrongs of his actions. All he really wanted to do was run the gangsters out of Hollywood. He also wanted to rid Hollywood of Communists, but to him that was of secondary importance to bringing law and order to the streets and to the film industry itself. While his efforts to aid the HUAC were obviously appreciated, his efforts to inform the FBI of Mafia activity seemed to have no effect.

14

Undercover in Hollywood

Jim still had a career to resuscitate. Lew Wasserman of MCA took over as his agent, and a deal was done with RKO, 20th Century-Fox, United Artists, Warner Brothers and Universal to each make five James Stewart films.

The first picture in this deal was *Magic Town* for RKO, who had released *It's a Wonderful Life*. RKO was not one of Hollywood's biggest studios, although neither was it the smallest. Its strength lay in films with modest budgets and modest star names. Some stars who rose to greater things, like John Wayne and Robert Mitchum, had made their names in RKO films. But the studio was also known as a place for the bigger stars to step down to. For James Stewart to be making a second consecutive RKO film, when the first had failed, was not a sign of good things to come.

That second film, *Magic Town*, was filmed and released in 1947 – in fact that and *It's a Wonderful Life* were his only films of that year. Jim played a cynical, fast-talking public relations man. He discovers that the small, uncorrupted town of Grandview is such a pure representation of the heart of America that its own community-based opinions and forecasts have accurately reflected events in America for some fifty years. Seeing his chance to make quick

James Stewart at the age of two, riding his tricycle in Indiana, Pennsylvania.

© Bettmann/CORBIS

Left: Stewart's third film, *Next Time We Love*, was with the woman he loved for so long, Margaret Sullavan (1936, Universal).

Opposite: Stewart had an early supporting role opposite Jeanette MacDonald in the operetta *Rose Marie* (1936, MGM).

Right: The legendary Fonda–Stewart friendship began in 1932 when the aspiring actors worked at the same theatre in Cape Cod. _{SNAP/Rex}

Opposite (top): In Frank Capra's *Mr. Smith Goes to Washington*, Stewart was pitched against the nasty men of power (including Claude Rains), this time in the American Senate (1939, Columbia).

Opposite (bottom): It was the high society wedding of any year: Stewart, Cary Grant and Katharine Hepburn in *The Philadelphia Story*, for which Jim won the Best Actor Oscar – and doesn't he look surprised (1940, MGM)?

Above: Stewart was highly decorated for his courageous efforts in the US Army Air Force during the Second World War. Time Life Pictures/Getty Images

Stewart's first film after the war, *It's a Wonderful Life*, with Donna Reed, was a flop in its day, but now it's the quintessential Christmas film (1946, RKO). RKO/The Kobal Collection

Jim and Gloria were married on 9 August 1950 at Brentwood Presbyterian Church, Los Angeles. Their six hundred guests included stars such as Spencer Tracy, Gary Cooper and Ray Milland. SNAP/Rex

Stewart was the named star of *Winchester '73,* with Stephen McNally (right) as Jim's murderous brother, but the real star was the rifle itself. The film marked the beginning of Stewart's career as a major Western star (1950, Universal).

The happy family: Jim and Gloria with his stepsons Ronald and Michael, from Gloria's first marriage, and twin daughters Kelly and Judy, born in May 1951. SNAP/Rex

Playing a doctor on the run from the law for murder, Stewart was hidden behind clown make-up all the way through *The Greatest Show On Earth*, co-starring Charlton Heston (1952, Paramount).

There wasn't a dry eye in the house by the end of *The Glenn Miller Story* in which James portrayed the great band leader, with June Allyson as his devoted wife (1953, Universal).

Stewart starred with Grace Kelly in his second Hitchcock film, *Rear Window* (1954, Paramount). <small>SNAP/Rex</small>

Wearing the same lucky hat as in the previous three Anthony Mann Westerns, Stewart was at odds with the self-appointed sheriff and cattle rustler John McIntire in *The Far Country* (1955, Universal).

Below: The violence of the Mann Westerns reached its zenith in *The Man From Laramie*, and Stewart performed his own stunts (1955, Columbia).

Starring Stewart and John Wayne together for the first time, the John Ford Western *The Man Who Shot Liberty Valance* was an unhappy experience for many involved, including Woody Strode, far right (1962, Paramount).

Below: There's a snake up in that thar tree, making Carroll Baker hug closer to Stewart in this scene from *How the West Was Won*; the still is signed by Jim himself (1962, MGM-Cinerama).

The first in a trio of comedies directed by Henry Koster, *Mr. Hobbs Takes a Vacation* saw Stewart as the harassed husband to lovely Maureen O'Hara (1962, 20th Century-Fox).

Below: Almost the last good, solid James Stewart film was *Shenandoah*, with Phillip Alford as his youngest son returning home from the Civil War in a tear-jerking ending (1965, Universal).

Stewart and Henry Fonda in the comedy Western *The Cheyenne Social Club*, a difficult film for Jim to make because during filming he learned his stepson Ronald had been killed in the war in Vietnam (1970, National General). © John Springer Collection/CORBIS

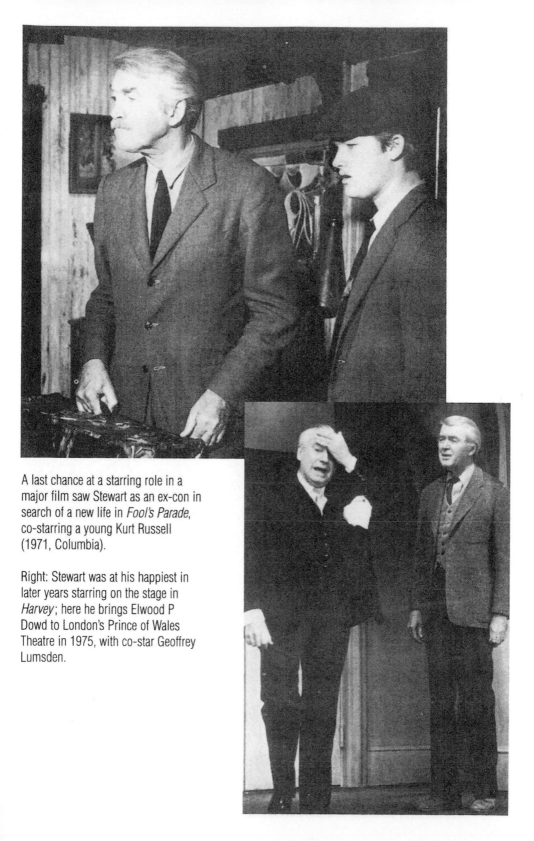

A last chance at a starring role in a major film saw Stewart as an ex-con in search of a new life in *Fool's Parade*, co-starring a young Kurt Russell (1971, Columbia).

Right: Stewart was at his happiest in later years starring on the stage in *Harvey*; here he brings Elwood P Dowd to London's Prince of Wales Theatre in 1975, with co-star Geoffrey Lumsden.

Jim and Gloria enjoyed forty-four years of marriage until Gloria's death in 1994. GLO/Rex

money, he poses as an insurance agent, makes notes of the town's opinions on a variety of topics, and sends his findings to a clearing house. His accuracy in predicting national trends earns him big money, but it also threatens the town's innocence. And so he has a change of heart and helps Grandview to return to its former state.

It was in essence a Capra-style picture, which is not surprising as it was produced and written by Robert Riskin, who worked on the screenplays of *It Happened One Night, Mr. Deeds Goes to Town* and *You Can't Take It With You*. But the film was a bigger disaster than *It's a Wonderful Life*. Most people involved blamed the failure of the film on its director, William Wellman, who was at his best when dealing with action pictures. But fault also lay in Riskin's attempt to create a Capra picture without Capra, and with the studio. RKO excelled at making *film noir* (often starring Robert Mitchum) and inexpensive action pictures (often starring Wayne); *Magic Town* was neither.

Jim got little joy from making the film. 'There wasn't much being offered to me after the war . . . and I kinda took whatever I was offered,' he said. '*Magic Town* seemed like a good idea but it didn't help . . . and part of the problem was *me*. I just wasn't convincing . . . just like the film.

'What was a pleasure, though, was getting to spend time with Robert Riskin and his wife Fay Wray . . . you remember her? The actress from *King Kong*. We all went to the premiere of *Magic Town*, and it was a disaster. Even the suit I wore was a disaster. After I arrived at their house, they kept kind of avoiding me . . . and then they opened all the windows. It turned out that I'd put too much cleaning fluid on my suit, and it smelled so much they could hardly breathe. But I couldn't smell a thing. I got to wondering how many other people I'd nearly choked to death with my clean suits.'

More critical than his suit crisis was his career crisis, and he sought a way to salvage it – and himself. 'I felt I needed to do something to prove . . . only to me . . . that I could get some satisfaction as an actor. So I took off to New York to do *Harvey* on Broadway.'

It was a move that many in Hollywood thought professional suicide. He wasn't doing the play because he had been offered the leading role and a chance at Broadway stardom. The role had been played successfully since 1944 by Frank Fay, who simply wanted a break for the summer of 1947. The producers had asked Bing Crosby to fill in for Fay, but Crosby didn't want to be anyone's understudy. So they asked Jim, and he accepted. 'There was all this talk about Jim being reduced to an understudy,' said Burgess Meredith. 'But it was a shrewd move.' It was also a way of escaping the terrible atmosphere in Hollywood over the witch-hunts.

Going to New York in the summer of 1947 to do *Harvey* was a welcome relief from all the political heat back in Hollywood. The Pulitzer Prize-winning play by Mary Chase featured the exploits of Edward P Dowd, who manages to escape from reality by spending his time in a bar, talking to an invisible six-foot rabbit called Harvey. Dowd's gentle but erratic behaviour convinces his sister to have him committed, but his sincerity and conviction not only persuades the asylum staff that it's his sister who needs committing, but also convinces the asylum director that Harvey actually exists.

The critics, who had come to associate Frank Fay with the role of Dowd, were not kind to Jim, finding his style unsuited to the kind of 'hokum comedy' the play appeared to require. However, the play, which had not been doing so well recently, suddenly started pulling in capacity houses. Burgess Meredith believed that Jim actually saved the play from closing, because it continued to do well when Frank Fay returned.

Jim said, 'It's important for an actor to get back to the stage, and I wasn't having any luck in the movies, so I took the job. It was a wonderful play, and I kinda liked the way Edward P Dowd looked at life. He was saying that there are a lot worse things in life than sharing a drink with an invisible six-foot rabbit. And after the war, I had to agree with that. And I liked being back on the stage. That was in 1947, and I guess I've had this friendship with my invisible white rabbit ever since.' (Jim was referring, in 1975, to the fact that he had made the film version in 1950, had gone on to do a television movie in the 1970s, had returned to the play on Broadway, and was now bringing it to the London stage.)

After his summer stint on Broadway, Jim returned to Hollywood to make Henry Hathaway's gritty, fact-based drama *Call Northside 777* for 20th Century-Fox. He played a cynical reporter who is asked by his editor (Lee J Cobb) to investigate a personal notice in the newspaper that offers $5,000 to anyone with information on a killing that took place eleven years earlier. He reluctantly accepts the assignment and discovers the ad was placed by an elderly woman (played by Kasia Orzazewski), eking out a living by cleaning, who has saved for years to try and prove that her son (Richard Conte) was innocent of a murder charge. The sceptical reporter investigates the murder and with just one piece of evidence is able to clear the accused, but the real killer is never found. The story was based on the experiences of reporter James P McGuire, who won a Pulitzer Prize for his efforts to prove convict Thomas Majczek innocent of murder.

The film presented a new tougher image for Jim, honed under the direction of one of the toughest directors in the business, Henry Hathaway. Hathaway injected an almost semi-documentary style, filming on location in Chicago, although it never really lost its melodramatic touch.

When it opened in 1948, critics were split. *Variety* thought the film 'registers with a mild impact . . . has a faltering pace, an uneven realistic focus and only a thin dramatic point', and it was equally unimpressed by what it called 'Jimmy Stewart's jarring and unpersuasive performance'. Bosley Crowther of the *New York Times* disagreed, calling the film 'a slick piece of melodrama that combines a suspenseful mystery story with a vivid realistic pictorial style and which is winningly acted by James Stewart'. The London *Observer* wrote, 'Mr Stewart has really got under the skin of a journalist. It is a fine performance, all the better because it has no obvious tricks of showmanship, and he gets splendid help from Henry Hathaway's direction.'

The shame about *Call Northside 777* is not that it's a bad film, but that it's a very good film which is now largely forgotten. Viewed today, it comes as a pleasant surprise to see James Stewart playing a dramatic part and showing he didn't care too much about a general lack of warmth or charm in the character which audiences had come to expect from him. But that was what drew Jim to the film: 'I had the chance to play someone who was not Mr Smith or George Bailey. He doesn't do what he does because it's right, but because it makes for a good story in the newspaper. And he does it reluctantly . . . only after he is badgered by his editor. I liked the sceptical approach the character had, and his sarcastic remarks.

'That wasn't anything like the real fella [James P McGuire] at all. He was a truly decent man, and he was on the set to give his advice, which was very useful. But, like so many films based on true events, this one had a lot of dramatic licence because the writers, the producer and the director all thought it would make for better story-telling. Once I decided that the screen story had merit, I was drawn by the chance to play an entirely different kind of character.'

Hoping that his career tide had turned, Jim made his first film with Henry Fonda in 1947, *On Our Merry Way* for United Artists. The film also featured Burgess Meredith, who helped to instigate the project. Meredith told me:

'The film was supposed to be called *A Miracle Can Happen*, and it originally revolved around the story of a church minister, played by Charles Laughton, who is having a crisis of faith. One night a boy comes to him and persuades him to see his dying father. The minister complains but goes to see the man, and he learns that the child had died years before, and so the minister's faith is restored.

'My idea was we build an anthology around that tale which asked how a child could affect lives. I would play a reporter who asks that very question. I told this idea to Jim and Hank, and they liked it and said that they'd like to play a couple of jazz musicians, so we got our screenwriter John O'Hara to write it for us. And we got John Huston to direct it.

'It all went wrong with certain delays, and then Huston had to go off and work on another project, and so did Hank. Hank came back, but Huston said he'd lost interest in the picture and so George Stevens came in and shot some of it. We also had King Vidor and Leslie Fenton direct scenes.

'I produced the film with Benedict Bogeaus; in a way he was the senior producer. I was just the one who had the idea and wanted to do it. He was worried about the changes in pace and style of the film, which I have to admit were there. But it became a fascinating experiment to see if all that talent could make something different and remarkable, if a little off-the-wall for its time. It had stories with comedy, like the scenes with Hank and Jim, and then there was this serious story that was central, as far as I was concerned, about the church minister. But in the end Bogeaus decided to take out the whole of the Charles Laughton segment, and the title was changed from *A Miracle Could Happen* to *On Our Merry Way*, and it was a stupendous failure [when released in 1948].'

It was a bigger disaster for Jim, as he discovered when he heard that the *New York Times* was publishing an article called 'The Rise and Fall of James Stewart'. Ignoring the success of *Call Northside 777*, the writer of the piece had zoomed in on the failures of *It's a Wonderful Life*, *Magic Town* and *On Our Merry Way*, and it suggested that his stint as a replacement actor in *Harvey* was just an example of how desperate he was to work. Even Jim began to believe that he might well be dying, if not already dead, professionally.

Stewart had been writing up his own dossiers on the Hollywood gangsters. He also drew up a list of names in the film business who associated with them. They included actress Wendy Barrie, who had co-starred with Stewart in *Speed* in 1936, George Raft, Cary Grant, Gary Cooper, writer and producer Mark Hellinger (who wrote and produced the classic gangster picture *The Roaring Twenties*), Howard Hughes (who had become Bugsy Siegel's silent partner in the Flamingo hotel and casino in Las Vegas) and Lana Turner. Also on the list was Frank Sinatra.

'Jim's biggest problem was how to warn his friends to dissociate themselves from the likes of Bugsy Siegel without blowing his cover,' said Gloria. 'He passed on his dossier on the gangsters to the FBI, but the list of names he held back for himself. That list was really for him alone to work on because he didn't want any of his friends to be considered criminals simply by association.'

Over the next few months, Stewart took every opportunity to speak to the people on his list. 'His plan,' said Gloria, 'was simply to tell them all that he'd heard that the FBI were keeping tabs on them, and that they'd better stay away from Benny Siegel and his cronies.'

Not all of them needed his advice. Wendy Barrie had enjoyed an affair with Siegel. But, as she explained to Stewart, she had finished with him several years earlier when she was told by George Raft that Siegel was cheating on her with famed gangster moll Virginia Hill. Raft had told her that having an affair with Siegel was 'playing with fire', a move which had almost cost Raft his life, for when Siegel found out he set out to shoot Raft dead. Raft, who knew how to calm the killer with soft words, such as calling him 'Baby Blue Eyes', talked Siegel out of it. When Raft told Stewart this, Jim roared with laughter. 'The vicious killer is just Baby Blue Eyes!' Raft and Stewart had never been friends, but that day they both had a laugh at Siegel's expense.

Stewart warned Raft that the FBI were watching everyone who had contact with Siegel, but Raft told him, 'It's too late for me to pretend I don't know Benny. When he goes down, it'll be the end of me too. But make sure the others know.'

While Stewart took every opportunity to speak to the others on his list, somebody let Siegel know what was going on. 'Jim never knew who it was,' said Gloria. 'But he thought that somehow someone said something careless to Virginia Hill, and she told Siegel. He was always positive it was neither Cary Grant nor Gary Cooper. It might have been Mark Hellinger or Sinatra.'

Siegel went looking for Stewart, and when he found him, Stewart thought it was the end for him. 'He wouldn't give Siegel the satisfaction of terrorising him,' said Gloria. 'He stood up to Siegel. But Siegel just laughed and said, "Jimmy boy, the FBI will never touch me." Jim didn't know what that meant at the time. Only much later did he learn that Hoover, whom Jim had always admired so much, was being blackmailed by the Mafia.'

Stewart had believed that if Siegel was permanently removed by the FBI, the Mafia in Hollywood would disintegrate. Ironically, the Mafia took the matter out of Stewart's – and the FBI's – hands. On 20 June 1947, Bugsy Siegel was killed at the Los Angeles house he shared with Virginia Hill. He had been shot to death by a Mafia hit man; Siegel's crime was not repaying the millions of Mob dollars he'd borrowed to build the Flamingo hotel and casino in Las Vegas. The local police investigated the matter while the FBI remained at a discreet distance. When police went to speak to George Raft, he told them, 'I don't know who killed Benny. But I tell you this; when they killed him, they killed me too.' After

Siegel's death, Raft's career quickly went into decline.

Cary Grant was one of the first to hear the news of Siegel's death. Al Smiley, Siegel's closest associate, who had been in the house when Bugsy was killed, telephoned Grant with the news. Grant gave his condolences, but said he couldn't guarantee to be at Siegel's funeral. In fact Grant, like Howard Hughes and Gary Cooper, made sure they were unavailable to pay their last respects at the funeral.

Now that his friends were free of Siegel's influence, Jim sent his report on the Mafia to Washington. He received a call from Hoover thanking him for his diligence. 'I hope my report will make a difference,' Jim told Hoover. 'You can be sure that it will,' Hoover replied. But Hoover had no intention of using the file, and it was probably destroyed.

However, Jim had a copy, which turned out to be useful when news of Siegel's death made the American public aware for the first time that organised crime was a reality. It prompted the first real investigation into the Mafia, led by Senator Estes Kefauver who set up a special committee. This began sitting in December 1950 and its hearings were televised live across America. 'Jim took great satisfaction in watching the Kefauver Committee hearings,' said Gloria, 'because he made sure they got a copy of the report he had sent to Hoover. But he didn't want his name coming up in the newspapers and the Mafia knowing about it, so he handed the report to [actor] Robert Montgomery who was going to report on the hearings on the radio.'

Montgomery was a former president of the Screen Actors' Guild who had worked with a number of other people, including James Cagney, to have two prominent members of the Mafia, Willie Bioff and George Browne, arrested and imprisoned in 1941. He ensured Jim's report reached the committee.

'When Jim watched Virginia Hill being questioned by the Kefauver Committee,' recalled Gloria, 'he took a great sigh of satisfaction because he had drawn up quite a dossier on her.'

Jim continued to write reports on the Mafia in Hollywood, including profiles of people like Mickey Cohen and Johnny Roselli. Each time he sent in a report, Hoover would call him and thank him personally. And then nothing more was ever heard of those reports.

*

Jim was again drawn into Frank Capra's ongoing investigation by the HUAC. In accordance with the Screen Directors Guild's anti-Communist policy, Capra, as a Board member, signed an affidavit in 1948 to say he was not a Communist. But when, in 1950, the whole of the SDG was required to sign the loyalty oath, Capra was one of several prominent directors who protested (other directors included Clarence Brown and John Ford, who were definitely not Communists). 'What I objected to,' said Capra, 'was the blacklist that the loyalty oath would result in.' His objections resulted in a further addition to his HUAC file stating that 'Capra, Frank, supports revolt against loyalty oath in Screen Directors Guild.'

Despite the growing suspicion that Capra was a Communist, he was never called to testify before the HUAC. However, six members of the SDG were secretly questioned about the blacklist by HUAC investigators. It is probable that Capra was one of them; James Stewart had been called upon to persuade Capra to answer questions. 'I know that Jim met with Capra and told him that he personally had vouched for Capra's loyalty, but Capra had to answer questions himself or face being called before the HUAC in public,' said Gloria. 'Jim knew they had that file on Capra and that it looked very bad for him. So Capra met investigators at the Drake Hotel in Los Angeles.'

After giving testimony, Capra went on what he described as 'a holiday on his ranch'; in fact this was virtually his retirement from the film industry. 'I lost the heart for making films in Hollywood,' said Capra. 'Then I was asked by the Defence Department [in 1951] to work as part of their VISTA project, which was a top-secret think-tank. My job was to make documentary films, and I felt in this way I could prove my loyalty.'

But it did not prove to be as simple as that. The previous investigations on Capra conducted by the HUAC, Army Intelligence and the FBI surfaced, and the FBI was instructed to conduct a new investigation of him. Capra was told his appointment to VISTA was on hold and he was presented with a letter of charges which he had to answer. All the past accusations were listed. He presented the letter to Stewart, who wasted no time in writing to the Defence Department, testifying to Capra's loyalty to America.

A number of other prominent Hollywood actors and directors

also wrote letters, but Stewart did more than just write. 'He went straight to J Edgar Hoover and he got into quite a rage while there,' said Gloria. 'It was one time when he couldn't control his temper, and it really shook Hoover up. Fortunately Jim got control of himself and basically went into a controlled monologue, speaking on Capra's behalf. He told Hoover, "You asked me to do a little work for you, and I've been happy and privileged to do it. But now I'm really putting my own neck on the block. I'm putting *my* reputation on the line in defence of this man who is a friend of mine and a good American. So I'm asking you to give this fella a break . . ." and Jim went on and on, and finally Hoover was won over.'

There were many others, such as John Ford, who wrote on Capra's behalf, but Capra himself credited Jimmy Stewart with being the one who got the Defence Department to clear his security for Project VISTA in 1952. 'I know Jim had some influence with Hoover,' said Capra, 'but it had to be more than I ever imagined because I was told, "You can thank Major Stewart." I said, "Do you mean James Stewart?" All they said was, "Major Stewart personally vouched for you, and that means more than the references all the movie directors and movie stars have sent." When I asked Jim about it, he just said, "Aw, Frank, I only did what you made me do when I was Mr Smith." I think it made a difference that Jim was a real war hero.'

It also made a difference that Stewart had urged Capra to undertake some undercover work for the FBI in Los Angeles, and it seems likely that Stewart may, at this time, have revealed to Capra the full extent of his own undercover work for the FBI.

When the 'unfriendly witnesses' – those who became the Hollywood Ten – were called to Washington in the autumn of 1947 to answer the charge of contempt, Hollywood's liberals formed themselves into the Committee for the First Amendment (the CFA), which opposed the charges. Its members included John Huston, Humphrey Bogart, Gene Kelly, Billy Wilder, William Wyler, Burt Lancaster, Judy Garland and Edward G Robinson.

Eddie Robinson may not have known it then, but he was being labelled a 'Red'. So was Jose Ferrer, who told me, 'Just the innuendo that you might be a Communist was enough to have you put on a blacklist. Well, not a blacklist, but a greylist. I became aware of this when I was working with John Huston on *Moulin Rouge* in 1951, and I was warned that I would never make another film. The fact is I was and am politically left-wing, but I was never a Communist. Neither was Eddie Robinson, but the same thing happened to him. He had it worse than I. He was a Jew, and there were prominent people [in the HUAC] who were anti-Semitic. To be a Jew to these people was almost as bad as being a Communist.'

John Rankin of the HUAC was such a person. In 1951, in response to the protest from the CFA, he gave a now-famous speech to the House of Representatives which supposedly shed light on the actions of the CFA: 'I want to read you some of these names. One of the names is June Havoc. Her real name is June Hovick. Another one is Danny Kaye, and we found out his real name is David Daniel Kamirsky. Another one is Eddie Cantor, whose real name is Edward Iskowitz. There is one who calls himself Edward Robinson. His real name is Emmanuel Goldberg.'

The speech made little impression even on Hollywood's most conservative citizens, including James Stewart. He was, according to Gloria, particularly 'furious' at having his friend Edward G Robinson's name slandered. As far as Jim was concerned, the HUAC was trying to paint Robinson a deep red. To many others, including Jose Ferrer, John Rankin was suggesting that the Jews were as bad as the Communists.

'Many of the studio heads were Jews,' said Ferrer, 'and at the first hearings in Hollywood, they [the HUAC] hauled the studio heads over the coals for giving work to Communist actors and screenwriters. The studios very quickly co-operated with the witch-hunters. I heard there were some of the more right-wing community in Hollywood who were angry at Rankin's speech, including John Wayne, Ronald Reagan and James Stewart. But it seemed to me that none of them were upset that Eddie Robinson was being whipped for being a Jew. They just didn't like him being called a Communist.'

Not every Hollywood liberal believed the right-wingers were anti-Semitic. John Huston told me, 'I never heard Wayne or Reagan say anything that was anti-Semitic, but I heard them say things that were anti-Communist and anti-liberal. James Stewart I never really knew that well, but I heard that he had something of a problem with people who were not entirely Gentile or white middle-class Christians. Joe Mankiewicz, who knew Jimmy Stewart better, told me that Stewart would never make it into the Ku Klux Klan but neither was he at ease around blacks – and I think that might include Jews.'

Henry Fonda, always a Hollywood liberal, said, 'Jim is a true conservative, and that's his view. Just because it isn't mine, it doesn't make him wrong. Even if I think I am right – and I do! I don't have any problem with anyone of any colour, and neither does Jim. What he does have is a different attitude towards them, and that's just his upbringing. But anyone who ever says he persecuted anyone for being a different race or colour is a liar.'

I have heard Jim's views on racism debated by several people, and can only conclude that while he may not have been entirely without prejudice, as suggested by Woody Strode, it was only by a matter of degrees. I have seen Jim talking to a black woman – a film publicist – and I didn't notice any difference between the way he spoke to her and the way he spoke to me.

But whether or not he was concerned about anti-Semitic slurs against Eddie Robinson by John Rankin to the House of Representatives, what certainly concerned him was the accusation that Robinson was a Communist. Jim went straight to the FBI and demanded to know what the allegations were against Robinson. He said to them, 'If Eddie was a Communist, don't you think I would have told you?'

Jim was shown a slim file which noted that Robinson had been a member of a group called 'American Youth for Democracy', which the FBI considered to be a Communist sponsored organisation. He had also loaned $2,500 to screenwriter Dalton Trumbo, one of the Hollywood Ten. Jim demanded, 'Is that all you've got?' He was told that they were still investigating Robinson, but suggested that Stewart do the same 'to see if they could all come to the same conclusion'. Jim told them, 'All right. And the only conclusion we'll come to is that Eddie is no Communist.'

Jim went to see Robinson, who by now was feeling the effects of being greylisted. 'I can't get any work,' he told Jim.

'What am I going to do?'

'What you're going to do is prove to them that you're not a Communist,' Jim told him.

'How can I prove that?'

'Prove to them you're a loyal American. All they want from you is to go before the [HUAC] committee and tell them the names of those you know are Communists.'

'Oh no,' said Robinson. 'I can't do that.'

Jim said, 'But you know all the same Communists the rest of us do. Just give 'em the same names everyone else has.'

Robinson asked Jim if he'd named names. Jim couldn't admit that he'd been gathering information for the HUAC, even though many in Hollywood had openly given names to the committee. Said John Huston, 'There were mainly two kinds of name-givers. There were those who admitted to having been Communists but were now repentant and ready to name other Communists, and there were those who were never Communists but knew the names of those who were.

'It didn't matter if you were a reformed Communist or not; if you got up on the stand and named names, you were guilty by association. You were seen to be just trying to save your own neck. There were still a lot of liberals like myself who might not want an informer working for them. The only way to get past that was to meet members of the HUAC in private and tell them what you wanted to say, and then nobody knew. And that made for a bad climate in Hollywood. You were often wondering about people, like Jimmy Stewart, and asking yourself, "Did he name names in private?"'

There is no record of Stewart ever meeting HUAC members in secret to name names, and that is because he probably never did. He had another method, and one which he saw as being a part of his patriotic duty. It had nothing to do with trying to save his career. When Jim gave the FBI or HUAC representatives lists of names, they were of *known* Communists, and not *suspected* Communists. He never gave names in person; he only ever gave typed lists. Edward G Robinson had appeared on none of these lists.

Jim continued to try to persuade Robinson to go before the HUAC and give testimony. Robinson finally gave in, and he sent a request to the HUAC to appear before them. This he did in 1950, bringing with him piles of documents. 'He felt humiliated and he thought he was vindicated,' recalled Jose Ferrer. HUAC representative Francis E Walter announced:

'This Robinson hearing was a good thing. The time has arrived when we should find out what influences have been at work in Hollywood, who was responsible for the charges of Communism, and who is not a Red.

'I think we should offer everybody who has ever been accused an opportunity to come before us and clear his reputation of these charges. I favour a full and complete investigation of the charges and rumours.'

Jim was delighted with the result, and Robinson, although clearly embarrassed by his experience, thanked Jim for 'helping to save' him. But it was not enough for some quarters in Washington. Robinson's hearing came in for an assault by Republicans in Congress, who attacked the 'bill of health' the HUAC had given him because no witnesses had been called. A new hearing was demanded so evidence could be taken from anti-Robinson witnesses. When Jim heard this, he told Robinson, 'There's nothing to worry about. There are no witnesses to testify against you.'

Robinson wasn't convinced, and he called upon Joseph Roos of the Community Relations Committee (an organisation which represented Jewish positions to the Gentile community) to help. Roos, who defined his job as 'an investigative reporter for movie stars', went through the cheque stubs of many known non-Communist stars to prove to the HUAC that they too gave donations to the 'American Youth for Democracy', and that the fact that Robinson had made a donation in no way proved him to be a Communist.

In fact, no 'anti-Robinson' witnesses could be found. Jose Ferrer, who was also allowed to go before the HUAC around the same time, said, 'They had me and Eddie Robinson, and put us both in the position of having to defend ourselves, and it was for him, as it was for me, a humiliating experience.'

Jim, however, felt justified in persuading Robinson to testify. But it was at a cost; major studios became wary of hiring Robinson.

Jim felt sure that it would only be a matter of time before Robinson would find his career on track again. But when Robinson's career continued to struggle, Jim began to question whether he had been right in persuading him to go through the indignity of appearing before the HUAC. His conclusion was that there had been no other way for Robinson to clear himself, but still feeling partly responsible, Jim went first to J Edgar Hoover. In a personal meeting at Washington, Jim outlined Robinson's dilemma. Hoover told Stewart, 'I don't see what I can do about it.'

Jim told him, 'You're the head of the FBI, the greatest law enforcement agency in the world. I was honoured to be asked by you for my help in this matter, and I've done my best. I was happy to do my duty. But there's an innocent man whose life is turning upside down because he had the guts to stand up and say that despite the accusations, he was not a Communist. Now I think the least his country can do for him is to help him when he's down.'

Hoover gave Jim vague promises, enough to send him back to Hollywood thinking he had accomplished his mission. But it didn't take long for Jim to realise that Hollywood was still not forgiving Robinson for a sin he never committed in the first place. 'Just to be accused was enough,' said John Huston.

A lot of actors found that to be true, but for now Jim was only interested in helping Eddie Robinson. In desperation, he eventually went to Cecil B DeMille (with whom Stewart was to work in 1950 in *The Greatest Show on Earth*) and asked the most staunch right-wing conservative film director in Hollywood to give Eddie Robinson a break. This DeMille did, casting Robinson in *The Ten Commandments*. The fact that DeMille would cast Robinson in an important role in such a major picture sent a message to the whole of Hollywood, and Robinson's career was saved.

While it's possible that Jim told Frank Capra about his work for J Edgar Hoover, it's certain that he told at least one person, the one man he felt he could trust the most – Henry Fonda. It was a huge mistake. 'The only person who knew – the only one Jim confided in – was Henry Fonda,' said Gloria. 'And that led to an almighty rift between the two that lasted for years.'

It was no secret that in 1948 James Stewart and Henry Fonda had some kind of argument and did not speak to each other for a number of years. Said Gloria, 'Most people speculated that it was over politics. Both Jim and Hank said it was a political argument because of their different beliefs. But it was worse than that. Much worse. Jim thought the one person he could confide in about his secret work for the FBI was Hank. He was so wrong.'

When Jim told Fonda that he was helping the FBI, Fonda exploded. He accused Jim of being 'an informer'. The description did not sit well with Jim, who tried to explain that his main reason for working for the FBI was to run the Mafia out of Hollywood.

Fonda told him, 'You stupid son of a bitch. The FBI haven't even been able to run the Mafia out of Chicago. They're sure as hell not going to run them out of Hollywood.'

'I have Hoover's word,' Jim told Fonda.

'What good is his word?' argued Fonda.

'He's the head of the FBI, for God's sake.'

'And then I suppose you're going to help him run all the Communists out of Hollywood.'

'And what's wrong with that?'

Gloria told me, 'They went at each other in the most heated argument they'd ever had. Hank was a liberal who believed everyone had a right to their own politics, even though he didn't like Communism himself. And Jim believed the Communists were a real threat. They'd never agreed on politics, and for the most part they agreed never to discuss politics. But this was different. This time Hank was accusing Jim of being an informer, which is a dirty word, however it comes out. The row almost came to blows.'

Jim's rage surfaced during the argument, and Fonda prepared to defend himself. But Jim checked himself, held back the punch he was going to land on Fonda's chin, and stepped away. Both men were shaking, partly through rage, partly through fear. They had come as close to physically fighting as they ever would – and Gloria was convinced that Jim would have inflicted terrible damage on Fonda if he had not managed to get control of himself. Shaking, sweat breaking out across his forehead, his teeth clenched, Jim told Fonda, 'Don't you ever call me an informer again. There's only one goddamn thing that I am, and that's a patriot.'

Both men stood down, turned their backs on each other, and walked away. 'They didn't speak again for several years,' said Gloria.

In 1948, Fonda left Hollywood and returned to New York to resume his stage career. During the early years of her marriage to Jim, Gloria saw the pain he suffered over the breakdown in his friendship with Fonda. She said, in 1979:

'Jim was devastated at losing his best friend. It just ate him up. Many times I told him, "Give Hank a call." But Jim couldn't bring himself to do it. He said, "When I've done what I have to do, when I can look Hank in the eye and tell him that Hollywood is free of those gangsters, then I'll call him. I want him to know that I did the right thing."

'Jim was amazing during those years. People knew he and Hank had had a bust up. But they didn't know why. With anybody else, Jim just seemed like his usual self. He didn't give anything away to anyone. But with me, he could show his real emotions.

'Jim knew that those who openly boasted about their complicity with the HUAC faced a backlash. Adolphe Menjou boasted that he conducted investigations on behalf of the HUAC and that J Edgar Hoover was a very close personal friend. That didn't do him any good at all. People didn't like the idea they were being spied on, even if the spy had no Communist affiliations at all, because the merest innuendo could damage someone's life and career. A lot of people turned their backs on Menjou, and his career went downhill.

'I think Ronald Reagan's career was damaged because he was a known informer of the FBI, which is perhaps why he turned to politics. There were a lot of people in Hollywood working as FBI informants. Jim knew he had to keep his FBI connection a secret. I don't know if to this day he has ever told anyone else apart from Hank Fonda. I am sure he didn't. And I know that he wished he'd never told Hank.'

15

Gloria

In search of a career-saving project, Jim accepted, with some reluctance, an offer to star in what seemed like a sure-fire Alfred Hitchcock thriller, *Rope*. The film was an adaptation of a play inspired by the infamous Leopold–Loeb case, when two well-educated men from Chicago committed murder for the thrill of the act and to demonstrate what they perceived to be their superiority over the rest of society.

John Dall and Farley Granger played the two young men who commit what they think is the perfect crime. They celebrate by serving supper, neatly laid on a chest in which they have hidden the body, to the victim's relatives, friends and the killers' former teacher, played by Stewart. He becomes the investigator when he suspects what the boys have done, and manages to chip away at their initial confidence to reveal the shocking truth, part of which is that it was something in his teachings that inspired the killers to act.

Jim had trouble accepting that he was right for the role of a man who, although the hero, is also the villain. 'This professor was the one who unwittingly inspired these two killers,' said Jim, 'and I found that frightening at first. That was something dark and sinister . . . I'd never done anything like it. But Hitchcock persuaded me to do it because he said that James Stewart is the last person on earth the audience will expect to be the instigator of such a horrific crime. And as an actor, that intrigued me . . . to explore a dark side intrigued me. So I did it.'

Warner Brothers paid him a lofty $300,000 to make *Rope*. But Jim began to wonder if it was worth the fee because the picture was difficult for everyone to make. It was especially difficult for Jim, whose confidence in his own abilities and his viability at the box office were well and truly shaken.

Part of the difficulty was Hitchcock's idea to split the film into uncut ten-minute takes. Usually, even in 1948, takes rarely lasted longer than a minute or two, while in today's fast-edited films, very few movies have takes that last even as long as two minutes.

To accomplish this feat, and to keep the camera moving for a complete ten minutes to maintain visual interest, lengthy rehearsals were needed. But much of the time was taken up with getting the camera into the right place at the right time, and for parts of the set to be moved out of shot to accommodate the movement of the camera. This technique tested the patience of the whole cast, not least of all Jim's. He complained to Hitchcock, 'The only thing that's getting rehearsed around here is the *camera*.'

The strain on Jim began to manifest; and it wasn't only the strain of filming. The stress that came from being Hoover's most secret of agents in Hollywood drove him literally to drink. 'I never knew Jim to drink as much, *ever*, as he did when making *Rope*,' said Burgess Meredith.

Jim told me, 'I couldn't sleep at nights after a day's shooting on *Rope*. Just to do a ten-minute take is hard enough because there are always noises that ruin the sound, like the props and set walls being moved . . . and we were having to do them over and over. I'd never found making a film so difficult.'

Gloria knew that not all of Jim's problems had to do with making the picture. 'He'd lost Henry Fonda, and he was under pressure from the FBI, *and* he was trying to do the best job he could for them without betraying his own sense of integrity . . . which was seriously in jeopardy,' she said. 'I think he would have coped better if he'd just been able to make a film where he learned his lines, turned up on time and had a little fun. But no one had fun on *Rope*.'

Hitchcock tried another innovation with *Rope*, shooting it in 'real time' so that the film's eighty-minute running time actually represented eighty minutes. This was considered a terrible idea by the critics when it opened in September 1948. *Variety* picked out the good and the bad in the picture: 'Hitchcock could have chosen a more entertaining subject with which to use the arresting camera and staging technique . . . James Stewart, as the ex-professor who first senses the guilt of his former pupils and nibbles away at their composure with verbal barbs, does a commanding job. John Dall stands out as the egocentric who masterminds the killing and ghoulish wake. Equally good is Farley Granger as the weakling partner in crime.'

Jim felt the picture 'didn't work', and yet somehow the film stands up better today than it did when released. What makes the film so compulsive is that the viewer is urging Stewart on to solve the crime; this was a formula which made the TV series *Columbo* a success. But in 1948, audiences and critics preferred a whodunnit rather than a picture where they already know who did it.

The film had another problem; its homoerotic subtext with which Hitchcock enjoyed teasing the audience. The actual case of Leopold and Loeb established that they and their victim were homosexuals, and Hitchcock saw no reason to make his characters any different. But the strict censorship of the day forbade any such thing, and the film inevitably ran into problems in some states and cities of America, getting banned altogether in Chicago. It was also banned in West Germany until 1963, and then shown only after major cuts.

Relief came for Jim when he was recalled to New York to give Frank Fay another break from *Harvey* for the 1948 summer season. The play was something Jim was falling ever deeper in love with, and this time round he even managed to get some good reviews.

Then it was back to Hollywood for what was an ego-bruising experience. He accepted second billing to Joan Fontaine in *You Gotta Stay Happy*, a somewhat prophetic title considering what was going on in Jim's life and career. The film, produced by Fontaine's husband, William Dozier, featured her as a millionairess who jilts her husband on their wedding night and persuades a pilot, played by Stewart, to take her with him on a business flight to California. She finds herself on board a cargo plane in the company of a young married couple, a casket with a dead body, frozen fish, a crook on the run, and a chimpanzee that smokes cigars. Stewart falls for Fontaine, and only discovers she is wealthy when he crash-lands, effectively losing his business. He is saved when she buys him a new four-engine cargo plane.

'That wasn't such a bad film,' reflected Jim. 'Joan was a nice person to work with . . . although she didn't much like her sister [Olivia de Havilland] so we steered clear of her as a subject. Joan was pregnant at the time, and she shouldn't have been doing some of the stuff she had to do. She did a scene where she had to leap off a hay wagon, and she had some trouble . . . pain in the tummy. They got her to hospital. I went to visit her. She said I was the only one from the picture who came to see her. I don't know how true that was . . . I guess if Joan said so, it must be. Not even the director [H C Potter] went to see her.'

Gloria pointed out an ironic footnote to all this: Joan Fontaine had a daughter who grew up to marry H C Potter's son – and Fontaine refused to go to the wedding. Said Gloria, 'I don't know what that says about anything . . . except that Hollywood people are the craziest in the world. I've got one of the few sane actors for a husband.'

The film didn't overwhelm the critics. It was another variation on *It Happened One Night*, and a clear attempt to copy Capra. That was why they brought in Jimmy Stewart, even if he was second-billed. The film came and went quickly, did moderate business, and is now largely forgotten. However, when seen today, it is an entertaining ride, and Jim is good, if not remarkable. It was the kind of part he could do with little effort to make it work (or it *seemed* he expended little effort), and he enjoyed the chance to just learn his lines, turn up on time, do a few short takes and feel generally at ease.

But the film was not a career-saver. Being demoted to second billing meant he was on his way down, and he didn't know if he would ever find his way back up again.

While trying to save his career, and while trying to deal with the political and – as far as he was concerned – the criminal activities in Hollywood, Jim was also gradually sorting out his own personal priorities. He had been seeing an RKO contract player, Myrna Dell. It was what Burgess Meredith referred to as 'a casual romance'. Jim always laughed off any suggestion that there was anything serious between them.

According to Meredith, their relationship began when actress Sylvia Sidney invited Dell to a party she was throwing for John McClain, a much respected theatre critic of the New York *Journal-American*. Sidney suggested Dell choose between Jimmy Stewart and another actor as a date. Dell chose Jim because he was her favourite actor. Jim picked her up from her home and they arrived at Sylvia Sidney's house. A man opened the door and Jim behaved as though he recognised him, pumping his hand and saying how wonderful it was to see him. When Jim stopped shaking his hand, the man, who looked embarrassed, said, 'May I take your coats?' He was the butler.

Jim confirmed the story for me, and explained, 'I was suffering from hearing loss by then, and I often misheard what people said. When this fella opened the door, he said something . . . I don't know what he said . . . but it just seemed to me that he *had* to be the theatre critic.'

Jim's gradual hearing loss was something that caused him endless misunderstandings over the years. He recalled, 'Somebody told me something, and I thought they were saying, "Louis B Mayer said hello." So I said, "Please say hello to Mr Mayer when you see him next." They said a lot louder, "You misunderstand. I said Louis B Mayer is *dead* – did ya know?"'

Jim rarely joked about his hearing loss, but he enjoyed telling me this story: 'I was flying out to Africa with Gloria, and there was a little turbulence . . . nothing that worried me. A stewardess came up to me and said, "Excuse me, Mr Stewart, but you used to be a pilot, didn't you?" I said, "Yes. Still am." Then I thought she said, "Our pilot has passed out and we need you to fly the plane if you'd care to come up to the cockpit." I said, "Waall, I don't know. Can't the co-pilot fly the plane? Don't you have emergency procedures?" And Gloria, who'd realised my mistake, said, "No, Jim. She said that the pilot would be pleased, if you wanted to see how they fly the plane, to welcome you to the cockpit."'

As well as trying to deal with the problems caused by his hearing loss (which he believed he inherited from his mother), Jim began to consider trying to change the way he spoke by hiring a voice coach, thinking that might help his ailing career. He put forward this suggestion to numerous people, including Burgess Meredith and Myrna Dell, in order to gauge their response. They all told him that there was nothing wrong with his voice. He only needed to find a decent script.

Although he was seeing Myrna Dell, it was evident to those who knew him best that he was never going to allow things to get serious between them. It was nevertheless equally obvious Jim was hoping to find someone he could marry. 'When you're almost forty, life means more than just a book full of girls' telephone numbers,' he said. 'To me, being married is about having the security of a permanent relationship, and that's what I needed at that time. I needed to put down roots.' One thing he knew for sure was that he wouldn't marry an actress: 'I've seen a high mortality rate in a lot of Hollywood marriages. Too often both partners have their own careers and have to live apart so much.'

Gloria Hatrick was the perfect choice, although Jim never knew it when they first met, and Gloria certainly didn't think Jim was what she considered to be much of a catch. 'I was at the actor Keenan Wynn's house for a Christmas celebration [in 1947],' she told me. Gloria then was an attractive 31-year-old socialite, recently divorced from millionaire Edward McLean Jnr. 'I was just leaving when three drunken men arrived – Johnny Swope, Bill Grady and James Stewart. And James Stewart was very different from the gentle, sober James Stewart I'd seen on the screen. He had always been my favourite actor, so you could say I was somewhat underwhelmed by what I saw that day. Jim can't remember our first meeting – probably because he was too drunk.

'A few weeks later I was having lunch at Romanoff's restaurant with my two sons, and in walked Jim with some friends, and he never even acknowledged me – which is not surprising since he couldn't remember meeting me the first time because he was so drunk.'

They didn't meet again for several months. Then, in the summer of 1948, a story hit the newspapers that claimed Jim had proposed marriage to Myrna Dell. The wedding, it was claimed, would take place as soon as Jim returned from New York (he had by then taken over from Frank Fay for his second stint in *Harvey*). Both Jim and Myrna laughed off the speculation.

On his return from New York, Jim was invited to Gary Cooper's house for dinner. It turned out to be a ploy hatched by Cooper and his wife Rocky to try and match Jim with a prospective partner. They had selected Gloria Hatrick, and when they told her that she was going to be sat next to James Stewart, she immediately protested. 'I wouldn't have gone at all, but Gary and Rocky convinced me that I had not met the *real* Jimmy Stewart,' she said. 'They insisted that we would find much in common.

'Jim didn't know me from Eve. What took me by surprise was how shy he was. He hardly said a thing. And *that's* what first attracted me to him. After dinner, Leland Hayward insisted Jim and I go to Ciro's with him for a little dancing. Jim was a very good dancer. He seemed more at ease dancing than he was talking. I knew he was getting interested in me when Leland tried to cut in and Jim waved him off.

'He wanted to see me the next day, and suggested we play golf, which is a sport I enjoy, and so we had our first date on our own. Jim didn't admit that he didn't actually like golf; he only went because *I* said I liked it. After that we saw each other regularly. He loved my two boys, Michael and Ronald, who were only two and three years old.'

Burgess Meredith said he knew immediately that Jim was more interested in Gloria than he had been in any woman for a long time: 'He was always talking about her, how great at golf she was, what a great dancer she was, what great kids she had, and how this huge dog she had always jumped on him with glee when he arrived.' When Jim had first read the script for *The Philadelphia Story*, he'd assumed he was being offered the part of the man who marries the society girl. Now he was actually dating the society girl.

Gloria was born in Larchmont, New York, to Edgar and Jessie Hatrick. Edgar had earned his fortune pioneering early documentary films, newsreels, promotional films and movie serials. In 1908, he was hired by media tycoon William Randolph Hearst to run the

Hearst Metrotone News company and produce *News of the Day*, which provided audiences of silent films with one of the first filmed weekly news programmes. During the First World War, he worked for the US Government Information Service, producing the first documentary footage of the conflict to be seen by the public.

Gloria – like her brother and sister – enjoyed the best education in the top schools, including the Finch College for Women on the Upper East Side of Manhattan. As a young, tall, slim, attractive woman, she worked as a model, a dance instructor and a fashion designer.

She turned down the opportunities to go into acting that her father's connections offered, but she enjoyed the company of actors. She was blessed with a wonderful sense of humour that ranged from charming sarcasm to plain silliness. She was described by Burgess Meredith as 'a very gutsy broad', although I think the term 'broad', which perhaps induces images of a lively girl from low society, did not do her justice. She was a well-educated and intelligent lady, but she enjoyed life to the point that she might not necessarily fit snugly into the category of a 'lady' in the more accepted genteel manner. There was nothing genteel about Gloria, but neither was there anything common about her. She was her own woman with an assertive but never arrogant personality.

When her husband, Edward McLean Jnr (they had met at a function for Cosmopolitan Pictures, which was owned by Hearst), announced that he was leaving her for one of the Vanderbilts, the news came as no surprise to her. She had long known of his extra-marital affair. 'I didn't want to make things too easy for him when he told me he was leaving,' she told me. 'I was doing a crossword, and he was trying to tell me his intentions. I would say, "5 Down, *'philanderer'* seven words, the first letter is *'b'* and the last letter is *'d'*. Now just what could that be?" Finally he said, "Look, I'm going to divorce you." I said, "Just as long as you're the one who goes to Reno." As long as I got a good settlement so I could raise my two boys, he was free to go. And I was free too.

'It wasn't easy being a single mother with two boys aged two and three. Most single mothers didn't go out. I *did*. I was not going to miss out on a life, but I also made sure that my boys were okay. If I went for dinner to a restaurant, they came too. I took them to some parties, and everyone would dote on them. But it was Gary and Rocky Cooper who said to me, "Come to dinner and meet Jim, but *don't* bring your boys." A single mother with two children doesn't get the best of the catch usually . . . but I did. I got Jim. When he found out I had children, he wanted to meet them. And he was great with them right from the start.'

Jim's acceptance of Gloria's children and her gutsy nature provided Jim with a glimpse of his future. He told me, 'I thought to myself, "Jim, you might never find a better one than this girl" . . . and I was right. So I decided I'd better ask her to marry me.' When he fell in love with Gloria, he cut right down on his drinking.

He maintained there was another good reason for deciding to marry Gloria: 'She had a German shepherd dog called Bello who always leaped on to me when I arrived. Gloria said he was just being friendly . . . but this huge dog seemed to want to take my head off. So I decided I'd better marry Gloria to ingratiate myself with Bello.'

Gloria just had one niggle about Jim: 'He was always tight with his money. I thought with me he might loosen up a little. But he didn't. I kept saying, "Let's go out to eat at a restaurant," and he kind of fumbled and mumbled and said something about why spend money in a restaurant when I – *I* – could cook. Finally I said, "Let's go to a restaurant, and *I'll* pay." His sense of pride as a man over-came his sense of prudence, and he finally took me out to dine. When *You Gotta Stay Happy* had its premiere, Jim asked me if I wanted to go. I said, "If we go to the premiere, does it mean you're actually going to feed me as well?"'

When Gloria told me this story over dinner, Jim raised a hand and said, 'All right now, Gloria, I think you'll find I'm paying for this meal, so you can quit with the . . . you know what I mean.' He looked at me and said, 'If you were constantly being photographed by newspapermen every time you went out with a beautiful woman to a restaurant, wouldn't you get a little tired of it?' That was his explanation of past events, and my reply to him was, 'If I went to dinner every night with a beautiful girl, they could take all the pictures they want.'

He replied, 'You say that now but you . . . you . . . just you wait and see.'

As I pointed out once to Gloria, I never found out if that was true. To which she replied, 'What do you mean? You've been eating out with *me*.' And I replied, 'Yes, you're right – but nobody knows me, so nobody wants to take my picture.'

'Well, they damn well should,' she said, which goes to illustrate the humorous verbal fencing Jim and Gloria enjoyed, and the rather special lady Gloria was. But then, Jim was pretty special too.

Whether or not Jim was resisting eating out with Gloria at restaurants to avoid being photographed, or just because he didn't like spending his money, he had changed his ways by the time they were married because they had begun frequenting a restaurant in Beverly Hills called Chasen's. They continued to eat there two or three times a week, unless they were out of the country, until the restaurant closed down in the 1990s.

In between romancing Gloria and working secretly for Hoover, Jim still had his career to consider. Help came from an unexpected source – his original studio, MGM. He never expected to work there again, especially now that his star seemed to be on the wane. They offered him his first biographical film, *The Stratton Story*. It told the story of baseball star Monty Stratton who, at the height of his career, trips during a hunting expedition and accidentally shoots himself in the leg. The leg is amputated, and Stratton goes into depression. Inspired by the sight of his baby son taking his first steps, Stratton straps on an artificial leg and learns to walk. Eventually he learns to pitch a ball again; encouraged by his wife, Ethel, he returns to baseball and wins his first game.

Director Sam Wood and Monty Stratton wanted James Stewart to play the part, and no one else. Louis B Mayer not only *didn't* want Stewart at his studio, he didn't want to make the film at all. According to Jim, Mayer told Wood, 'How do you think people will feel watching this man with one leg? They will feel it's a disgusting sight.' Mayer also mentioned that baseball pictures almost never succeeded.

Nevertheless, he finally gave the go-ahead, but insisted that Van Johnson play Stratton. Johnson recalled for me in 1982, 'I got on really well with Monty Stratton, and I think he liked me, but I just couldn't pitch the ball in a way that pleased him. He said to me he hoped I wouldn't be offended but he was going to ask Mr Mayer if Jimmy Stewart could play the part. I wasn't offended because I didn't want to look ridiculous on the screen, but I said, "How do you know Jimmy Stewart can pitch a ball?" He said, "I don't, but Sam Wood told me that Jim will practise time and again until he can." I liked Jimmy and didn't mind if he got the part. I knew Metro would find something else for me to do, so I said, "Go ahead, Monty. And good luck." I wished Jimmy luck too.' Stratton personally went to Mayer and demanded that Jimmy Stewart play the part. Mayer, who needed the film to get started, gave his permission – reluctantly.

Donna Reed, Jim's co-star from *It's a Wonderful Life*, was cast as Ethel Stratton. She was one of the few people I ever met who ended up disliking Jim. In 1984, she recalled, 'Van Johnson was cast as Stratton, but something happened and they cast Jimmy. I liked Van but I was thrilled when they announced Jimmy was going to do it. I thought we were pretty good together in *It's a Wonderful Life*. But Jim asked that they take me off the picture too, and they replaced me with June Allyson. When I asked why, I was told that Jimmy was fighting for his professional life. I said, "What do you think *I'm* fighting for?' And I was. I didn't work for MGM again. The pictures I made got worse, except for *From Here to Eternity* [for which she won an Oscar as Best Supporting Actress], and my career never did recover. So I'm mad at Jimmy for wrecking my career.'

Jim admitted that it was his choice to replace Reed with Allyson: 'I had to have a hit, and as much as I liked Donna Reed . . . and as good an actress as she is . . . which she proved in *From Here to Eternity* . . . the sad fact is that on *It's a Wonderful Life* we just didn't have any chemistry . . . on screen *or* off. We just didn't hit it off. And I think the film suffered . . . it was one of the weaknesses in the film. Capra thought so too. He once said to me, "Jim, if only we could have had someone like Margaret Sullavan or Ginger Rogers, but your wife in the picture has to be so *ordinary*, and you can't cast Margaret or Ginger to play ordinary women." I felt just so bad about Donna not being in the [Stratton] film . . . but I needed someone who was going to play a woman who was going to be a hundred and ten per cent supportive of her husband . . . and I wasn't convinced Donna could pull that off, because we just didn't hit it off. Things like that show up on the screen. And I feel guilty.'

He asked for June Allyson because he knew that she had made a success at playing the girl-next-door in a succession of films. Her reputation was also one of an easy-to-work-with, sweet-natured girl. As Jim put it, 'What you saw of June on the screen was what you saw off the screen. She was the sweetest actress, and we made a good screen team.' They would go on to make three successful films playing husband and wife. In fact, it got to the point that their screen chemistry was too convincing for many members of the public, who came to believe they really were married.

Gloria said, 'When some members of the public approach Jim, and I'm with him, and he introduces me as his wife, they are shocked and say, "Did you and June Allyson get *divorced*?" I sometimes jump in and say, "Jim's a bigamist. He's married to me *and* June." They go away puzzled, and Jim gets annoyed because he thinks they'll never come and watch another of his films.'

In preparing for the role of Stratton, Jim took time to learn how to pitch a ball properly, as coached by Monty Stratton himself. He also learned how to walk in a way that convinced the audience he had a false leg. 'These things are important,' he said. 'You don't have to actually know how to pitch a ball, but you have to *look* like you know. The better you can actually pitch a ball, the more convincing you'll be. And Stratton was a genius with the ball, so I had to *look* like I was a genius with the ball too. Or the picture wouldn't have worked.'

As it was, the film did work, and audiences loved it. It took $4 million in 1949 on its first release, making it MGM's biggest earner of the year. Jim's career had suddenly stabilised. He wasn't exactly back on top, but he wasn't going further down.

The word that Jim was romancing socialite Gloria Hatrick began to spread, and newspaper columnists, who'd been bewildered at Jim's lack of interest in famous actresses lately, began mentioning the couple in their columns. Soon, Gloria's name was known widely as James Stewart's prospective bride. Some suggested the wedding would take place in February 1949, with the venue being somewhere in Mexico. In fact, the wedding was finally set for 9 August 1949, to take place in Los Angeles at the Brentwood Presbyterian Church. However, unkind columnists suggested that Jim, at the age of forty-one, was perhaps a little old to be getting married and starting a family.

MGM were obviously pleased enough with Stewart in *The Stratton Story*, even before it had been seen by critics and public, to put him to work opposite Spencer Tracy in *Malaya*. In this potboiler of an adventure, Jim played yet another newspaperman, this time teaming up with soldier of fortune Spencer Tracy to smuggle rubber out of Malaya during the Second World War. Jim said he did the film 'so I could work with Tracy again. The first time I worked with him, he was still a rising star at Metro, but by the second time he was a major star – I mean *major* star.' But it wasn't the happy experience he had hoped for:

'The trouble with Tracy was, he had become a real pain in the derrière. He kept threatening to walk off the picture. He'd insisted he wanted to do an action picture, and so MGM got him this picture. I said to him, "What's eating you, Spence?" He said, "That son of a bitch who's directing this garbage" – only he didn't use the word "garbage". He was talking about Richard Thorpe, who did a lot of stuff at MGM because he was quick and he saved the studio money. He did just about everything in one take. He did a lot of action pictures that way. That was okay by me. I can do the one-take thing if there's nothing interesting to play as an actor.

'So I said to Tracy, "But, Spence, you don't need more than one take. You get it right first time, every time." He said, "You think so?" I said, "Sure." He said, "I'm so glad they got *you* on this picture. I said I'd only do this garbage if they cast you in it." Waall, I knew that wasn't entirely true, because he was already cast and *I'd* agreed to do the picture because *he* was in it. I was still relegated to second billing, but with Tracy as the star, I didn't mind.

'The producer [Edwin H Knopf] came to me and said, "Tracy is saying he's going to walk again." I said, "What do you think I can do about it?" He said, "He likes you. You're his best buddy on this picture. I want you to make sure he doesn't walk."

'I thought about it . . . and so I started talking to him about the two of us taking a trip abroad . . . since I was his "best buddy" on the picture. I began bringing in travel brochures and talking about going to India or Greece or anywhere in Asia or Europe. Waall . . .

he seemed really excited about this . . . and when the picture was over, I said, "Have you got your passport ready and your bags packed?" He said, "What for?" I said, "For our trip abroad." He said, "Why, I wouldn't go across the street with you, you son of a bitch."

'I asked Katy Hepburn how she put up with him. She said, "Whenever he got mad and called me a bitch or something worse, I always just came back with, 'And you're the sorriest son of a bitch I ever knew.' And he'd laugh, and that would be that. They say fight fire with fire. I fought Spence with Spence."

'After his outburst, I decided to steer clear of him for a few weeks . . . and then I called him and we got together . . . and I said, "Tell me, Spence . . . why did you call me a son of a bitch?" He looked surprised and said, "I never called you that. I never *would* call you that." I said, "Yes you did . . . when we finished on *Malaya*." He said, "Oh *that*! Jesus, Jim, *everybody* was a son of a bitch on that picture . . . including *me*." And that's just the way Tracy was. I said, "Well, Spence, do you want to come to this son of a bitch's wedding?" He said, "Of course I do, you son of a bitch."'

Gloria had a little addition to that story: 'When Tracy called Jim a son of a bitch, Jim got mad. But *mad*! He grabbed Tracy, who was much shorter but stockier, and said, "I ought to punch you right in the mouth." That temper of Jim's isn't something even Spencer Tracy wants to see the worst of. And Tracy said, "Oh yeah! Go on, take your best shot." Jim knew he could knock Tracy out. Tracy had been drinking, so it wasn't going to take much to knock him out. Jim just got a grip on himself, let go of Tracy, pushed him away, and said, "You were nice to me when I first started, and I'm not forgetting that. But you ever call me a son of a bitch again and I'll knock the holy crap out of you." I think Tracy, who wasn't usually afraid of anything or anyone, felt really bad about what he'd said to Jim . . . once he'd sobered up. He tried calling Jim, but Jim was still so steamed up, he wouldn't take his calls for a few weeks. Jim has the patience of a saint – he really does – but when his patience runs out . . . and it takes a hell of a lot to make it run out . . . you'd better watch yourself.'

*

Gloria hadn't met Jim's family even in the final weeks leading up to the wedding. She knew that she and Alex were going to clash when she heard that Alex was arranging for the wedding guests to provide something a little out of the ordinary as wedding gifts. She told me:

'Someone called me and said, "Did you know Jim's father is asking the guests not to bring wedding gifts but to donate pews to the Brentwood Presbyterian Church?" I was furious. I went to Jim and told him and asked him what the hell was his father doing. He was trying to calm me down and said that he'd sort things out with his father. I think it was the nearest I came to cancelling the wedding. It wasn't as though I *needed* any gifts. I just was not going to have *anyone* being so presumptuous about *my* wedding. But Alex got his way.

'I only met Jim's parents a couple of days before the wedding. Alex was definitely relieved that Jim had found a wife, and he was even more relieved that I wasn't an actress. But he had reservations, and I didn't care. He told me, "I understand you've been married before." I said, "Yes, just the once." He said, "Nobody in the Stewart family has *ever* been divorced." I wasn't sure if it was an accusation or a warning, so I said, "Mr Stewart, I can assure you, I don't intend to marry again just so I can get another divorce."

'I was always a heavy smoker, and I lit up in front of him. He looked at me as though I had just committed the vilest sin you could think of. He said, "Miss Hatrick, you *smoke*." I said, "Yes, I do. Would you care for one?" Jim was pacing around like an expectant father. Totally on tenterhooks. When I offered Alex a cigarette, Jim nearly died. Then Alex said, "Do you go to church?" I replied, "Only for funerals and weddings, so only a few days to go before my next visit." Jim's jaw dropped to the ground. He thought all hell was going to break loose.'

Peace was maintained, and the wedding took place on schedule at Brentwood Presbyterian. Six hundred guests attended. As Gloria noted, 'They were sitting on a lot of pews that had my name on them. That didn't help my nerves . . . even though I'd been down the aisle once before. I was so nervous, I just shook the whole time.'

Among the stars there were Spencer Tracy (on his best behaviour), David Niven, Gary Cooper and Ray Milland. Henry Fonda, of course, was missing. 'Hank would have been Jim's best man,' said Gloria, 'and I know it broke him up that Hank wasn't there – it was going to take some time to heal those wounds. Later, we found out that Hank was just as heart-broken. Jim had a lot of great friends fortunately, and Bill Grady [the MGM casting director] was one of the best, so he was best man.'

Missing from the wedding were Gloria's estranged parents; Edgar had left his wife for an affair with an actress thirty years younger than he. But their absence had nothing to do with their separation: Gloria's mother was in a New York hospital recovering from an operation, and her father was in a Colorado Springs clinic with a disease of the lung.

Jim and Gloria began their honeymoon at Ojai Valley in California for a week, then went to Akron, Ohio, where Jim had a commitment to officiate at a soapbox derby, and then on to Honolulu for a month. But the honeymoon was interrupted when Gloria's father died. Gloria and Jim flew to New York where she and her sister Ruth arranged the funeral.

Then the newlyweds returned to Honolulu where they met up with Helen Hayes and her husband, Charles MacArthur. In 1977, I interviewed Helen Hayes on the set of *Candleshoe* at Pinewood Studios. While talking about her participation in the film version of *Harvey* and her friendship with Jim, she told me: 'We had lost our daughter Mary who had been ill with polio. That sort of tragedy just destroys your life, and Charles and I were trying to mend our broken lives in Hawaii. When Jim and Gloria were there on their honeymoon, Jim called us at our hotel and insisted they take us to dinner. We kept saying that we were just being a burden on them and Gloria would say, "What rubbish. Now we'll meet for breakfast tomorrow at nine."

'And then we'd have more meals with them, and they took us everywhere they went on the island, and we went deep-sea fishing. They just insisted we go everywhere with them, and we *knew* they were supposed to be having their honeymoon on their own, and we knew that Gloria was mourning her father, but they just wouldn't take no for an answer. And they helped my husband and I pull our lives back together.'

When the honeymoon was over, Jim and Gloria moved into a house on North Roxbury Drive in Beverly Hills, where they would spend the rest of their lives. Gloria tore down the weeds in the overgrown garden to indulge her passion for growing vegetables, and Jim became probably the only actor in Hollywood who took regular deliveries of garden produce to the casts and crews of the films he was working on.

From the moment Jim married Gloria, he was never just a stepfather to Gloria's boys, Ronald and Michael. While their real father was away most of the time living the life of a playboy (according to Gloria), Jim took on the role of the boys' actual father. 'It just seemed to me the natural thing to do,' Jim told me. 'I felt like a father with two boys, and to me they *were* my sons – so I think they always looked upon me as their father.' Gloria confirmed that her boys did look upon Jim as a real father: 'They loved him and he loved them – and that's what fathers and sons are all about.'

Not everyone, least of all Alex, was convinced that the marriage would survive. Henry Fonda believed he understood (by 1976 when I interviewed him) why the marriage was such an unexpected success: 'Jim had come from a small town in Pennsylvania, but he had made his home in Hollywood, and you can't get two more contrasting towns. He loves both homes, but he chose to live in Hollywood because that's where the work was. And he *likes* the life in Hollywood. More importantly, he's got Gloria, who kind of regiments his life but without all the moral and religious overtones he had in Indiana. She makes decisions, and he goes along with it. I think it makes his life easy for someone to say, "We're gonna do this or that," without there being some moralistic purpose. It's being done because it's *fun* – the kind of fun Gloria likes. And if he needed a little spiritual uplift or just a taste of the simple life, he could always go and visit his folks back in Indiana. So Jim had the best of both worlds.

'Just because Jim and Gloria aren't exactly cut from the same cloth doesn't mean she isn't the right woman for him. Clearly, she is – and has always been – and will always be. She keeps him active, you know. Always has done, as he grew older. She refuses to give in to old age. He even pulls her leg every time she gets her latest tuck.' (Being as young as I was in 1976, I didn't know what a 'tuck' was, and didn't like to ask. Of course, as I later discovered, it was a face-lift. The one thing I can say about Gloria is, if she was having face-lifts, it didn't show. She never had that stretched-face look. If she was vain, she wasn't stupid.)

Gloria was well aware from the time she accepted Jim's proposal of marriage that she was marrying into a profession rife with broken vows. Despite her outgoing confidence, she began married life with hidden insecurities. She told me:

'When you marry a leading man in Hollywood movies, you're marrying a man who is going to be spending much of his time with some of the world's most beautiful women, and that's going to be the cause of some insecurity for any woman. There was a period during the early years of our marriage when I was really quite afraid that he would come home from work and announce that he'd fallen in love with his latest leading lady and was leaving me.

'You know, Jim isn't really Mr Smith, or George Bailey or Elwood Dowd. I think there are lots of bits of Jimmy in those parts and all those parts are a part of Jimmy's personality. But Jim is a red-blooded American male and he likes to see beautiful women. Before we were an item, he was seeing plenty of beautiful girls. He *loves* women. He can tell the difference between a beautiful girl and an unattractive girl. He knows if a girl attracts him. The thing about Jimmy, though, is that he didn't go around falling in love with every girl he went out with. He somehow held back from allowing himself that luxury . . . until he met me, I'm very happy to say.

'Of course, I knew he was always in love with [Margaret] Sullavan and *that* was never going to turn into anything, so the chances of him falling for anyone else and making anything of it were remote – although that's clearer in hindsight, of course. What I now know – what I must have always known – is that when Jimmy made a commitment to me, it was a commitment he took as seriously as the oath he took to his country when he enlisted. That's simply the moral thinking behind the man, and it may have to do with his religious beliefs or not, although I think it's just what he always was back in Indiana. And he brought that morality with him to Hollywood – although he did manage to sow some wild oats while he was a bachelor.

'So, yes, I was worried to begin with, but the truth is, right from the beginning, he never once gave me cause to be suspicious or jealous in any way. I could never be jealous about Sullavan, even. In fact, there's something immensely typical about Jimmy loving a good female friend so much that, despite their history way back when, he was never going to have an affair with her because it was simply against his principles. She was married, usually to one of his best friends. And then he got himself a wife – who happened to be me – and he was not going to get romantically involved with Sullavan, even though I know – though he has never admitted it to me – he always loved her. But I think while the love he had for her began as a real boy–girl kind of thing, it developed over the years into a deep affectionate friendship that he would never have destroyed in a million years for the sake of lust.

'I think it would be true to say that Jim actually has gone out of his way many times to be particularly attentive to me. The more beautiful and glamorous his leading lady was, the more attention he paid to me. I asked him once why he did that, and he said, "Because I want you to never feel anything less than the most special thing in my life." The romantic Jim that people see in his films is the real him.

'Now, if I'd wanted, I could have said, "Jim, you don't have to do that," but I *liked* it. So I let him be as attentive as he could be whenever he felt the need. But I suppose after I was secure enough not to feel threatened, all that attention he lavished on me made *him* feel better.'

16

Keeping All the Balls in the Air

Darryl F Zanuck, production chief of 20th Century-Fox, had wanted Jim to play Doc Holliday in *My Darling Clementine* but had failed to convince the film's director, John Ford, that Jim could play a Western character. Undaunted in his belief, Zanuck cast Jim as real-life mail rider and army scout Tom Jeffords in *Broken Arrow*, and gave him top billing.

Filmed in glorious Technicolor in the spring of 1949 in the Coconino Mountains in Arizona, and directed by Delmer Daves, *Broken Arrow* was the true story – with plenty of dramatic licence – of how Jeffords conducted the peace agreement between the Apache tribes led by Cochise, played by Jeff Chandler, and the United States government in 1870. Although the film was a sincere effort to show Native Americans in a sympathetic light, it sold itself as a love story – Jeffords falls in love with an Indian girl, played by Debra Paget.

Jim liked to recall an incident during filming: 'We were shooting in the Coconino Mountains in Arizona, and after about a week, an old Apache fella walked into our camp and said that there would be a terrible disaster if we didn't strike our camp right there and then. Waall . . . we took the decision to take his advice . . . and not many hours after we got out of there, a wall of water hit the area where we'd been camped. Some of our crew and actors would've been killed for sure . . . and many said that the old Apache fella must've had an omen. But the old Apache just said, "No. It was just the annual melting of the snows."'

The film's producer, Julian Blaustein, told me in 1989, 'Our film was ahead of its time. It was the first Western to show the Native Americans – we don't call them Indians anymore – as people and not as savages. Jimmy Stewart liked that idea. I think he took the film because he was trying to establish himself after the war, but he really liked what we were aiming for.'

In regard to the suggestions that Jim had racist values, Blaustein said, 'I never knew Jimmy to do or say anything that was racist. What he did say was that the Indians had been so badly treated by the white settlers and later by the American government that there would be distrust and hatred between the races for decades. Even today it exists. Perhaps the thoughts that Jim has about being an American – that it's time to put away all that hate and that the Native Americans mustn't keep trying to separate themselves from the rest of American society – are the kind of thoughts that make him sound racist. He doesn't mean to be; I know that. But he thinks the same about African Americans. He thinks they shouldn't segregate themselves. He doesn't believe there should be ethnic minorities, that we should all be Americans. But to Jim it's a bit like the child who grows up thinking there is a monster under the bed. When you're an adult, you *know* there's no monster under the bed, but you can't help feeling a little anxious about it. And I think Jimmy has always been a little anxious about the ethnic minorities.'

Although the film is now considered a major Western and was indeed a success when released in 1950, Zanuck had doubts about the picture when Delmer Daves delivered his final cut. Zanuck disliked the way the actors portraying Indians had been allowed to speak their lines in a clichéd slow and broken manner, and he was also unhappy with many of the action scenes. He called for major retakes and supervised a major re-editing of the whole film, which took so long that it was not ready for release before Jim had another picture in the can and premiered. That film, *Winchester '73*, was to change Jim's career for ever, turning him into one of

Hollywood's major Western movie stars alongside John Wayne and Gary Cooper.

In the summer of 1949, Jim's agent, Lew Wasserman, met with the chief of Universal Studios, William Goetz. Wasserman told Goetz that Jim was eager to make a film version of *Harvey*, for which the film rights had been acquired by Universal, but Goetz quickly lost interest when Wasserman said that Jim's salary had to be $200,000. Although a major studio, Universal was not as rich or powerful as MGM or Warner Brothers, and the salary Wasserman was asking for was too high.

However, Goetz had a property he wanted to make with director Fritz Lang. Called *Winchester '73*, it would be a fairly modest production, shot in black and white. Goetz suggested that Jim could do *Harvey* if he starred in *Winchester '73* and agreed to make them both for a percentage of the profits and no up-front fee. Wasserman consulted Jim. The benefit of a percentage deal was that Jim stood to earn a lot more than he might otherwise have been paid – but only if the films were successful. And if they did make him a lot of money, it would be paid over a matter of years while the films continued to do the rounds and bring in a steady profit. As Jim noted, 'Getting a lot of money over a period of time rather than a lot of money in one go meant you didn't have to pay a shock amount in tax.' He agreed the deal, and he went to work on *Winchester '73*.

Jim played Lin McAdam, who wins a handsome Winchester '73 rifle in a Dodge City marksmanship contest. His murderous brother, Dutch, played by Stephen McNally, steals the rifle. It subsequently passes through various hands before finding its way back to Lin, who embarks on a manhunt for Dutch. Jim said, 'I liked the script of *Winchester '73* straight away. I had a tough character to play for once. I liked the idea of a man who was *driven*. It gives the character shades of light and dark. And those Westerns I did . . . at Universal in the fifties . . . were all like that.'

The Westerns that Jim referred to were all directed by Anthony Mann, who took over *Winchester '73* when Fritz Lang pulled out. Said Jim, 'I was trying to find a way to re-establish myself as a leading actor – or any kind of an actor. And Tony Mann was trying to make headway in his career. We had the same ambitions at the same time, so we were lucky at the same time. So much of this business is luck. You either get lucky or you don't. I got lucky.'

Aaron Rosenberg, who produced *Winchester '73* and most of the ensuing Stewart/Mann films, said:

'What Tony Mann brought to that first film was the element of making the rifle itself an essential character. It was the thing that brought all the other characters together. It was quite episodic, but that kept the audience interested in wondering where the story of the gun would lead to, and who it would affect.

'He also brought out something in James Stewart that hadn't really been seen before. It was an almost manic rage that would suddenly explode. The audience felt it knew Jimmy Stewart from the Capra films, and there was an element of the familiar Stewart in *Winchester '73*. But there was an underlying toughness that hadn't been seen much before. And then Stewart's character would just go into a violent rage which was a fresh approach, not just for Stewart, but also for the Western. Here was a hero with flaws.

'Tony Mann said he liked the idea of making the audience wonder if there was something that was latently psychotic about the Stewart character, and that theme developed over ensuing Westerns, especially in *The Naked Spur*.

'When Jimmy was first trying on his wardrobe, Tony Mann would pick and choose until he got just what he wanted. The most important part of Jimmy's wardrobe was the hat. Many people think a cowboy hat is a cowboy hat. But there are many shapes and sizes, and a hat can say a lot about the personality of the person wearing it. Mann tried any number of hats on Stewart for about two months before they found the one he finally wore.'

That hat became a regular piece of wardrobe in all their Westerns together. Said Stewart, 'Wearing the same hat . . . that was just a quirk. I felt it was kind of a good-luck piece.' With typical self-deprecation, he added, 'It certainly got a good notice in the first picture . . . actually better than *I* did.'

'Stewart and Mann had a good working relationship from the start,' said Rosenberg. 'Tony Mann thought he was Henry Hathaway or John Ford at times with his tendency to get tough with actors. I don't think Mann was a naturally tough mean bastard like Hathaway and Ford. But he never tried it on with Stewart. Stewart was always anxious to do well, completely co-operative and a very skilful actor indeed. He always wanted to give the best performance he could. He wasn't satisfied with just being effective, as a lot of other film stars were happy to be. It mattered to him. And Tony Mann responded to that because Mann wanted to be a great director, like Ford, and not just a good craftsman, like Hathaway. So you had two men actor and director wanting to be the best they could.'

As with learning to pitch a baseball for *The Stratton Story*, Jim practised using a Winchester '73 until the rifle looked like it was a part of his character. 'It's always important to me to get the technical things right,' he said. 'If you play a character who's an expert with a rifle, you better at least *look* like you're an expert. So I practised not just firing the gun, but learning how to hold it in such a way that it looked like it was the most natural thing in the world for me to walk down the street with a rifle in my hand. I was lucky to get an expert from the Winchester Arms Company to show me how to fire it, how to hold it, how to load it, how to do everything that made me look like I could really do it. And by God, I think I could do it by the end.'

Rosenberg recalled, 'Jimmy Stewart practised with that rifle until his hands were sore. That devotion to the work impressed Tony Mann – and it impressed me. Tony said to me, "I believe we can really go places with Jimmy in other films." It all began so promising, that partnership.'

Winchester '73 introduced a new friend into Jim's life – his name was Pie, and he was a horse. Jim told me:

'There was a gal named Stevie Myers whose father was Roy Myers, who'd supplied horses for the old-time Western stars like Gene Autry and Tom Mix. Now Stevie raised horses for films, and so I went to her ranch and she brought out about six horses. They were all big critters, just kind of moseying around. Then I saw a horse that was in a barn and he was peeking out of the entrance, like he was watching what was going on. He seemed to know something the other horses didn't. He had personality. He seemed intelligent, whereas horses are usually pretty dumb, like those other horses roaming around.

'I said, "Who's that?" and she said, "That's my horse. His name is Pie." I said, "Would you mind if I just got on him?" She said, "Sure, you can get on him and you can try to ride him, but I never give him to anyone else because he's thrown a number of guys who've tried to ride him."

'Waall, I rode him, and he didn't try to throw me, and I just fell in love with ol' Pie right there and then. And I guess he liked me 'cos he didn't try to kill me. So Stevie let me borrow him for every Western I made. What a wonderful horse. Even when he got older, and we were riding with a pack of other riders on horseback, he'd want to race out in front, even if we weren't supposed to. He seemed to enjoy what we were doing. I'd swear that horse had looked out at me from that barn because he wanted to make pictures with me. I would have bought him, but Stevie wouldn't sell him because she loved him too. But she always let me use him. For twenty years, me and Pie made Westerns together.'

Universal Studios used its many up-and-coming contract players in bit parts in the film, including Tony Curtis (billed as Anthony Curtis) as a young cavalryman, and Rock Hudson as a Native American. As Hudson recalled to me in 1980, 'You didn't audition for parts like that. You were just told to do them and you did them or you didn't get paid. The funny thing is that now *nobody* would think to cast me as an Indian.'

Universal also had Shelley Winters on its books and gave her the role of Lin's fiancée. 'You couldn't make a Western in those days without having a romantic subplot,' said Rosenberg. 'Tony Mann hated putting in those romances because there really is no place for them realistically. But that's what the studio said the audiences wanted.'

Shelley Winters told me, 'I didn't know what the hell I was doing in that picture. I always figured that there were all these guys running around trying to get their hands on this goddamn rifle who should've been trying to get their hands on *me. That's* what the film should have been about as far as I was concerned. But that doesn't make for a good Western, I guess. In the end, nobody remembers me being in it,' and she pointed to me and added, 'except you.'

Released in July 1950, the critics generally agreed that *Winchester '73* was an exceptional Western and that Jim was good in it. As the New York *Herald Tribune* noted, Stewart looked 'as if he had been doing nothing else throughout his illustrious career'. *Variety* noted, 'Stewart brings real flavour and appeal to the role of Lin, in a lean and concentrated portrayal.'

The public also approved, and its success, as Wasserman had hoped, provided Jim with a steady income for a long time. With audiences eager for more Western action with James Stewart, Fox released *Broken Arrow*, which also did well.

Jim was out of the saddle for his next picture, *Harvey*. Howard P Dowd is a man who lives in his own dream world. This struck a chord in Jim who admitted, not for the first time, 'I'm a dreamer. I know I am. Always have been. I daydream a lot . . . I go into my own head. I don't think it's an escape. I like life. But I like to dream. If a man doesn't have dreams, he has nowhere to go, it seems to me. So I find it difficult to keep my mind on one thing. I know people get alarmed when they see me drift off. They think I'm worrying about something . . . or I'm unhappy. But I'm something of a loner . . . I like to be alone. Not lonely . . . but just being on my own . . . and I like to let my mind take me somewhere else. Maybe that's how I keep my sanity.'

Surprisingly, Jim was dissatisfied with the film version of *Harvey*, despite its success in 1950, which, like *Winchester '73*, provided him with a steady income over a number of years: 'I really discovered during filming that the play was better as a play . . . not as a film. I'm delighted audiences liked it . . . and still do. I get remembered for that picture almost as much as I do for *It's a Wonderful Life*.'

Variety didn't entirely agree with Jim, saying that the play 'loses little of its whimsical charm in the screen translation'. It added, 'Stewart would seem the perfect casting for the character, so well does he convey the idea that escape from life into a pleasant half-world existence has many points in its favour.' *Time* said, 'Dowd takes on the coloration of Stewart's movie personality; the gangling awkwardness, the fumbling apologetic gestures, the verbal false starts.' The *New York Times* thought, 'Mr Stewart is disarming of all annoyance. He makes Elwood a man to be admired.'

Jim was critical of his own performance: 'I think I played Dowd a little too cutesy, a little too dreamily. I wanted to have another go, so I did years later.' But he had to wait until the 1970s to get it the way he wanted, in the 1972 television film.

Jim was definitely on a roll again, his career saved largely by taking to the saddle, and by talking to a six-foot invisible white rabbit. At Fox, he was in *The Jackpot*, playing an ordinary middle-class married man who wins $24,000 on a radio quiz show. Consequently, his family life is turned upside down. Based on the real-life misadventures of a Rhode Island family, the picture was a good comedy, ideally suited to Jim's talents at playing bewildered fathers and husbands, and was a modest success in 1950.

He stayed on at Fox for *No Highway in the Sky*, which reunited him with Marlene Dietrich. This film, at least, was done for the up-front salary 20th Century-Fox was paying. Dietrich, now a faded star, played an actress travelling with Jim who is an aviation scientist. He discovers that the plane he has designed, in which he and Dietrich, among others, are passengers, has a fault that threatens their safety. After landing for a stopover, and with the pilot unwilling to listen to his warnings, the scientist sabotages the aeroplane so it cannot take off. A subsequent inquiry proves he was justified in his actions.

The film was shot in England in the late autumn of 1950. Gloria went with him for the three-month shooting schedule. According to Gloria, Jim hated making the film. He felt awkward working with Dietrich, and the fading star was causing considerable problems for the other actresses, including Glynis Johns as a stewardess, by trying to hog the camera. 'Dietrich's problem,' said Gloria, 'was that she was so much the ageing movie star that she didn't even get the character Jim played to fall in love with her – he fell for the stewardess, who was much younger and prettier.'

The only joy in Jim's life during this time was when Gloria discovered she was pregnant. After staying with him for the first two months, she had to return to Los Angeles – adding to his misery. Jim recalled the film as being so stressful that it aggravated his appendix, or so he thought. 'I was getting pains in my lower stomach,' he said, 'and I just *know* it was the film that caused it.

Turned out to be my appendix. I had an emergency operation and was in hospital for two weeks while the actresses slugged it out.'

Jim's stay in hospital made him even more miserable. Gloria was unable to return to England, having discovered that she was having twins and advised that a flight across the Atlantic was unwise.

Kenneth More, who co-starred in *No Highway in the Sky*, recalled the experience of working with Stewart and Dietrich: 'We were shooting out on a runway in a bitter wind in December. James Stewart had come out of hospital and gamely stood and froze with the rest of us, waiting for Marlene Dietrich to come out of her trailer. She always had to look absolutely perfect, and as soon as she stepped out into the wind, her hair, which was pretty well lacquered anyway, would blow out of place and she had to go back inside. Finally Jimmy said, "This has gone on for long enough," and he strode over to her trailer and went inside. About five minutes later, he reappeared with Marlene in tow. I have no idea what he said to her, but it worked; it got her out so we could get on with the scene.

'Marlene wasn't a bitch, but she did think only of herself. Jimmy thought of himself too, especially since he'd only just come out of hospital, but he was also thinking equally of everyone else. We were all freezing, and Marlene was holding everything up, and Jimmy Stewart took charge and sorted it.'

When the film was at last finished, Jim returned home to Gloria. They waited for the arrival of their twins. Jim was the more anxious of the two; Gloria recalled, 'Jim was paranoid about how he would get me to the hospital in time because he was so unsure of his ability to drive me to hospital and get me there in one piece. He began to rehearse the journey, driving to the hospital from home. He timed himself so he knew exactly how long it would take. It was like the way he learned to do things technically in a film. Driving me to hospital was a technical thing he had to learn to do. And one time he got lost and had to stop at a gas station to ask the way.'

Jim admitted that driving anywhere by car was not his greatest strength: 'I'm a terrible driver. I can fly a plane because somehow that's like living a dream. But driving a car for me is just reality, and I can't seem to concentrate. Gloria wouldn't even let the children be in the car when I drove. *I* don't even like being in the car when I drive. I'm just filled with terror when I'm at the wheel. I'm convinced I will crash into something. It's a huge relief when I make it home and into my garage.'

But despite all of Jim's attempts to make the day of the babies' delivery as smooth as possible, there was a sting in the tail to this story. Said Gloria, 'In the end, it was all a waste of time because I had to be taken by ambulance when problems developed. I had some complications and the girls had to be delivered by Caesarean.'

It was 7 May 1951 when their non-identical twin daughters, Kelly and Judy, were born. Their arrival was sadly overshadowed by the serious condition the Caesarean had left Gloria in. 'I almost died,' she told me. 'They couldn't stop the bleeding. They operated on me three times and I had five blood transfusions. Jim got so worried that he was going to lose me that he got his church minister to pray with him at home.' This was a subject that neither Gloria nor Jim ever discussed with reporters. Gloria was able to tell me a little about it, although it was obvious that the whole episode was a nightmare she was distressed to recall. She asked me not to bring it up with Jim, and I complied.

But there was another tale which she had much more fun relating – of the day she left hospital: 'The babies had been home a month by the time I was allowed to go home. When they said I could go home, Jim said, "Don't worry about a thing. I know the route between here and home like the back of my hand." That didn't fill me with confidence. He said, "I'll go and get the car and bring it round to the entrance, and you go down in the elevator and I'll meet you there."

'I was taken down to the lobby in a wheelchair with all my luggage and all the flowers I'd been sent. And there I waited. After twenty minutes the nurse said to me, "Where is he?" I knew the answer. I said, "He's forgotten." She said, "How could he forget?" I said, "*He* can. Take me back upstairs. He'll phone." So she took me back up, and sure enough he phoned. He'd simply got in the car and driven straight home, and didn't remember he was supposed to collect me until he got home.'

Gloria did not object to Jim's insistence that their twin girls, as well as Michael and Ronald, were raised with the same Presbyterian values that he had grown up with. Gloria told me, 'I figured that none of it had done Jim any harm, so I saw no reason for our children not to have the same virtues as Jim. Of course, what you don't realise when your children are young is that they are all individuals, and they will all be different. Judy and Kelly were very different from each other, and Ronald and Michael were different. That's what makes a family interesting – or they'd all be Jimmy Stewart clones and that would have driven me *mad* – much as I love him!

'But what he taught them – what I hope they found valuable – was that you are not entitled to everything in life. You have to take the bad with the good, and you make the most of it. And he taught them not to rely on their father being a famous Hollywood movie star and think that gave them a free ride. They had to earn anything they wanted. And I agree with the philosophy.'

Hollywood fame and riches did, however, allow Jim and Gloria certain benefits many working-class Americans could never afford. Their children had a nanny, a French-Canadian called Irene DesLierres. 'The children called her Mamselle,' said Gloria. 'She was a wonderful lady who was very firm with the children, but she had a sense of humour that the children enjoyed. As for having a nanny, or a governess as she liked to be known, Jim had worked hard for the money he made, and he believed in using that money to give our children the best in life. But they still had to learn they couldn't just expect things on a plate. They had to learn to work for what they required – or desired.'

Emulating his own father, Jim treated his children to as many outings as his work schedule would allow. They often went on picnics when the children were still young, and Disneyland was always a big hit with the whole family. But in a town where parents who were actors often *acted* the roles of devoted parents, neither Jim nor Gloria tried to pretend they were America's ideal family. Burgess Meredith noted, in 1980:

'Gloria is a good woman, a good wife and a good mother. She could have played "Mommie Dearest" like Joan Crawford and put on a false face of a picture-perfect mother, but she was a very pragmatic woman and she didn't spoil the children – and she didn't bother to be *seen* to be spoiling the children. She didn't mollycoddle them. But she always made sure that such things as birthdays were happy days. When one of the children had a birthday, Gloria – and Jim –

would throw them the best fun kind of parties. And as the children grew up, they made sure their mom and dad had great birthday parties too.

'Birthdays and anniversaries are important to Jim and Gloria. Normally they are not sentimental – that is, not *falsely* sentimental. Jim always buys Gloria something special on her birthday and on their anniversary. And when Jim has a birthday, Gloria puts on truly elegant parties for him.

'As far as being a father is concerned, Jim was never a man to show all his emotions – or his deepest emotions. He loves his children, and he must have a way of showing it that only they see because they know he loves them. When the children need his love, they've got it. But he doesn't put on a show.'

When the children were young all the fan magazines of the time were keen to present the Jimmy Stewart family as the perfect American family. As Gloria put it, 'We were the Disneyland family – with nothing out of place. I'll say we were a good family – a *nice* family – but God, we were never *that* sweet or we'd have all been sick all the time!'

Jim's next film was Cecil B DeMille's circus extravaganza *The Greatest Show on Earth*. Jim had romantic reasons for doing the film: 'When I was a kid and the circus came to our town, I always wanted to run away with the circus. It's every kid's dream. When I heard that DeMille was going to make this big circus film, I asked if I could play the clown, and Mr DeMille said I could.' The film was to be the biggest money-maker of 1952.

But the more realistic and pragmatic reasons Jim asked DeMille for a part in the circus picture had to do with being a struggling free-lance actor. Jim knew he was still battling to keep his career afloat: 'When you worked for a single major studio, an occasional flop didn't matter so much . . . because they'd keep looking for your next job for you . . . although not every actor liked that prospect because it lost them their freedom. But I was free . . . and struggling. When you freelanced, you were only as good as your last film so you tried to stay ahead of the game. When you made a turkey, you tried to get another film – a *good* film – finished before the turkey came out.'

Jim knew *No Highway in the Sky* was a turkey, and he was proven right when it was released in 1951 to only moderate business. So he tried to compensate by getting himself a part in the latest Cecil B DeMille epic. When he wired DeMille to ask for a part, it was an act of some desperation. As Charlton Heston, who co-starred in *The Greatest Show on Earth*, told me, 'Actors are not supposed to beg directors for a film part; they let their agents do the asking while actors sit in their ivory towers. Of course, that's not reality. I would guess that just about every actor at some time has begged for a part.'

By 1951, a DeMille film was an event, and actors were lucky to get a part in his pictures. Jim knew this, which is why he accepted DeMille's offer of a mere $50,000 as opposed to the $200,000 Lew Wasserman was demanding from studios for Jim's services. In fact, all the leading actors in *The Greatest Show on Earth* were paid the same amount. Heston, a Hollywood newcomer for whom this was only his second feature film, had no complaints: 'The best thing that happened to me early in my career was to do the DeMille circus picture. It wasn't the greatest film ever made, but it was the most seen picture that year [in 1952] and won the Best Picture Oscar. Every actor in the film should have been delighted at the exposure it gave them. I knew I was.'

The screen story centred on the various dramas and romances that befall the members of the huge travelling circus. The circus boss, played by Heston, is in love with his female trapeze artist, played by Betty Hutton. She is being wooed by a male aerialist, played by Cornel Wilde, who in turn is attracted by the elephant girl, played by Gloria Grahame.

Jim's part of a clown called Buttons provides the interesting subplot of the film. He is really a doctor accused of murder, having performed euthanasia, and is in disguise as a clown while on the run from the law. He wears his clown make-up throughout the entire film. Heston said:

'Jimmy Stewart had the best part in the film. Jimmy's skill as an actor was most evident behind that clown make-up because the make-up has the clown smiling permanently, yet Jim was able to convey every emotion his character had through that make-up – and it takes a very good actor indeed to be able to do that. It just so happens that Jimmy Stewart is not only a very good actor, but a *great* actor.

'He had a nice line in humour, which is essential when things start to go wrong as it did for me early in filming. Now this was only my second film, so I was pretty green. I did a scene where I had to pull up in my jeep, jump out and hop over the circus ring. I did the first part of the shot perfectly, pulling up in the jeep, jumping out – and then I tripped over the circus ring. Jim was there, looking down at me, and he said, "Well, Chuck, it can only get better from here." He became a good friend. I have the highest regard for him. I only wish we could have worked more together.

'I did have an interesting experience with him once – at a function for Princess Margaret of England. Jim sat between myself and the princess, and I couldn't hear what she was saying, so Jimmy related every word she said to me. Hence I had a conversation with Princess Margaret as played by Jimmy Stewart, which is a bizarre and very funny thing! And because Jimmy is hard of hearing, I couldn't be sure that what he told me was exactly what the princess was saying!'

To delight audiences and fill in for the lack of plot, the film was packed with actual circus performances and, most notably, a spectacular train crash in which the circus boss is badly hurt. Buttons reveals his true vocation by saving the boss's life and is then arrested by the police, who have long been on his tail. *The Greatest Show on Earth* is now badly dated but remains barely watchable, if only to observe Jim's skill as an actor.

Feeling he had spent much of 1951 making a film that would at the very least be a box-office smash, he took, with some reluctance, the leading role in MGM's biopic *Carbine Williams*. It was the story of the North Carolina metalworker David Williams. After an FBI agent was killed during a raid on the still which Williams ran as a sideline to supplement his meagre income, Williams was imprisoned for thirty years. During his long sentence, Williams used his metalworking skills to design an automatic rifle that became the M1 carbine. The Army discovered the new rifle, adopted it, and Williams received a pardon.

'You don't go into a movie expecting it to be . . . not very good,'
said Jim. 'It's usually only when you're making the film you start
to realise that things aren't going too well.' This must have been
true of *Carbine Williams*. It seemed to have much to say about the
American penal system, as did the film *The Birdman of Alcatraz* ten
years later, in 1962. But *Birdman*, an independent production, had
a realistic quality in John Frankenheimer's direction, and a strong,
gritty performance by Burt Lancaster. *Carbine Williams* had a
distinct lack of realism or grit. This was due to the studio's policy
regarding its trademark glossy style, the film's direction by Richard
Thorpe, who never made a film that strove for realism, and the
casting – even miscasting – of Jim, who hummed and hawed his
way through the part like a Jimmy Stewart caricature.

But *Carbine Williams* was the least of his problems. In
November 1951, a Hollywood magazine began recirculating the old
rumours that Stewart and Fonda were homosexuals, and suggested
that Jim's homosexuality was the reason he had waited so long to
get married. Finding a ready-made family, it suggested, was the
ideal cover-up.

Jim chose not to reply to the accusations. At home he fumed and
raged, according to Gloria, but he decided publicly to keep quiet.
He was still not in touch with Henry Fonda, who remained in New
York. Fonda, too, was aware of the lies, but he was also counselled
to ignore them.

Stewart was just managing to resuscitate his career, while
learning to cope with family life and at the same time dodge the
cruel barbs thrown at him by sections of the Hollywood press. Life,
in his own words, was 'just getting harder while you're getting
older . . . and that doesn't seem fair. I think of a circus performer,
keeping all the balls in the air . . . and the longer you do it, the more
you get tired.'

17

The Anthony Mann Years

In 1952, Jim was back on the Western trail with Anthony Mann for their second big outdoors venture, *Bend of the River* (also known as *Where the River Bends*). After the success of *Winchester '73*, Universal gave producer Aaron Rosenberg the go-ahead to make this next Western in Technicolor.

This time, Jim had a darker streak to his character, being a former outlaw called Glyn McLyntock (sounding not unlike Lin McAdam from *Winchester '73*) who is trying to redeem himself from his outlaw past. Beneath his bandanna, he hides the scar from an unfinished hanging. By chance, he comes across a lynching and saves the very man who had previously rescued him from his hanging. That man, Emerson Cole (played by Arthur Kennedy), joins up with Glyn to help a group of pioneers struggling to make it through the wilderness to Oregon. They fight off the elements and Indians before the pioneers can settle. When Glyn realises that Cole has not changed his ways and tries to stop him from extorting money from the settlers, Cole and his newly acquired gang capture Glyn and leave him on top of Oregon's Mount Hood. Glyn swears revenge with what have become classic lines: 'You'll be seeing me. Every time you bed down for the night, you'll look back in the

darkness and wonder if I'm there. And some night I will be. You'll
be seeing me.' Glyn tracks the gang, killing them one by one until
only Cole is left. They fight it out in the fast-flowing river which
finally sweeps Cole to his doom.

Filming in Oregon and on Mount Hood, Anthony Mann used the
spectacular backdrop to enhance the story. Beginning as the tale of
a modest wagon train, it becomes a bleak tale of revenge in which
the natural elements – chiefly the river – become the cause of the
villain's downfall. Said Rosenberg:

'I think Tony Mann used the background – the mountains, the
wilderness, the rivers – in such a way that they became a part of the
story, as essential as the characters. They enhanced the characters. I
think he was more successful in this than John Ford. And he tapped
into that edge that Jimmy Stewart had. People wondered if the last
part of the film was about Jimmy Stewart seeking revenge or just
bringing a criminal to justice. They asked that because they found
it hard to accept that Jimmy Stewart could be driven by revenge.
But vengeance makes a more powerful story for a Western than the
one about the good guy getting the bad guy. That's what made
Jimmy and Tony such a great team.

'Tony Mann helped to create that Western image of Stewart's.
Mann's style was more realistic than Ford's. In fact, Mann, I think,
really created the authentic, tough, violent kind of Western. Jimmy
Stewart didn't wear a white hat; he wore a grubby sweat-stained hat.

'Mann wanted him to look like he'd not had a bath in months.
He got Stewart to keep his stubble every day. If he didn't look dirty
enough, Tony Mann would pick up a handful of dirt and throw it
over Jimmy, who'd stand there and say, "Go on, Tony, mess me up.
I still look too clean."

People often say that the partnership of John Ford and John
Wayne helped to define the Western after the war. I think, with the
exception of *The Searchers*, they created a West that never seemed
quite real. Too romantic. But Mann and Stewart defined the
Western in more modern terms. It was hard, it was uncompro-
mising, it was never black and white. Those films changed the
Western for ever.'

Rock Hudson was among the cast, as a quick-on-the-draw gambler who helps Glyn and Cole retrieve supplies stolen from the settlers. He recalled:

'Tony Mann liked Jimmy an awful lot because Jimmy was a big star and Mann tapped into something in Jimmy's personality that nobody had explored before. I worked with John Wayne [in *The Undefeated* in 1969] and Duke would only play Duke. But Jimmy wanted to be a *good* actor. You could see he wanted to be a *very* good actor, and I learned from that. I wanted to try to become more than the beefcake star the studio wanted me to be. Jimmy inspired me to want to be a better actor.

'He's known to be a *gentle* man, and he is, but you don't want to get him mad. Out on location in Oregon, everyone was given a lunch box. It had sandwiches, some fruit, some juice – and suddenly somebody yells out, "They're crawling with maggots!" And a lot of these lunch boxes did have maggots in, and Jimmy just went *crazy*. I mean, *mad as hell*. He was yelling at Tony Mann and at the producer, "Who the hell have you hired to poison us with this goddamn garbage? The cast and crew are working our butts off and we expect a hell of a lot better than *this*!" And he threw the lunch box at Rosenberg, who promptly fired the caterers that day, and the next day there was a new caterer on location. So I learned from that too. Be nice, but when you're treated like garbage, give 'em hell. I never knew Jimmy Stewart could give anyone hell, but he could.'

Like *Winchester '73*, the film was weakened by a romantic subplot. The leading lady this time was Julie Adams, whose only purpose in the film, as the beautiful daughter of one of the settlers, is to provide a love interest for Jim. 'Jimmy never felt comfortable about his love scenes,' said Rosenberg. 'He felt he was too old for a young girl like Julie Adams.'

Gloria recalled that Jim's only interest in making the Anthony Mann Westerns was to 'delve into his dark side and discover if he was the actor he believed himself to be. He wanted to put miles between Mr Smith and those anti-heroes of the Mann Westerns. He wanted to do good work, and he felt that the contrived love stories took away from the strength those pictures had.'

It seems that Jim made certain demands to either eliminate any love interest for his next Anthony Mann Western, or find a way to make it a more integral part of the picture, and Mann heartily agreed. In fact, it was Metro-Goldwyn-Mayer who came to Anthony Mann with a story they wanted him to direct called *The Naked Spur*. It told of a bounty hunter who wants to collect the $5,000 reward on an outlaw's head so he can buy back land lost to him during the Civil War. With unwanted help from a gold prospector and an Army deserter, the bounty hunter captures the outlaw and the girlfriend who accompanies him. On the journey back, the outlaw sows the seeds of distrust among his captors until both the prospector and the deserter are dead. The girl helps the outlaw to escape, but he betrays her before the hunter kills him. The hunter and the girl, thrown together by circumstances, are left to make the trek home – to *his* home. It was a tough, violent Western in which the eventual romance between the bounty hunter and the girl are a natural part of the story.

Mann was eager to accept the assignment, insisting that Jimmy Stewart be cast as the bitter, violent, almost manic bounty hunter. It was to be the best, most influential Western Mann and Stewart made, inspiring later Western directors including Sam Peckinpah and Sergio Leone.

It was also possibly the smallest cast ever assembled for a major Western. Apart from an Indian war party, the only actors were Jimmy Stewart, Robert Ryan as the outlaw, Janet Leigh as his girl-friend, Ralph Meeker as the Army deserter, and Millard Mitchell as the gold prospector. The other main character was the bleak back-drop of the Colorado Rockies, which was as integral to the story as any of the characters.

'I think that film stands out today [in 1979] because it was ahead of its time,' said Jim. 'It's kinda like the films of Clint Eastwood. None of the characters was all good or all bad. Not even Janet Leigh's character. Even Robert Ryan had his moments when the audiences kinda liked him. But he had to be the meanest of them all so his fate could be justified. But most of all . . . I liked me. I was this man who was . . . it was like he was *possessed*. He had a demon that *drove* him. He had a violence that was driving him *mad*. I don't know if it's true, but I heard that Clint Eastwood was influenced by that film . . . and by my performance in it. Yeah . . . I liked me in that one.'

Ralph Meeker (speaking by telephone from Los Angeles in 1985) told me:

'We didn't have the comforts of a studio. It was all shot on location. We were a small cast, but every one of us had a strong personality. Even Janet Leigh could hold her own against us rough fellas. I'd heard from Jimmy that Anthony Mann could get tough with actors, but he didn't push any of us around. I'd heard that Jimmy often stepped in when Mann laid into a bit-part actor, but because none of us were bit-part actors, he laid off of us. Instead, he took his anger out on some of the crew.

'But I've often found that the best action directors are tough. They really push you. I could tell that Jimmy not only admired Tony Mann but he liked him an awful lot too. They had a tremendous rapport. Jimmy said to me, "Wait and see how Tony works on location. He's the best. I mean *the* best." What made Mann so brilliant was his ability to pick a backdrop that might be green and lush or barren and stark, or a rushing river, and he could put his actors against these backdrops, and it all became *one*. And when we wrapped on any given exterior set, Jimmy would wink at me and say, "See, I told ya!" Tony Mann could shoot on location better than any director I ever knew.'

Both Jim and Mann were able to work for MGM because their contracts at Universal were non-exclusive. But it was back to Universal for their next one, a contemporary action drama called *Thunder Bay*. Jim was eager to do it, but Mann was not. Jim and Dan Duryea played two ex-GIs who set out to find oil off the Gulf of Mexico and to assure the local fishermen that their livelihood will not be affected. In the process, the oilmen find love with Joanna Dru and Marcia Henderson respectively. Aaron Rosenberg said:

'I did the film because I was under contract to Universal and they told me to do it. Jim did the film because he was developing an interest in oil exploration and was – or became – a partner with a

Texas oilman. So he wanted to deliver a message that oil explor-ation and production did not affect the environment. Tony Mann did the film just because Jim wanted him to do it, but Mann always complained that there just was no story worth telling in the script we had. And I had to agree with him, but I was stuck with it as much as he was.

'Jimmy was one of Hollywood's biggest stars by then. Universal just wanted a Jimmy Stewart picture, and that's the story they gave us. Tony Mann didn't want to do it. I didn't want to do it. Jimmy did. I have to say that Tony did his best but the story was too weak. He just ended up putting the camera where he thought it would go best and hollering "Action!" Tony was a pro. He'd always try his best, even if he didn't feel like it. The funny thing is, although the picture wasn't up to much, it did very well at the box office. People liked to go and see Jimmy Stewart in almost anything where he got to play the amiable hero who slugged the bad guys. When the film was released [in 1953] it was a huge hit, simply because it was a Jimmy Stewart picture.'

An even bigger hit was *The Glenn Miller Story* which immediately followed. Perhaps the most famous of all of Stewart's biographical films, this one saw Jim don glasses, play a trumpet and learn just enough of the band leader's mannerisms to pull off a reasonable impression of Miller, but still with many of Jim's own much imitated characteristics to keep his legions of fans happy.

It reunited Jim with June Allyson, who again played his on-screen wife. Although they would make only three films together, with *Strategic Air Command* to come the following year, in the minds of audiences Stewart and Allyson became as inextricably linked as screen partners as were John Wayne and Maureen O'Hara. Allyson has recalled that many times fans approached her in public and asked her where her husband, Jimmy Stewart, was. Not wishing to disappoint them, Allyson generally told them that he was merely busy elsewhere that day.

Once more, the director was Anthony Mann, and once more he was unhappy with the material. 'Tony Mann wasn't at his best with that picture,' said Aaron Rosenberg, again producing. 'He thought it too sentimental – and it was. But for good reason, I thought.

Glenn Miller was a much loved band leader – a music star – who died when his plane was brought down during World War Two. Tony said to me, "The studio wants me to make the audience brim over with emotion when Miller dies. Well, by God, I *will*." And he did. At the end of that film everyone who ever saw it has ended up in tears. And it wasn't falsely sentimental. Mann really proved his professionalism, I thought, by giving the film integrity at its very end, even if he had been forced to make it a Jimmy Stewart vehicle with comedy, romance and all the elements that make for a good human interest story, 1950s Universal Studios/James Stewart style. You have to please the men who pay your salary.' It also delighted audiences and was the studio's biggest money-maker of the year.

The final weeks on filming *The Glenn Miller Story* were marred by tragic news. In July 1953, Jim's mother, Bessie, suffered a heart attack. She was taken to Indiana Hospital and placed in an oxygen tent. Jim immediately returned to Indiana and paid for specialists from Pittsburgh and New Castle to treat his mother. He kept vigil by her bedside and noted a slight improvement in her condition. But it was only a brief respite. She deteriorated, and a week after the heart attack she died, aged seventy-eight.

Her death sent Alex into a depression which he tried to drown with heavy drinking. Seeing his father spiralling downwards, Jim invited Alex to stay with him and his family in California. Alex stayed over a number of times, but he still had the store to run in Indiana.

When back home, Alex telephoned Jim at least once every week. 'It was a bad time for Jim and Alex,' said Gloria, 'because Alex would call us when he got up at around four or five in the morning, and neither of us much appreciated being woken up at that time. Jim told him time and again not to call so early, and they'd get into an argument.

'Jim made sure he called Alex every Sunday, but Alex would just continue whatever the argument had been during the week. It was hard on Jim, but he knew it was hard for his father losing Bessie. What was worse was Alex was always telling his friends and neighbours that his son would help with whatever problem they had because Jim had money. Jim just mostly ignored all this, otherwise he would have been spending all he earned on helping his father's troubled friends.'

*

After *The Glenn Miller Story* wrapped, Alfred Hitchcock called Jim and said he wanted to make another film with him, *Rear Window*. Jim said, 'I was intrigued by the story – a man is confined to a wheelchair with a broken leg, and he has nothing to do but watch what happens in the apartments . . . and then he sees a murder take place. What's he gonna do about it? That's an intriguing idea for a story and for an actor.'

However, according to Joshua Logan, Jim was not immediately attracted to the film. He couldn't see himself working with Hitchcock again after the problems and disappointment of *Rope*. And when he heard the story and Hitch told him that it would be shot on a single set, Jim was even more doubtful. When Hitch told Jim that he was casting Grace Kelly as the leading lady, Jim knew he was in trouble. Gloria's good friend was the former Mrs Ray Milland – she'd been Kelly's godmother. Then Ray Milland had an affair with Grace Kelly, and that put Grace in Gloria's black books.

'So I think Jim was looking at the film too *personally*,' said Logan. 'I mean, every director has the occasional bad picture, and it's unfortunate that Jim was in Hitchcock's failure [*Rope*]. But I knew about the property and I told Jim it was a good idea for a film. Leland Hayward told him the same thing. So Jim rethought the proposition and decided to do it . . . and because it was such a big success, Jim never admitted he turned Hitchcock down at first. He also got over any problem Gloria had about him working with Grace Kelly – who was known as a bit of a man-chaser before she became Princess Grace – by making sure he paid Gloria *extra* attention when he was filming.'

Jim's worries over the technical aspects of filming on a single set were quickly laid to rest. A lavish set was built, consisting of over thirty apartments, all of which were seen only through windows except for the one where Stewart's character lived. Hitchcock had learned from his mistakes making *Rope*, and he worked out his technical details in pre-production so the filming went relatively smoothly.

But at home, all was not quite as smooth. As Logan said, Jim paid a lot more attention to Gloria while filming *Rear Window*. But the reasons for this were not lost on Gloria. She told me that she was afraid for her marriage because she knew that Jim was attracted to Kelly. She also knew that *every* man was attracted to Kelly, and she reasoned that it was only natural that her husband find the cool blonde actress attractive. It didn't help, however, when Jim would come home and go on at length about Grace Kelly's virtues as an actress. He had often raved about Margaret Sullavan, but Gloria had learned not to fear what she knew was a love that never had a chance of evolving. But she was insecure where Kelly was concerned. She did not confront Jim about it. But, as she confided to me, she felt that if ever there was a time when Jim might have left her, it would have been for Grace Kelly.

In retrospect, she realised she was wrong, but it didn't help when Jim accepted an offer from Joshua Logan to appear with Kelly in *Designing Woman* (released in 1957), which Logan was to direct. Said Logan:

'I knew that Jim and Grace had chemistry on screen and that I wanted that chemistry to work for me in *Designing Woman*. Jim was – well – *ecstatic* about working with Grace again. I don't think Gloria was. But then Grace announced her retirement from the screen to become Princess Grace of Monaco, and when I told Jim that we could get Lauren Bacall to replace her, he immediately lost interest. It had nothing to do with Bacall. He had simply wanted to work with Grace Kelly again. In the end, I didn't direct the film; Vincente Minelli did. It starred Bacall and Greg Peck. Jim told me he wished he'd made the film with Bacall because he liked it, and it was a success. He pulled out of it for emotional reasons, and he regretted it.

'I don't really know for sure if Jim would have strayed with Kelly. I can't believe he would because his love for Gloria was so strong. But Grace, you know, could seduce a man with just a look from those big warm eyes. I don't think a man could help himself where she was concerned, and I wouldn't have blamed Jim if he'd been trapped by her charms. He often talked about how warm she was, and that playing a love scene with her was . . . not unexciting. But I think, knowing Jim as I do, he would have fought the devil and won. I *like* to think that. But who knows?'

After Grace Kelly died in a car accident in 1982, Jim told me:

'I could see why many of her leading men fell in love with her. You only had to play a love scene with her to know why. She has such lovely, warm eyes, and by golly she was just so darned appealing.

'You know, actors often say that when they do a love scene they are only acting . . . that kissing is only acting. That's like saying breathing is only acting, or walking is only acting. It's something you do to make a love scene work, and when you kiss, you *kiss*. I think Gloria knows this well enough, and I'm a dedicated husband to Gloria . . . but I'm not *dead*. If you have to kiss someone you don't like, then you act your heart out to try and make it work, but that's when there are no sparks, no chemistry, and it shows. But when you like kissing someone, the audience feels that warmth. I can spot actors and actresses who kiss but don't get along. And I can tell when they're both having a good time for just that short space of time. If I'd been of a mind, I could have been one of those fellas who fell for her when working with her. But I'm too darned sensible for that. You have to wisely pick and choose the pastimes you enjoy when you're an actor if you want to stay sane in this business. Flying I thought was a good idea. Wanting to carry on kissing the leading lady when I had a wonderful wife at home was a lousy idea. It's not just a question of what's morally *right*, but also what's just plain *sensible*.'

In 1953 Jim was back in the saddle again with Anthony Mann directing and Aaron Rosenberg producing. Borden Chase, who wrote *Winchester '73* and *Bend of the River*, had scripted another hard-hitting Western, *The Far Country*. Jim played a cattleman who, with his partner (played by Walter Brennan), drives his herd into Canada but has the herd stolen by a self-styled lawman (John McIntire). Again there was some needless romance, provided by not one but two girls, Ruth Roman as a saloon keeper and Corinne Calvet as a French-Canadian girl, both vying for the hero's affections. While making *The Far Country*, Jim learned a lesson that, he felt, explained what made a film special to people:

'I've learned that it's not always the whole movie that impresses people . . . [or] makes some kind of impact on them. It's often just single moments. I remember when we were up in the mountains in Canada shooting *The Far Country*. We were having lunch, and this guy came into the camp we'd set up, and he saw me, and he came over and said, "You Stewart?"

'I said, "Yeah."

'He said, "I saw you do a thing in a picture once. Can't remember the name of the picture, but you were in a room and you said a poem or something . . . that was good."

'That's all he said. And I knew what he meant. He was talking about a scene in *Come Live With Me* in 1941 . . . and he couldn't remember the title, but he had never forgotten that one thing . . . it didn't even last a minute on screen. And *that's* what's so great about the movies. If you're good and God helps you and you're just lucky enough to have the kind of personality that comes across on camera and off the screen, you can give people a little tiny piece of time which they'll never forget. And that's really something, to have that impact on people's lives.

'Movies can have an impact on people's lives. This means you have a certain obligation in what you do. But it also means that you touch the lives of people all over the world, and you don't know them, but they know you. They come up to you and they say, "I feel as though I know you," and I don't mind that because they say, "You seem like a friendly kinda fella," and that's fine with me.'

Of all the Stewart/Mann Westerns, *The Far Country* is the weakest, and both Mann and Rosenberg knew it. 'We spent months in post-production trying to fix the bits that didn't work,' said Rosenberg. 'It had some real flaws in it that just were not evident when we were filming it. I think we all thought we could just turn out another Western as good as the others, and we were wrong. Although we filmed it in 1953 and into 1954 [in the Canadian Rockies and Alberta's Jasper National Park], it didn't get a release until 1955.'

Anthony Mann was determined to remedy the situation by coming up with a superior Western. He abandoned Rosenberg, Universal and Borden Chase to work with producer William Goetz at Columbia on a screenplay written by Philip Yordan and Frank Burt. They came up with *The Man From Laramie*. But before Jim was available to do that film, there was something of a more personal nature he was interested in at Paramount.

Jim's deal with Paramount to make *Rear Window* allowed him to make a second film of his choosing for the studio, and he chose *Strategic Air Command*. His reason for doing the film was as a piece of propaganda for the United States Air Force wrapped up as entertainment. General Curtis LeMay of the real Strategic Air Command also wanted the film made; and with James Stewart, who held the post of Deputy Director of Operations of the Air Force Reserve, as the star, Paramount was able to benefit from the full co-operation of the Air Force.

The problem was, the film had little entertainment value. There was just a slight plot and therefore little to draw in an audience's emotions. Its director, Anthony Mann (who did the film as a favour to Jim), saw this from the beginning as the film's inherent weakness. Jim played a character pretty much based on himself, that of an officer in the Air Force Reserve who is called up because of a shortage of Strategic Air Command pilots. Apart from the fact that he leaves behind a baseball career, has a wife (played by June Allyson), and fulfils his duty until a shoulder injury puts him out of action, there was little else to fill the screen time of 115 minutes, except for impressive footage of aircraft taking off, in flight, and landing.

For Mann, the only reason to make the film, apart from helping his friend Jimmy Stewart, was a chance to work in the large-screen format of VistaVision, which gave a clearer picture than that of CinemaScope. Despite being one of Jim's least entertaining films of all time, his star power was enough to make it a box-office hit.

Jim was enjoying hit after hit and his deal with all the studios now gave him a percentage of the profits. Along with the profits he enjoyed from numerous investments, including oil wells, he was becoming a rich man.

Jim was shocked when he received news from Alex. Now a remarkable eighty-one, he was marrying a 78-year-old widow, Anita Stothart – little more than a year after Bessie's death. She was the aunt of Ruth Dingman, Alex's immediate neighbour. Gloria said that Jim didn't like Anita. She swore, which Jim didn't like hearing from a woman – or even a man, come to that. And she drank. And Jim knew the one thing his father didn't need was a wife who drank. Gloria said that Jim's sisters, Virginia and Mary, didn't like Anita either. But Alex had found a renewed vigour in his life and he and Anita worked out their wedding plans. When asked to make a public response to the news that Alex was to be married, Jim replied, 'Dad sure picked a good one. It sure is wonderful.' But, said Gloria, Jim really thought his father had 'gone crazy'.

Nevertheless, Jim agreed to be his father's best man. The wedding took place at the home of the Dingmans on 12 December 1954. It was something of a farce. To start with, all the fuses in the house were blown when the television and movie news people plugged their lighting equipment into the Dingmans' electricity supply. Then the organist, who was a recovering alcoholic, accepted champagne before the ceremony had begun, and before long he was so drunk he fell into the fireplace.

Gloria particularly remembered that a radio reporter sneaked in and said to her, 'Do you think your husband would remarry if you died first?' This sent Jim into a rage. He grabbed the reporter, oblivious to the film and TV cameras, took him outside and decked him with a right hook. Gloria recalled that the cameramen were all frustrated because none of them were quick enough to capture the event on film.

Jim paid for the honeymoon, which took Alex and Anita to Washington, New Orleans, and then to Jim and Gloria's home for the Christmas holidays. Gloria said, 'Jim never got to like Alex's new wife. He always referred to her as "the bride". I would say that, as much as Jim loved his father, things were never really good between them after that. Mostly, Jim tolerated his father out of respect, because Jim believed you should have respect for your father at all times, even if you don't like what he'd done or said.'

Anthony Mann couldn't wait to finish with *Strategic Air Command* and start work on *The Man From Laramie*. Neither Jim nor Mann knew that this would be their last collaboration.

Inspired by Shakespeare's *King Lear*, and filmed in Cinema-Scope, it was Mann's most ambitious film to date. In a story set against the bleak landscape of the New Mexico wilderness, Jim yet again played a character bent on vengeance. He is looking for the man who sold a consignment of guns to the Indians, enabling them to slaughter a cavalry detachment that included his younger brother. His search brings him to the kingdom of a cattle baron (played by Donald Crisp) whose empire will be inherited by either his psychotic son (Alex Nicol) or his rational son (Arthur Kennedy). The film was extremely violent, being full of beatings and killings that, as filmed by Mann, were far more brutal than anything else seen in American films at that time. In one scene, Stewart is shot through the hand at close range by the psychotic son.

At the age of forty-six, Jim was trying to get the most out of the strength and vitality he still had. In a famous scene from the film, Jim had ropes tied to his hands and was dragged through the sand and even through a campfire. He recalled, 'I felt it was important to do the stunt myself. It was a terribly dangerous scene to do but . . . it would look better if the audience saw that it was really me being dragged . . . and Mann, who usually let me do my own stunts, said that this was really a rough thing to do, and that it was too dangerous and they'd use a double. I didn't give up . . . I just kept on insisting . . . and finally he agreed but he still wasn't happy.

'Waall . . . we shot the scene . . . in *one* take. That's all it took. And Mann was as relieved as I was when I got up and walked away unscathed from it. And it was a scene everyone remembers. It wouldn't have worked half as well if they'd used a double. I guess I made Mann a nervous wreck for a short while.'

The Man From Laramie was a big critical and box-office success when released in 1955. The fans and the studios wondered what James Stewart and Anthony Mann would do next. No one could have guessed that within a year of *The Man From Laramie* being released, they would have a major falling out and would never work with or speak to each other again.

Ironically, it was around this time that an old friend came back into Jim's life. Since their argument in 1948 over Jim's involvement with the FBI and the House Un-American Activities Committee, Henry Fonda had been in New York.

18

Friendships Renewed and Destroyed

Henry Fonda had gone to New York in 1948. There he starred on Broadway in *Mister Roberts*, directed by Joshua Logan who had written the play in collaboration with Tom Heggen. The play and Fonda had been a smash hit. After its long run finished on Broadway, Fonda toured it through to 1952, when he returned to New York for another play, *Point of No Return*. He followed that successful run with *The Caine Mutiny Court Martial* in 1954.

Having shunned Hollywood and movies, it was the chance to do *Mister Roberts* as a film that brought Fonda back to Los Angeles. Gloria Stewart couldn't recall what precipitated the reunion between Fonda and Jim, but it happened some time in 1954. Her best recollection is that Fonda simply turned up at their home holding a box containing a kit for a model aeroplane. No words were exchanged. Jim simply offered Hank his hand, and Fonda shook it. Then Jim led Fonda into the house, they found themselves a spare room, and they sat down and began putting the plane together.

Fonda told me, 'After Jim and I had cross words about politics, we didn't speak for a long time. Finally we agreed to disagree but not to discuss politics ever again.' Gloria said that Jim told her they never actually said they would never discuss politics again. They just somehow knew they never would, and for the rest of their lives, they never said a word to each other that was political.

From the moment the two friends were reunited in 1954, they just continued their lives where they left off. The only thing that was different was that Hank had remarried; his new wife was Susan Blanchard, the stepdaughter of Oscar Hammerstein. Fonda's marriage to Frances had suffered due to the touring he did with *Mister Roberts*, and while the rift grew, Frances suffered with clinical depression. Matters were not helped when Hank met and fell for Susan Blanchard early in 1949. In April 1950, Frances Fonda committed suicide. In December 1951 Fonda and Susan were married.

Jim had been very fond of Frances, and the news of her death shook him. Gloria knew that he disapproved of the way Fonda had treated her, but when the two friends patched up their differences, Gloria knew that it was not only politics they would remain silent about; they would never discuss personal morals either. Jim simply would not judge Hank, as much as he disapproved of Fonda's lifestyle. He valued his friendship with Fonda so much that, having mended fences, he was not – *ever* – going to break them down again by pitching in with his thoughts and opinions about Fonda's private life.

For a long time Jim had avoided doing anything on television. 'In those days,' he said, 'you were either a movie actor or a television actor. You couldn't do both. Doing television was considered a comedown.' Nevertheless, in 1955 Jim did his first TV work, in the CBS anthology series *G. E. Theatre*. He did it only as a favour to Ronald Reagan, who hosted the Sunday evening series. NBC had decided to schedule the popular Western series *Bonanza* at the same time as *G. E. Theatre*, threatening its rating. Lew Wasserman, who was agent for both Jim and Reagan, persuaded Jim to do a guest spot on Reagan's show. The result was a thirty-minute Western, written by Borden Chase, called *The Windmill*, in which he played a poverty-stricken rancher.

Jim returned to help Reagan and his TV series again in 1957 with an appearance in *Trail to Christmas*, a Western version of *A Christmas Carol*; it also marked Jim's debut as a director. But there was more to Jim's aiding Reagan than mere professional courtesy. Jim continued to be active in his secret work to break the crime lords who still infiltrated many areas of Hollywood. The Kefauver investigation into organised crime, begun in 1950, had ended up making little difference because J Edgar Hoover was able to divert the public's attention away from the hearings with his dire warnings about Communism.

Since the death of Bugsy Siegel, Jim had been keeping tabs on the gangsters who took over the rackets. One of these was Mickey Cohen, who was allowed to rise to become one of the biggest mobsters in Los Angeles because of corruption in the Los Angeles Police Department. Cohen didn't involve himself in the film business but he was running the Mafia-sponsored rackets.

Ronald Reagan was Jim's go-between with the FBI, so Jim never had to meet with anyone from the Bureau. Hoover continued to thank Jim for his help and encouraged him to continue. Jim thought he was safe from any harm while he maintained his anonymity, but Gloria had cause to be worried. 'Jim wouldn't give up what he considered a holy quest,' she told me. 'I did have concerns that the hoods would find out what he was up to and do something about it. And we had our children to think of too. But Jim was just too clever. I know he would have liked to have led a raid on Mickey Cohen's home, just like a real FBI agent. It was a crime in itself that Hoover was letting Jim play out this masquerade with no intention of doing anything about it.'

Jim was also responsible for bringing to the attention of the FBI the name of Johnny Rosselli, the official Hollywood liaison and one of the most trusted lieutenants of Sam Giancana, the most powerful of the Mafia bosses. The CIA, though, already knew Rosselli well. Rosselli had two main functions: while he worked with the CIA on covert operations, providing Mafia hitmen for use by the agency, he was also in Hollywood looking for struggling actors and actresses for the Mafia to 'sponsor'. Such stars would then be in debt to their sponsor. This had long been a secret part of Hollywood business. Early clients had included Cary Grant and Gary Cooper, and later ones included Frank Sinatra and Marilyn Monroe. Both Giancana and Rosselli were allegedly involved in the deaths of Marilyn Monroe and President John F Kennedy.

Jim knew all about Rosselli and continued to pass on details to the FBI via Ronald Reagan.

As Deputy Director of Operations for the Strategic Air Command, and also for his status as a movie star, Jim was invited by President Dwight D Eisenhower to be the main speaker at the Veterans Day observances at Arlington National Cemetery, Virginia, in 1956. Jim was proud to accept the invitation.

After the success of *Rear Window*, Paramount was keen to have Hitchcock and Stewart make another film. Jim agreed, and Hitchcock decided to remake his 1934 thriller *The Man Who Knew Too Much*. Jim played a doctor on vacation in Marrakesh with his wife (Doris Day) and son (Christopher Olsen). He witnesses a murder and learns of an assassination attempt scheduled to take place in London. Before he can tell the police, his son is kidnapped by the plotters and threatened with death if the doctor does not keep quiet. And so the doctor and his wife follow the leads to London to foil the plot and save their son.

The Man Who Knew Too Much was a big hit when it opened in May 1956, and Paramount and Hitchcock began preparing for a follow-up, *Vertigo*. But before that, Jim had a film which he simply *had* to make. Warner Brothers had given Leland Hayward the green light to make *The Spirit of St. Louis*, the story of Charles Lindbergh's record-breaking flight from Long Island to Paris in 1927. Hayward was trying his hand at producing films and had won a three-picture deal with Warners; the first had been *Mister Roberts* and the third was to be Hemingway's *The Old Man and the Sea*.

Henry Fonda recalled, 'Warners was, like all the studios at that time in the mid-fifties, making smaller profits. Then Leland Hayward came to them with his proposition, which Jack Warner thought would give his studio some much-needed prestige. My only interest was *Mister Roberts*, which I felt if anyone was going to do, it ought to be *me* since I'd played the part for so long on Broadway.'

When it came to the casting of Charles Lindbergh, Jim begged Hayward to give him the part. Said Fonda, 'Warners didn't even want to cast Jim in the role because Jim was twice the age Lindbergh was when he made his historic flight.' Lindbergh was twenty-five when he made the flight. Stewart was forty-seven. Joshua Logan said, 'I knew they wanted a younger actor, John Kerr, who would have been the right age. Kerr was really unknown then, and his career was quite short. He refused to play Lindbergh because he didn't agree with Lindbergh's right-wing politics. Maybe he made the right decision for the wrong reasons because the failure of the film might have ended his career before it got going.'

Stewart recalled, 'I was smart enough to know I was twice Lindbergh's age. Hayward really pitched hard to get me the role. Jack Warner just wouldn't hear of it to start with, which I can understand. So Warner made Hayward break the news to me that I didn't have the role, which really disappointed me. But I wanted the part so badly, I went on a diet to get rid of the few measly pounds middle-age had bestowed upon me. I'd never dieted in my life. I became so thin that Gloria really got worried about me. She said I looked ill. But still Warner wouldn't budge. So I said to Hayward, "Tell Jack Warner I'll dye my hair."

'What finally got me the part was Jack Warner's own desperation to get the part cast. The studio had spent a great deal of money on pre-production and getting Billy Wilder to write the screenplay. Warner was counting the cost and seeing it mount up, and they *needed* an actor with some muscle at the box office, and thank God I had some muscle at that time. So finally Jack Warner gave me the part so they could get going because the budget was just going up and up, and they needed to get the results on film.'

Billy Wilder not only wrote the screenplay but also directed the film. He had decided that to simply tell the story of the flight would hardly hold an audience's interest, so he wrote a screenplay that revealed much of Lindbergh's life before the flight, told in flashback. Stewart recalled:

'Billy Wilder wanted to do the film because Lindbergh was one of his heroes. Leland Hayward wanted to do the picture because Lindbergh was also a hero of his. We all wanted to do the film for the same reasons . . . and I guess maybe that's not always the best reason to do a picture. Wilder's challenge was to get a good script. My job was to work on the character. I studied Lindbergh's mannerisms. I listened to the way he talked and watched how he walked. I tried to inject some of it into the character, but always Wilder said,

"Don't bury yourself in the part. The public will be paying to see Jimmy Stewart." A lot of Lindbergh's personality was perhaps more inside of me than outside, but that helped me as an actor.

'I also did a lot of flying in the picture. The studio wouldn't risk allowing me to do too much flying in case I crashed and that would be the end of their picture. I wasn't allowed to fly during any filming. But Wilder could at least get close-ups of my taxiing the plane.

'What I really wanted to do was fly the plane when they shot Lindbergh landing in Paris. I wanted to fly the plane and land it and feel how Lindbergh must have felt when he landed to the cheers of the waiting crowd. But they said I couldn't do that. Wilder said to me, "I admire your dedication and I understand your desire."

'I said to Wilder, "I think you need to demonstrate your dedication." He said, "What do you suggest?" I said, "Oh, I dunno . . . just a little something . . . like *wing walking*." He said, "I'll do it." And he did. For ten minutes he stood on the wing of a plane in flight.'

During filming, Stewart got to meet his boyhood hero:

'We were filming at Long Island when Lindbergh arrived to visit the set. I was thrilled to meet him at long last. I don't think he ever got used to the idea of being a celebrity . . . because he was a very quiet, very insular kind of man. He didn't have much to say and there wasn't too much time . . . although I would've liked to have talked to him at great length . . . but he just had enough time to take a look at the recreation of his original plane we were using, which Lindbergh seemed to like a lot.

'And before I could say very much to him, he was gone. But he did call me at home one late afternoon . . . around five . . . and he had just arrived at the airport and asked what Gloria and I were doing for dinner. So I told him we were going to Chasen's Restaurant – where we always ate – and he said, "Okay, I'll be there in about twenty-five minutes."

'So we met him at Chasen's, and he was very pleasant, but he was obviously a little shy and it was taking time for us to get to know him . . . but we didn't have long together because Paul Chasen came up to us and said that he was very sorry, but somehow word had got out that Lindbergh was there with James Stewart and about forty newspapermen and cameramen were waiting outside. So Lindbergh just said, "Do you have a backdoor . . . and would you get me a taxi?" So then he thanked us and said goodbye, and he left . . . and that's the last we ever saw of him.

'I know that Billy Wilder was never happy with the whole project. There was never a proper script to begin with. Wilder got to work on the screenplay and brought Wendell Mayes in to try and make it work. Leland Hayward was also putting in some kind of contribution. Wilder knew the story of just the flight was not interesting enough so he put in a lot of earlier stuff about Lindbergh's days as a young barnstormer. Wilder was at his best with comedy and I know he felt this kind of picture was wrong for him – or he for it. So he added a piece of fiction about Lindbergh teaching a priest to fly so he could get nearer to God! It was just a touch of comedy.'

Stewart felt that Wilder's genius managed to express itself through the director's invention of a fly that gets caught in the plane during the flight. 'Wilder couldn't have me flying all that time without saying a word, and he didn't want me – or Lindbergh – just talking to himself. So Wilder decided that a fly would find itself on board, and Lindbergh would talk to this fly to keep himself awake.'

'That was a stroke of genius,' said Logan, 'because one of Jimmy's strengths as a screen actor is his whimsical nature. And having him talk to a fly was just pure whimsicality.'

Wilder filmed in as many authentic locations as possible, from New York to Nova Scotia, Newfoundland, the Irish Coast, across the Channel and to Paris. His insistence on location filming inflated the original budget from $2 million to $6 million. By the end of 1957, the film had only grossed a mere $2.6 million. It was described by Jack Warner as 'a disastrous failure'.

Fonda recalled, 'Of the three pictures Leland produced for Warners, *Mister Roberts* was the only one that did well. I felt sorry for my pal Jim because he was so personally and emotionally involved with *The Spirit of St. Louis*, and nobody went to see it. Jack Warner, I think, liked to blame the film's failure on Jim's age, but I don't think that was the problem. I really don't think the public thought of Jim as a middle-aged actor trying to play a young man. They simply liked Jimmy Stewart, and the reasons they didn't go to see him in *that* picture I've never really figured out.'

The film's failure was a blow and a mystery to Jim: 'It was a dream of mine to play Charles Lindbergh. He was my boyhood hero. Funny thing about that picture. Happens to some movies, like *It's a Wonderful Life* . . . just doesn't do well when first released. In later years, it takes on a sort of classic status. But at the time, *The Spirit of St. Louis* was just a disaster.'

Logan said, 'I think the real reason the film bombed was not because Jimmy Stewart was too old but because the film really had no interesting story. Nobody cared that Lindbergh flew from New York to Paris in record time. That just wasn't the interesting story about Lindbergh, although Jimmy thought it was. The interesting story would have been about the kidnapping and murder of Lindbergh's baby [in 1932]. As for the title, *The Spirit of St. Louis*; everyone thought it was a musical. They should have called it *The Lindbergh Story*, especially as Jimmy had done *The Stratton Story* and *The Glenn Miller Story*. Who the hell knew that St. Louis was the name of the plane?'

The Spirit of St. Louis was the first failure Jim had suffered at the box office in several years, although today it is considered a classic. And even before the failure of the film, Jim had become embroiled in a controversy that revolved around his status as a pilot and an officer in the Air Force Reserve.

In February 1957, the Air Force nominated three Reserve major-generals and eight Reserve brigadier-generals. The list had been approved by President Eisenhower. One of the names nominated for brigadier-general was James Stewart. Maine Senator Margaret Chase Smith, a member of the Air Force Reserve, began receiving protests from past and present administrators of the Reserve Officers Association that Jim was receiving unfair consideration just because he was a film star. Senator Smith investigated all eleven submissions and came to the conclusion that hardly any of them merited a promotion. But her greatest criticism was for James Stewart (though she also objected to John Montgomery, a colonel who had resigned from the Air Force after long service to take an executive job at American Airlines and later at General Electric).

She pointed out that Stewart had done only one fifteen-day tour (in 1956) as a reservist since the end of the war, and had worn his uniform on just eight occasions in peacetime. She also called into question his ability to fly any of the modern jet aircraft, and voiced her surprise that he continued to be Deputy Director of Operations for the Strategic Air Command. Meeting with Pentagon officials, she asked them if they believed that James Stewart should be made a brigadier-general on the basis of his starring role in *Strategic Air Command*. They said they did. She responded with, 'Then why don't you make June Allyson a brigadier-general for playing the female lead in the picture?'

At a Senate committee in August 1957, Jim's nomination was rejected by a 13–0 vote. Jim later reflected on the controversy, saying, 'I don't think Senator Smith was mad at me personally. I can understand when someone thinks a movie star doesn't automatically qualify for an important rank. But the fact was, nobody expected me to climb into a modern jet and fly it. That wasn't what the Air Force Reserve had in mind for me. They had me in line for the post of deputy director of the Office of Information – and that was something I had no trouble handling.'

The controversy, however, raged on. As far as the Air Force was concerned, the Senate's denial of Jim's promotion was not the end of the matter.

After the disappointment of *The Spirit of St. Louis*, Jim felt his next film would be a sure-fire hit. It was a Western called *Night Passage*, produced by Aaron Rosenberg at Universal. Once again Borden Chase wrote the screenplay, telling the story of two brothers, one of whom (played by Stewart) is decent, while the other (played by Audie Murphy) is an outlaw. The decent brother takes on the job of protecting a payload of $10,000 and the outlaw brother helps to steal it. Finally, the outlaw changes his ways and loses his life while saving his brother's during a fight with the robbers.

Anthony Mann had been chosen to direct the film. He worked on pre-production and, according to producer Rosenberg, shot some of the opening scenes. 'But Tony was not happy,' said Rosenberg:

'He didn't like the script. Compared to his other Westerns with Jimmy, it just didn't amount to anything – and I had to agree. After starting work on the film, Mann said to me, "I can't go through with this. I'm quitting." I said, "But you'll be letting Jim down. You'll be letting me down." He said, "I put up with making *Thunder Bay* and *Strategic Air Command*. I even did *The Glenn Miller Story* for Jim. But I will not make this trash."

'When Jim heard this, they had an almighty argument. All I know is, it got so bad that Tony accused Jim of wanting only to make a Western in which he could play his damn accordion – and he *did* play his accordion in the film – and Jim was so insulted, he never talked to Mann ever again.

'I expected Jim to quit the picture too. But he refused to walk away. For one thing, he had a lot of respect for Audie Murphy because of his outstanding war record. He also liked the idea of playing a hero for once in a Western. I think Jim had grown tired of playing the anti-hero – the man with hate in his heart and a rage that leads him to violence. He even got to sing a couple of songs ["Follow the River" and "You Can't Get Far Without a Railroad"], which was something else Tony Mann objected to.'

Universal gave the directorial task to James Neilson, who had been a stills photographer before producing television shows and was subsequently hired by Walt Disney in the 1960s to direct several family adventures. Neilson failed to save *Night Passage*; it was arguably Stewart's worst Western.

The rift with Mann hurt Jim. Gloria said that he mentally beat himself up for having fallen out with the director who had literally saved his career after the war. 'There was something in Jim that just wouldn't allow him to forgive Mann – and that's not like Jim. I think Jim felt that he was as responsible for Mann's success as Mann was for his, and he felt Mann owed him something. But he would have liked to have made amends. He just couldn't bring himself to do it.

'I think that if Mann, like Hank [Fonda], had just turned up on the doorstep with a model aeroplane they could make together, everything would have been fine. But neither man made the effort, and they never spoke again.'

With Anthony Mann out of the picture, Jim's career as a star of Westerns had peaked. He would never reach the heights of *The Man From Laramie* again. His career was also slowing down, and there were precious few good films left.

But he now had a new interest in his life. He had always wanted to go to Africa on hunting safaris, and during the 1950s he began making regular visits there with Gloria. Gloria, however, was more interested in animal conservation, and in time she managed to interest Jim, too, in conserving animals rather than hunting them. The subject would also become a passion for their daughter Kelly when she was older.

19

Times of Depression

In 1957 Jim was back at Paramount, working with Hitchcock in *Vertigo*. Jim played a cop who has become a private detective after his acrophobia (the correct term for a fear of heights; 'vertigo' refers to the sense of dizziness) causes the death of a fellow cop. Assigned to watch over a suicidal girl, played by Kim Novak, his fear of heights prevents him from saving her life. Yet when she seemingly turns up again, he gradually unravels the truth that the girl was murdered and another (also played by Novak) has taken her place to cover up the murder. The climactic scene sees the private eye overcoming his acrophobia to pursue the imposter up a church tower, from where she falls to her death.

Despite the happy collaboration between Jim and Hitchcock on *Rear Window*, there were tensions on the set of *Vertigo*. Hitchcock resented the fact that Jim had disliked the original screenplay and had insisted on a rewrite. Hitchcock was also frustrated at not being able to persuade Vera Miles to do the film and had reluctantly cast Kim Novak, under contract to Columbia, in her place. Jim had been forced to accept a film for Columbia, *Bell, Book and Candle*, in exchange for the studio loaning Novak to Paramount. Consequently, nothing Novak did satisfied Hitchcock, and the director seemed to blame Jim for having to settle for Novak in the part. Kim Novak told me:

'Hitchcock didn't like having me in his picture and he felt I was ruining it. It was only after the film was finished that I heard how much he thought I'd wrecked his picture. I felt I did a lot of good work in that movie, and I got some of the best notices of my career. But Hitchcock couldn't blame himself, so he blamed me.

'Thank God I had Jimmy Stewart with me in that picture. He treated me so well. I learned a lot about acting from him. When we had emotional scenes, he'd prepare himself. He wasn't like a lot of actors who could just get in front of the camera and do it all when the director yelled "Action!" And he couldn't just stop when the director yelled "Cut!" He had to prepare himself first by somehow going deep inside of himself, and you knew to leave him alone when he was like that. Then he'd say he was ready, and we'd do the scene. And when it was over, he wouldn't just walk away. He allowed himself to slowly come out of it. He'd hold my hand and I would squeeze his hand so that we both had time to come down from the emotion.'

The film worked well as a mystery thriller, but failed to convey the actual paralysing fear that people with acrophobia suffer (and I speak as a severe sufferer). Various camera tricks and editing tried to convey the fear, but for an audience to believe in it, the experience really has to be conveyed through an actor's performance. Jim succeeded on many levels in doing just that, but Hitchcock's camera trickery dispelled it. The film had only modest success – although in recent years it has actually become generally regarded as one of Hitchcock's best. In fact, of the four films Jim made with Hitchcock, only *Rear Window* stands out (which illustrates my opinion that Hitchcock is, arguably, one of the most overrated film directors of all time).

Somewhere during production of *Vertigo*, Hitchcock became dissatisfied with Jim, who was next due to star in Hitchcock's *North by Northwest*. Jim had only been offered the part because Hitchcock's first choice, Cary Grant, was unavailable. Hoping to delay the film until Grant became available, Hitchcock gave Jim numerous excuses for the hold-up, such as rewrites on the script and problems with the studio. Finally, Jim had to report to Columbia for *Bell, Book and Candle*. Hitchcock pretended he was sorry to lose Stewart, but it meant that he was at last able to cast Cary Grant in *North by Northwest*. It was typical of the director who once said 'Actors are like cattle'.

In *Bell, Book and Candle*, Kim Novak played a witch who sets out to lead a normal life and fall for a normal man. She puts a spell on her neighbour, played by Jim, to make him fall in love with her. Meanwhile her warlock brother, played by Jack Lemmon, writes a book on modern witchcraft, threatening to expose how his sister cast a love spell.

Jim knew he was wrong for the part. 'I was almost fifty and it just looked ridiculous having someone like Kim Novak choosing me for a husband,' he said. The irony was that Cary Grant, four years older than Jim, had originally been set to star in *Bell, Book and Candle*, but he had held off so he could do *North by Northwest*.

As Kim Novak remembered, Jim was often distracted on the set: 'He said he was having trouble with his two sons, who were teenagers. He was on the phone a lot, trying to sort out problems Gloria had with the boys. I don't think he was happy doing the film at all. He didn't seem to have the care and attention to performance that was there during *Vertigo*. He didn't prepare for scenes; he just did them and walked away when they were finished.'

If Jim was slacking in his technique, Jack Lemmon didn't notice. He told me, 'He was in total charge of his technique – even more than his directors must have realised. It just *looked* as though he wasn't in control. He really stammers off the screen, so on screen he uses that stammering but he kept it under control. So he knew when to stammer and when not to. He knew how to exploit that "Jimmy Stewart" mannerism. He's a very astute actor.'

Released in 1958, *Bell, Book and Candle* was not a great success. That same year, Anthony Mann's violent Western, *Man of the West*, did well and in 1959 *North by Northwest* was a big hit. Mann had originally intended Jim to star in *Man of the West*, but following their rift, he cast Jim's close friend Gary Cooper in the part. And Cary Grant, Jim's replacement in *North by Northwest*, was also a close friend. 'I was discovering for the first time – after all those years – that Hollywood was really a *cut-throat* business,' Jim told me. 'It wasn't my actor friends who were cutting throats. It was the directors.'

According to Gloria, Jim believed that had he been able to do *North by Northwest* and *Man of the West*, his career would have still been riding high. As it was, he had hit a slump – and it was one from which he would never truly recover.

In April 1958 Lana Turner's boyfriend, Johnny Stompanato, was fatally stabbed by Lana's teenage daughter, Cheryl Crane, at Lana's Beverly Hills mansion. Stompanato had often beaten Lana, and this time Cheryl, fearful for her mother's life, picked up a kitchen knife and drove it into Stompanato.

The name of Stompanato, or Johnny Valentine as he was also known, was not new to the FBI. Jim had compiled a short dossier on him as being one of Mickey Cohen's henchmen. When Lana began her affair with Stompanato, Jim had begged her not to pursue a romance he felt sure would end up in violence. But she ignored him, and Jim always felt it was a miracle that Cheryl had been able to stop Stompanato from probably killing Lana.

The file he had on Stompanato and Cohen was passed to Ronald Reagan, who passed it on to the FBI. But the FBI took no interest in it, even when Stompanato was killed. Jim accepted Hoover's excuse that it was down to the Los Angeles Police Department to deal with the case. The ensuing court case found that it was a case of 'justifiable homicide' and Cheryl was free.

Jim tried to warn Hoover that other lives might yet be lost because there were still too many gangsters in Hollywood, most of them linked to Mickey Cohen and Sam Giancana. Gloria told me, 'Jim was right. When Marilyn Monroe died, nobody dared to mention that the Mob was behind it. Jim won't talk about it, but he knew that Monroe was murdered by the Mob. Even then, Hoover told Jim that it was a matter for the Los Angeles police. Jim was delighted when Senator Robert Kennedy personally began investigating organised crime.'

What Jim didn't know was that Hoover would have nothing to do with Kennedy's investigation. Nor did he ever know that when Robert's brother, John, became President of the United States and

Robert became Attorney-General, the brothers tried to get Hoover out of the FBI because of his corruption. 'Jim used to say, "I don't trust the Kennedy boys," just because they were Democrats. Jim would say, "Why don't they just let J Edgar do his job and break up the Mob?" Jim just didn't understand – and nobody did back then – that Robert Kennedy was doing the job Hoover should have done years before. Jim always told Hoover, "You can count on me." And I think Hoover did.'

When Warner Brothers approached Hoover in 1958 to ask for full co-operation in making *The FBI Story*, he had one major stipulation: he wanted James Stewart to be the star. Jim told me, 'I was honoured that Mr Hoover thought that I should be the one to embody the FBI agent. I don't know what Jack Warner thought when he went to the FBI and asked for an official stamp of approval and was told, "Only if Jimmy Stewart is the star," but I was honoured . . . and grateful.' The film's director, Mervyn LeRoy, told me a slightly different version of events:

'When J Edgar Hoover heard that Jack Warner was going to make a film that supposedly told the "true" story of the FBI, he told Jim not to worry and that he would make sure Jim got the part. So when Jack Warner contacted Hoover in Washington and said, "See here, Mr Hoover, we want to make a film about the history of your wonderful organisation," and Hoover said, "You'll have my full co-operation – but only if Jimmy Stewart is the star, and we have full control over every aspect of the film," Warner had second thoughts. Not that he didn't want Stewart in the part, but he must have known that the picture wasn't going to be a Warner Brothers production. It was an FBI production – all the way.

'First off, Hoover went through the script with a fine-tooth comb, took out everything he didn't like and insisted other scenes be added. He also chose every member of the cast – not just Jimmy Stewart, but *everybody*, as well as the crew. Even I had to be approved. Even the extras had to be vetted. It turned out that in one scene there was an extra who was not considered "American", and the scene had to be reshot. Worst of all, I had two FBI agents accompany me the whole time.'

It may have been that Hoover wanted to repay Jim for all the work he had done for the FBI by forcing Jack Warner to cast him in the film. Or that Hoover had come to think of Jimmy Stewart as being the quintessence of an FBI agent. Hoover always had a romantic idea of what an agent should be – upright, moral, patriotic beyond question – and he came to see that notion in the form of James Stewart. There were stories of Hoover firing or reassigning agents who were found to be drunk, or having adulterous affairs. He even had an agent removed from Washington for carrying a copy of *Playboy*. Those were vices that Jimmy Stewart just did not represent; while his status as a war hero and an officer in the Air Force Reserve, as well his conscientious patriotism, were virtues that made Jim, in Hoover's eyes, the perfect FBI agent.

The film's story was something of a sprawling epic, following Jim's career as a fictional FBI agent as he took on the Ku Klux Klan, brought down gangsters like Dillinger and Baby Face Nelson, arrested Native American killers, rounded up enemy agents during the Second World War, and then captured Communist spies. 'Jim loved playing the part because he felt he was telling the story of the greatest law enforcement agency in the world,' said Henry Fonda. As for Fonda's own view: 'I thought it was a prime example of a state-controlled movie. I thought that's what they do in the Soviet Union.'

Clearly, it was a subject Jim and Hank never discussed. Jim said, 'You couldn't make the picture without Mr Hoover's assistance. It wouldn't have had the authenticity we were aiming for. I knew Hoover well. He knew about a lot of things . . . including picture making. I don't know how he knew about all that . . . but he did . . . and he loved being involved with that picture. I met him on a number of occasions, and he was always easy to talk to because he knew about so much. He just kinda put people at their ease.'

Apparently, though, he didn't put Mervyn LeRoy at ease. LeRoy said, 'I had to show Hoover the picture before virtually anyone else saw it. It didn't matter whether Jack Warner liked or didn't like it. Hoover was the one who had to like it. When I showed him the film, it was so terrifying, I was wet with perspiration all over. I was really worried when he didn't laugh at the humorous bits. But when it was over he said, "That's one of the greatest films I've ever seen." I almost cried with relief. Of course, it's not one of the greatest films ever made, but I did my best under difficult circumstances.'

Gloria told me that Jim was too easily impressed by Hoover, and he had never actually been officially released from his undercover work for the FBI – partly, she said, because his undercover work never was official. 'I think Hoover kept him kind of hanging on just in case he ever needed him. And I think that when Hoover said he wanted Jim to star in *The FBI Story*, he was also telling Jim that this was part of his ongoing commitment to Hoover and the FBI. That commitment only ended when Hoover died.'

Hoover died in 1972. By 1979, and certainly in the ensuing years whenever I met with Jim and Gloria, it became clear to me that Jim's once glowing admiration for Hoover had severely waned. Gloria said it was due to the revelations that Hoover had been keeping so many secret files on many Hollywood people, and the fact that Hoover's corruption had come to light. As Fonda put it, 'Hoover didn't like it when he heard rumours that Jim and me were a couple of fags, but *he* was a fag the whole time – and that's his business. But don't go around slinging mud when it sticks hardest to you. I thought he was a disgusting fellow – but I wouldn't say that to Jim.'

For some years, Jim found that wherever he went in the world, he had the watchful eye of the FBI taking care of him. He put it down to Hoover's gratitude for the work he did in *The FBI Story*: 'Almost wherever we've been, whether it was Spain or Italy or virtually anywhere, whenever we landed, we'd be approached by some man who would come straight up and say, "The Boss has asked me to check that everything is okay with you, and if you need us at any time, here's my card." I guess making *The FBI Story* will do that for you.' In fact, said Gloria, it wasn't making *The FBI Story* that earned Jim protection from the FBI the world over – it was having worked undercover for Hoover, especially during the years of the Communist witch-hunts.

While trying to keep his career from nose-diving, Jim had more personal concerns on his mind. Margaret Sullavan had become depressed, and as soon as he had heard about her troubles, he had offered his help. Said Gloria, 'Margaret was only in her late forties, but she was having trouble with her hearing. Jim understood because he had suffered from hearing loss ever since I'd known him. Margaret had been rehearsing a play that would have gone to Broadway, but she couldn't hear the cues. She became so anxious that she couldn't sleep, so her doctor gave her sleeping tablets.

'Jim gave her as much support and encouragement and advice as he could. He had learned to make sure he knew everybody else's lines and he had reached a point where in rehearsal he would watch rather than listen for his cues so he could go straight into his lines. But Margaret just found that too difficult, and she grew depressed.'

Jim worried endlessly about Sullavan, and even talked to Henry Fonda about the situation. Fonda didn't know what he could do to help, and felt guilty that he was unable to offer his former wife support. Gloria felt that Fonda's reluctance was due to Frances' suicide; he was afraid to accept that history could repeat itself. He was, said Gloria, emotionally unable to handle that possibility. But Jim never gave up on her.

Neither did the Air Force give up on Jim in their battle to have him promoted to brigadier-general. Since the rejection of his promotion in 1957, Jim had put in a lot more flying time with the Strategic Air Command. The Pentagon approved his transfer as chief of staff of the Fifteenth Air Force Reserve, and the application for his promotion was resubmitted in February 1959. Finally, in July 1959, Jim was reposted to the Reserve Information Services, thereby removing him from potential combat service for which he admitted he was no longer suited, and his promotion to brigadier-general was finally confirmed.

Jim was about to give what many considered to be his last great performance – in Otto Preminger's courtroom drama *Anatomy of a Murder*. Jim played a defence lawyer in a murder case that had, for its time in 1959, an unusual twist. The accused (played by Ben Gazzara) had killed a man who had raped his wife (brilliantly played by Lee Remick); Jim's lawyer was legally barred from using the rape as the cause of the killer's insanity because the rape was not legally proven to have occurred. The lawyer's only hope was to convince the jury that his client was insane when he committed the murder.

Gloria said, 'Jimmy loved the screenplay for *Anatomy of a Murder* and really wanted to give it all he'd got. Before filming we were off to India for a safari holiday, and he brought the script along. At night we'd settle down in our tent, and Jimmy would say, "Just going to study my lines for a while, dear," and I'd go to sleep. I'd wake up several hours later to find him still going over his lines. And the next night. And the next. He wanted to be absolutely sure he was ready when we got back.'

Stewart recalled, 'There was an awful lot of dialogue . . . long monologues . . . which I was kind of used to doing but not so many in one film. And as you get older it isn't so easy to remember all those lines. You kind of wish for a script with short, to-the-point lines. But this was a challenge for me. I think a lot of us have a secret desire to be a lawyer . . . or some kind of investigator who asks questions and slowly unravels the truth. The trick for this lawyer was to justify a murder. Usually the defending lawyer is trying to prove his client is innocent, but this was so different . . . and I needed to be able to understand what the lawyer was saying . . . what he was trying to do. And I had to make sure I knew my lines.'

Lee Remick recalled, 'Lana Turner was originally cast, and when Jimmy left for India, he thought she'd still be playing the part when he came back. But while he was away there was some kind of huge row between Turner and Preminger. And when he got back, he found she'd been replaced . . . by me.

'Working with Jimmy was a wonderful experience. I never felt as though we were the greatest of friends because there is a certain aloofness with Jimmy. I always felt that it wasn't that he was ignoring you or being unfriendly in any way – he was always polite, always warm, would always say hello and ask how you were, but then he'd be off somewhere inside of himself. He seemed to enjoy his own company – and I think that was because he was a true loner. Most of all, he seemed to be simply concentrating on his work. He'd be going over his lines, and you could read it all in his face. And there were times when he just seemed lost in something. George C Scott [who played the prosecuting attorney] would say, "Jimmy's in his time machine and he's back God knows when or God knows where, but he's lost in time." And I think Scott was right on those occasions.'

George C Scott told me:

'Jimmy seemed so much older to us "younger" actors, even though he was only about fifty. But already he was at an age when it seemed each week there was news that another of his friends – or just someone he'd worked with – had passed away. And you'd see him go into a sort of daze every now and then, just lost in some thought or other. Sometimes he just looked distant. But every now and again you'd see him smile. One day I asked him what he was thinking. He said, "Oh, just remembering." Now that I'm older than he was at the time, I understand, although I don't stop and dream as much as Jimmy did back then. I guess that's what he was doing really – dreaming. Daydreaming.

'I learned so much from Stewart. This was only my second movie, so I had a lot to learn. And whenever I was worried about something, or wasn't sure about even little technical things like how to perform for the camera and not *to* the camera, he'd show me.

'We had a lot of scenes where we each had long speeches in the courtroom, and either he'd be taking centre stage and doing a cross-examination while I sat at my table and made my objections, or it'd be the other way round and *I'd* have centre stage and he'd be at *his* table. I was very used to working in theatre and having an actor to talk to, but often in films when you have a close-up and you're having a conversation with another character, you don't always get the other actor to deliver his lines because for a while the camera is not on *him*. You often have some assistant director or grip or continuity girl reading their lines, and you just don't get the right responses to make your own responses as good as they could be. Of course, you learn how to do that after several movies. Then they turn the camera around for a new set-up so the camera is on the other actor, and you can go off and have a cigarette while the script girl reads your lines.

'But Jimmy didn't do that. When we did those long courtroom scenes and he'd finish doing a long piece when the camera was on him, he didn't leave the set. He stayed and delivered all his lines off camera while I had all my close-ups. He'd stand by the camera, in his lawyer's suit and totally in character, delivering his lines with conviction just for my benefit.'

Stewart was surprised by a lot of animosity he received from long-time fans: 'A lot of people wrote to me and said, "You let us down. I took my family to see a Jimmy Stewart picture and you're up there in court talking dirty and holding up a pair of women's panties." I was puzzled why so many people thought *Anatomy of a Murder* was in bad taste. I never understood why some people thought it was offensive. I thought we handled the whole thing very delicately ... *too* delicately by today's standards. And yet I think the film has as much impact today as it did then, so if anything it's the films of today that are offensive. The kind of part I had in the picture was the kind of part you just can't turn down, and if something like it came along and it was just as well written, and the character so interesting to play, I'd do it.'

Regarding Preminger's reputation as a cruel director (his nickname was 'Otto the Ogre'), Jim said, 'I had no problem working with Preminger. I'd heard all the terrible stories about him, about how he would chew an actor out for no reason other than to be a bully. But I never saw any of that.' George C Scott felt that Stewart was the main reason for the absence of Preminger's usual tirades:

'Actors – or men of any profession, race, creed or colour – don't come any *nicer* – and I hate to use that word but it's appropriate in this case – than Jimmy Stewart. Even when he got mad, which he did at times over something that tested his patience, he did it in such a *nice* way that you would be left wondering what had just happened. There was an actor who hadn't learned his lines properly, and when he blew take after take, you could see that Preminger was ready to chew him up and spit him out. And I knew that Stewart was just as mad, but all he did was say – very patiently – to Preminger, "You know, Otto, I spent my whole time in India learning my lines and I know I fluff them once in while, but I sometimes wonder if I should just have waited until five minutes before coming to the set before learning my lines – like some people seem to have done. Tell you what, Otto, why don't we take five minutes so *somebody* can learn their lines." And he said it without raising his voice. Just very even and very *Jimmy Stewart*, and you knew he'd made his point without ever raising his voice on even a single word, and the actor concerned was left feeling completely embarrassed. With me, I have to rant and rave, but by God, Jimmy just was so calm and almost *kind* about it all, his method had more impact than all my temperamental outbursts. And it also stopped Preminger from blowing up. Stewart just kept the whole situation calm.'

The film garnered good reviews – the last really good reviews Jim would ever receive. Bosley Crowther in the *New York Times* wrote, 'Slowly and subtly he presents us with a warm, clever, adroit and complex man and, most particularly, a portrait of a trial lawyer in action which will be difficult for anyone to surpass.' Campbell Dixon in the *Daily Telegraph* wrote, 'James Stewart makes the Clarence Darrow of the piece the embodiment of shrewdness and homespun charm.' *Variety* said, 'Preminger purposely creates situations that flicker with uncertainty, that may be evaluated in different ways. Motives are mixed and dubious, and, therefore, sustain interest. Balancing the fascinating nastiness of the younger players, there is the warmth and intelligence of Stewart.'

The two major flaws in an otherwise excellent film are the casting of real-life lawyer Joseph Welch who, as the judge, delivers a performance that is amateurish and unbelievable, and the excessive length. The latter was due possibly to the fact that the film was quickly edited in just twenty-one days to meet a release date of June 1959.

Nevertheless, Jim was nominated as Best Actor by the American Academy Awards, and the film received six other Oscar nominations, including Best Picture. But the Academy Awards in 1960 were dominated by the twelve Oscar nominations for *Ben-Hur*. Charlton Heston, nominated as Best Actor for *Ben-Hur*, told me, 'All the nominees were put together in a large group before the ceremony for a photograph, which is unusual. Jim was there, of course, and he came over to me and said, "Chuck, I hope you win." And he meant it. You can tell when someone you're competing with is just being courteous, but he was sincere.'

And Heston did win the Oscar. According to Gloria, although Jim had told Heston he hoped he'd win, it was Jim's way of protecting himself from disappointment. He kept telling Gloria, as they sat waiting for the announcement, 'I might win. I think I just might win. I have a good chance.' When Hugh Griffith was named as Best Supporting Actor for *Ben-Hur*, they knew that *Ben-Hur* was going to sweep the board – and it did, almost. It won eleven of its twelve nominations, including Best Actor.

However, Jim was named Best Actor at the Venice Film Festival in September 1959, as well as by the New York Film Critics. And the picture was named as best film of the year by *The Film Daily*. But for Jim, there would be no more Oscar nominations.

In the summer of 1959, Jim broke his own rule about never making a war movie and starred in *The Mountain Road*. In his own defence, Jim said, 'Technically, this was a film about events *before* World War Two . . . but to be honest, I was simply taken with the story of this officer in the American Army who finds that there's a whole lot more to commanding than just wanting to be in command. That's something I learned in the war . . . and I guess it struck a chord in me. Unfortunately, the film wasn't as good as I'd hoped it would be.' Jim played an American major who leads a squad of soldiers in China to commit sabotage to slow down the advancing Japanese. Released in 1960, the film is now largely forgotten and rarely seen.

On 1 January 1960, Margaret Sullavan died alone in a hotel room from an overdose of sleeping pills. It was probably suicide. Jim was devastated. 'He did become something of a recluse for a while,' said Gloria. She made him take a vacation, and for several months he considered retiring. 'He had lost the spark that had always been there,' said Gloria. 'I think that spark went out, not with the failure of his films, but with the death of Margaret Sullavan.'

Rescue came in the unexpected form of director John Ford. Having rejected Jim for the part of Doc Holliday in *My Darling Clementine*, Ford now offered Jim a Western, *Two Rode Together*. Henry Fonda, who had fallen out with Ford during the filming of *Mister Roberts*, told Jim to beware of him.

'I knew what Ford was up to when he put Jim in *Two Rode Together*,' said Fonda. 'Ford resented the success Jim had in the [Anthony] Mann Westerns. Ford really wanted Duke Wayne for the film, but for some reason Duke couldn't do it, so Ford turned to Jim. I told Jim not to trust Ford.'

But Jim was now eager to get back to work and hoped for success; most John Ford films, especially the Westerns, were successful. In this one, Jim, as a town sheriff, joins up with cavalry officer Richard Widmark to search for children and women who have been kidnapped by Indians. Its plot was similar to Ford's masterpiece *The Searchers*, but it lacked that film's sense of drama. Too much comedy lessened the film's impact, and it never reached anything approaching an exciting finale. It was clear to all that John Ford had lost his touch – or he was just a filmmaker who was unable to keep up with the times. The Jimmy Stewart/Anthony Mann Westerns had really changed the genre for ever.

Despite the failure of *Two Rode Together* on many levels, Jim was to work on two more Ford films, *The Man Who Shot Liberty Valance* and *Cheyenne Autumn*, curiously establishing him as a Ford regular. In fact, insisted Henry Fonda, Ford was using Jim partly to get back at him. 'I know Ford would have cast me in *Two Rode Together* if we'd still been talking, but we weren't, so he didn't. He once told me, as he was passing, "Who the hell needs you when I've got Jimmy Stewart?" I thought that was mean, not just to me, but to Jim.' Nevertheless, Jim was to look back on his three Ford films with nostalgia:

'I wasn't sure what to call him. Hank Fonda always called him Pappy. Duke Wayne called him Coach. Other actors had names for him – some affectionate and respectful, others definitely *neither*. So I settled on Boss. I felt safe if I always called him Boss.

'I'd hoped for something more than we got from our first picture together. You go with a director because of his history and his proven talent, and with Ford he'd made all those classic films . . . some were Westerns, some weren't. Some with Fonda, some with Wayne. But they were all memorable. Then I finally get to work with him and I quickly realised he wasn't really all that *interested* in the movie. He was just so *bad tempered* all the time.

'He also had a way of making his leading actors edgy with each other. I'd never worked with Dick Widmark before, and I liked him straight away. He doesn't come straight into your life like he's suddenly your best friend and you wonder how you ever got on without him, as some actors are wont to do. He kinda sizes you up, first . . . sees where you're coming from, and then he warms up. Ford took advantage of this, and he took me aside and said, "Watch out for Widmark. He'll try and steal every scene." So I said, "Thanks for the warning, Boss." Later I find out he took Widmark to one side and said, "Watch out for Stewart. He'll steal every scene." And that got things started with a certain kind of tension between Dick and me.

'But pretty soon Dick and I were having so much fun. But Ford wasn't having much fun, and he took it out on the crew. There was a scene where me and Dick had a long conversation sitting on a log by the edge of a river. I thought the scene would look just perfect if Ford had shot the scene so the river was behind us. That would have been a beautiful shot. But Ford felt mean that day and decided to shoot it from the river, so the whole crew had to wade into the river, which was freezing, and Dick and I were the only ones on dry land. I felt bad for the crew, and they were getting mad at Ford, and the whole atmosphere was pretty awful. The saddest thing was, the shot he got was just plain ordinary and he would have got a great classic Ford shot if he'd photographed it from the bank, with Dick and me against the river in the background. But he just wanted to make everybody miserable.'

Widmark remembered the making of *Two Rode Together* as being a lot of fun. He told me, 'I'm hard of hearing, Jim's hard of hearing and Ford was hard of hearing. Ford would be giving us direction and Jim would say, "What?" And I'd say, "What?" And Ford said, "What?" And we were like that most of the time – "What?" "What?"'

If Widmark was making an attempt to maintain a sense of nostalgia about John Ford, Jim did just the same, despite the problems Ford caused on the set: 'Ford and I had a run-in at the very start because he had a hat for me . . . and I had this hat of mine from the Mann Westerns . . . and we argued . . . and finally he let me wear my hat. But he said, "If we ever do another picture together – which I *doubt* – I want you to have "hat approval" in your contract."'

Jim was under no illusions about the outcome of *Two Rode Together*:

'I was disappointed with my first Ford film, which was why I wanted to have a second go later [with *The Man Who Shot Liberty Valance*]. Perhaps Ford had lost interest in movies, I don't know, but he never talked about his pictures at the end of the day. He liked to talk about his days in the navy, or about sport. And he never discussed what he wanted from a scene. I figured he must have known exactly what he wanted and didn't feel the need to explain it. I heard from Fonda and Wayne that was true of his earlier films. But by this time, I just don't think he knew quite what to do anymore. So he just put the camera down, and he tried to do a scene in just a first take if nobody screwed up. If he did take after take, he felt the actors lost their spontaneity. I told him, "I'm able to do take after take, Boss," and he said, "You actors always say that. I know what's best for you." All he really did was make actors feel edgy because if they did get it wrong in the first take, he flew into a rage – even with Duke [in *The Man Who Shot Liberty Valance*]. I'm not sure if he just enjoyed making the actors nervous or if it really did add something fresh to a scene.'

Filmed in the autumn of 1960, *Two Rode Together* was released to lukewarm reviews and box office in 1961. After completing the Ford picture, Jim felt his career was almost at an end. Henry Fonda told me, 'He was becoming more depressed. It was late 1960 when Jim said to me, "You know something, Hank? I don't know if I'll ever get another picture." And I said, "You too? That's exactly how I feel."'

Jim's depression worsened when he learned that Gary Cooper was dying of cancer. At the 1960 Academy Awards ceremony, held on 17 April 1961, Jim accepted an honorary Oscar for Cooper, who was too ill to appear in person. Jim choked as he said, 'We're all very proud of you, Coop . . . all of us are very proud.' Cooper died on 13 May 1961, and again it was a time for sorrow.

There was worse to come; in the summer of 1961 Alex was diagnosed with stomach cancer. For the next few months he was in and out of hospital. Finally, in December, he was sent home to die. The end came on 28 December 1961. Alex was eighty-nine. Jim and his two sisters were at his bedside when he passed away. Gloria told me, 'Jim asked the Presbyterian minister to read the 91st Psalm at the funeral. When they laid Alex to rest at Greenwood Cemetery, the minister read the Psalm. Jim just wept. After the death of his father, Jim stopped going to Indiana.'

On the evening of Alex's funeral, Jim strolled down to the hardware store to take one last look around. He remembered moments from his childhood, and he sat at his father's old oak desk. He opened a drawer and found inside the penny that had been flattened by President Warren Harding's funeral train. Jim had lost his penny, so he took his dad's. It was the one bright moment during those times of darkness and depression.

Prior to Alex's death, Jim had told him to leave everything in his will, which included a coal mine, to Virginia and Mary. Jim needed none of it. He had invested in oil wells and real estate, he co-owned ranches in California, Nevada, Texas and Hawaii, and he was continuing to receive his share of the profits from the numerous successful films he had made in the 1950s. For all other films, he received a six-figure fee. Alex had protested because he wanted to leave his son something. Jim told him, 'You gave me something that money can't buy. You gave me you.'

The hardware store was closed down. In 1969 it was demolished, and in its place stood the headquarters of the Savings & Trust Bank. Jim never lost that second flattened penny.

20

The Last Good Decade

Jim could have been forgiven for believing that he really would never work again. It was 1962 before he made his next film, John Ford's *The Man Who Shot Liberty Valance*. The film only got made because John Wayne had a contract with Paramount and persuaded them to let Ford make his picture. They agreed as long as the film had a low budget, was filmed in black and white, and most of it was shot in the studio.

The film is so lacking in action and exterior scenes and is so sound-stage bound that it almost looks like a filmed play. Yet it had an excellent cast, with Jim as the lawyer who arrives in the town of Shinbone to set up shop, only to find himself landed with the tag of being the man who shot Liberty Valance (played with superb villainy by Lee Marvin, before he became a major screen hero in *The Dirty Dozen*). Only later does the lawyer learn that a local cattleman (John Wayne) was really the man who shot Valance.

Ford played his usual games on the set, chewing out John Wayne, as he always did, for being a 'lousy actor'. And it was on the set of this film that Ford caused the tension between Jim and Woody Strode, accusing Jim of being a racist. Lee Marvin recalled:

'I didn't much care for Ford's cruel tactics. It never worked with me. I would have punched Ford in the mouth, and I think Ford knew that; which makes me wonder why he asked me back to do *Donovan's Reef*. Maybe he liked me for being the kind of guy to punch him right back. What I didn't get was how he could treat Duke [Wayne] so appallingly and make a fool out of Jimmy Stewart. Ford called Jimmy a racist. Jesus, *Ford* was a racist. He couldn't stand the English. He thought the IRA were heroes. But he didn't think that was being a racist. In my book it is.

'I asked Jimmy outright, "Do you have a problem with blacks?" He said, "Why, do you?" I said, "Of course I do. We've been kicking the shit out of them for hundreds of years, I'm pretty goddamn concerned they're gonna take it out on *me*." And he said, "Ya know, Lee, you're the first person who understands the way I feel. You bet I'm not keen to think how we've treated them and what they might do back if they had the power."

'Woody [Strode] heard us talking and he came over and he said, "If I heard you right, you're worried us black folk are gonna pay you white folk back for all the misery you caused us." I said, "We've got a valid point, don't ya think?" And Strode said, "If you'd stop thinking of us as avenging angels and start thinking of us as just people, we might all get along better. The trouble is, I can predict the time is coming when all hell will break loose between blacks and whites. After that, maybe we'll get along." And I saw his point, but Jimmy came back with, "Why do we have to fight about it? Didn't we free the black slaves in the Civil War?" And Strode said, "That wasn't freedom. That was oppression." And I could see that Strode had a point. But Jimmy just didn't get it.

'Man, we did a lot of talking about racial problems. I think Jimmy *did* have a problem about coloureds, but it was just his generation. Jesus, mine wasn't much better. Jimmy was better than a lot of his generation was when it came to Negroes. In fact, there was one actor who I won't mention who was waiting for Woody to arrive on the set. He cried out, "Where's the nigger?" I could see Duke was about to tear this guy's head off, but Jimmy got there first. I didn't know the guy could get so *angry*. He grabbed this actor by the shirt, tearing it, and he had to kind of get control of himself. But he was simmering – *boiling*. And he said, "Don't ever use that word around me again, or I might do something our director will regret because he'll have to replace you with an actor who's not all broken up and reshoot a helluva lot of expensive scenes." I liked Jimmy before that incident, but *after* it, I liked him a whole lot more.'

Jim preferred to recall his work on *The Man Who Shot Liberty Valance* with fondness. 'I sure liked working with Duke. And Vera Miles was a great gal. And Lee Marvin was a scary guy . . . you never knew if he was drunk or sober 'cos he always seemed the same to me – drunk *or* sober.' He also liked to recall that Ford won his battle over Jim's usual cowboy hat, which he'd worn in *Two Rode Together*. He said, 'He won out because in *The Man Who Shot Liberty Valance*, I didn't wear a hat at all . . . on *his* orders.'

The film was a success, to Jim's relief, but it still couldn't compare to the films he had made with Anthony Mann. The fact that Jim was the star of a successful Western, however, was enough for producer Bernard Smith and director Henry Hathaway to cast Jim in the Cinerama Western epic, *How the West Was Won*, in 1962.

The film spanned two generations of pioneers, with the story split into five different episodes. Three directors – Hathaway, George Marshall and John Ford – took on the mammoth task between them. Jim appeared in the opening episode as Linus Rawlins, a mountain man who gives up his wicked ways to settle down with Carroll Baker, whose parents and half her family have been wiped out when their rafts were caught in rapids. Henry Hathaway, who Jim hadn't worked with since *Call Northside 777*, directed the episode, which also featured Karl Malden, Debbie Reynolds and Walter Brennan.

Jim arrived at the hotel in Kentucky where the rest of the cast of the opening episode were staying in the summer of 1962. Carroll Baker recalled:

'I'd never met Jimmy Stewart, and didn't meet him until the first morning we would be filming together. I was quite nervous because he was a legend. I made sure I was up and ready and waiting at the car early so I didn't keep him waiting.

'The first sight I had of him took my breath away because he was all dressed in his buckskin and he just looked exactly like he'd stepped out of the pioneer days of the old West. I remember he seemed quite shy, and as we were driven to the location, he didn't say anything. And I couldn't think of anything to say. Finally, he said, "Carroll . . . have you ever played a game called Count the Cows?"

'I said "No."

'He said, "Waall, would you like to play . . . Count the Cows?"

'I said, "I don't know how to play it."

'He said, "Waall now . . . you just count all the cows on your side of the road, and I count all the cows on my side of the road . . . and when we reach the location, whoever has the most cows wins." So we played Count the Cows for the next hour, and by the time we arrived we were laughing and talking, and we were good friends. He just made me feel so comfortable.'

Filming took place at Paducah, on a small island where the Tennessee River meets with the Clark and Ohio Rivers. The island was infested by rattlesnakes, so Hathaway sent men in with shot-guns to kill the snakes. But some snakes managed to avoid getting killed. Jim recalled, 'Carroll and I were doing this love scene, and Henry Hathaway was directing . . . and I could see, out of the corner of my eye, this fella dodging about in the background. Henry was furious. He called, "Cut! What the hell are you leaping around for?" Then this fella said, "There's a snake up in that tree." And I looked up and on the branch right above us was this snake . . . just kinda watching us. Henry said, "I don't *care* about the snake. He's minding his own business. Don't you ever move around like that in shot again." And so we carried on with the scene . . . and Carroll . . . she was a bit frightened . . . said, "I'm not going to look up," and she kinda played the scene *extra* close to me . . . which must have pleased Henry.'

How the West Was Won was a huge success. But in many ways it seemed more like a farewell from James Stewart in a good role, giving a good performance at the age of fifty-four. 'I felt that the best of my work was behind me by then,' he told me. 'I liked what I did in that film. I wanted to do more. My character turned up as a dead body in the Civil War episode that Ford directed . . . and I said,

"Let me play the body of my own character." But Ford was just so grumpy and said that a double, who looked *nothing* like me, could do the part.'

Not being able to play his character, even dead, in the Ford-directed sequence disappointed him, according to George Peppard, who played his son throughout the whole of the second half of the film:

'Jimmy told Ford that it wasn't going to cost the studio any more to do the single shot because we were all on flat fees. An audience quickly forgets the name of a character, especially in a film like that with so many characters. He argued, and rightly so, that when the men carrying his body tell the doctor, "This is Linus Rawlins," a simple shot of Jimmy lying dead on the surgeon's table would have made all the emotional difference to the audience. But the guy they had playing him looked nothing like him. Ford just didn't like anyone coming up with good ideas.

'I had to do a scene where I talk about how my father once told me a story about the time he came face to face with a grizzly bear. The dialogue was something like, "Pa said, 'Waall . . . uh . . . I was going someplace but the . . . er . . . grizzly bear got there first.'" I'd not done a scene with Jimmy, but I wanted the audience to feel I'd really been his son and that we'd had times together. Now, everyone does a bad Jimmy Stewart impression, including me, and I thought if I could do the story of the bear in his voice, it would make all the difference. So I said to him, "Tell me this story and help me do it the way you would say it." So he sat with me and told this story a few times over until I had the rhythm of his speech about as good as I could get it.

'When we shot it, Ford yelled at me, "Who told you to use that stupid voice?" And I yelled back, "*I* decided because *I'm* going to make sure the audience remembers this is Jimmy Stewart who played my father." And Jimmy was grateful for that.'

Jim's next film couldn't have been more different to *How the West Was Won*. It was a likeable but overlong comedy called *Mr. Hobbs Takes a Vacation*. For the first time in his career, Jim was playing a man his own age, although he somehow looked older than his fifty-four years. He played a banker who takes his wife and young children, as well as his married daughters, their husbands and all his grandchildren, on a disastrous holiday in a run-down, rambling house on the California coast. Maureen O'Hara played his wife, and Henry Koster directed for 20th Century-Fox. Although not a great picture, it was successful enough in 1962 to warrant another Jimmy Stewart comedy directed by Henry Koster, *Take Her, She's Mine*.

Although partly set in Paris, this film was largely shot, for economic reasons, on the Fox backlot. Jim played the father of an activist daughter (played by Sandra Dee) who creates such havoc in his life that he ends up in jail, nearly drowns in the River Seine, and is accused of distributing pornography.

Jim actually enjoyed making the Koster comedies because they didn't require far flung and often arduous locations, and he felt comfortable playing a man his own age. And in 1962 Jim also made another television appearance, this time for John Ford, in *Flashing Spikes*, the story of ball-player Slim Conway.

The following year Ford asked Jim to appear in a cameo in what should have been a great Western, *Cheyenne Autumn*. The film was interesting for its sympathetic depiction of the Indians – critics have often described it as 'Ford's apology to the Indians' – and it had a real epic quality about it. But Ford was not the right director for this kind of mammoth project. He was old and grumpy, and his style outdated. He even decided to stick a useless comedy sequence that had nothing to do with the story, right in the middle of the film. It was this sequence that featured Jim, playing Wyatt Earp, with Arthur Kennedy as Doc Holliday.

Henry Fonda considered this to be another slap in the face by Ford. 'Ford didn't even think Jim could play a Western character when we did *My Darling Clementine*,' said Fonda. 'It's not sour grapes on my part because I wouldn't have wanted to do that stupid sequence in what was not a good film, but I knew that Ford was casting Jim as Wyatt Earp as if to say to me, "You're not the only Wyatt Earp in town." I know that Jim thought the whole sequence was a mistake, but he won't admit it publicly.'

Fonda was right: Jim preferred to look back on the experience as something that was pure fun. 'The thing about Ford was . . . he liked pulling surprises,' he told me. 'My last film with him, *Cheyenne Autumn*, had this scene where Arthur Kennedy and myself had to ride out of town in a stagecoach. And Ford wanted . . . I forget why . . . for Arthur and me to look kinda surprised. So he said to us, "Boys, I'm gonna ask the driver to turn the stage around and ride out the other way." And then he went to the driver and said, "Drive straight ahead." Waall . . . when we pulled out we sure *were* surprised . . . and so was everyone else who had to jump out of the way.'

The film lost money, and Ford's career was all but over. Jim's still had a little life left in it. He made his third and best Henry Koster comedy, *Dear Brigitte*, in 1965. He played an absent-minded professor who, among other things, helps his young son, played by Billy Mumy, meet film star Brigitte Bardot.

Just as Jim was thinking he would retire gracefully from the screen, he was offered an excellent script written by James Lee Barrett. It told of a family living in Virginia during the Civil War whose widower patriarch is determined to keep his sons out of the war. But the war takes away members of his family, and he can no longer sit idly by. The film was *Shenandoah*, the first of three films he made with director Andrew V McLaglen. Universal Studios, who made the film, considered it to be just a minor project, and McLaglen was left alone to make the picture on location in Oregon with no Universal executives checking on everything and inter-fering. McLaglen, who had graduated as a director from television, was to become known for taking as many short cuts as possible to get a picture made on time and within budget. But with *Shenandoah*, he took more time and care, and a lot of that was due to Jim.

Co-star Doug McClure told me, 'When you did a scene with Jimmy, and I had a few where it was just him and me, he would finish a take, and Andy would say, "That was perfect." Jimmy would say, "I think I can do it better," and Andy would say, "But you were perfect," and Jimmy would say, very slowly, very patiently, "Let me try it again." And so we'd do the scene again, and there was always an improvement, but it was so subtle that I couldn't see it until I saw it on film.' McLaglen recalled:

'Jimmy would ask for several takes, and each time he was consistent with what he'd done before, except that he'd always find a way to improve everything. For instance, if in take one he scratched his ear, he'd do the same on each subsequent take. A minor detail, perhaps, but he'd thought about the ear scratching as telling something about the character or what he was thinking, and he'd never fail to do those little things with each take. But always the scene got better until in the end Jim had got, and given you, all he could from a scene.

'He didn't mind being upstaged either, although I think he looked upon an actor who might upstage him as a bit of a challenge. He said, "I don't care what they do – they can pick their nose or whatever – just so long as it helps the picture." Well, in one scene we had Strother Martin, who steals every scene he's in, in every film he makes. He's just that kind of actor; he's impossible not to notice. He can be so damn funny. And Jimmy had this scene, and Strother was doing his usual stuff, and by the end of the scene, Jim knew that Strother was the centre of attention. Jim said to me, "Who did you say that fella was?" I said, "Strother Martin." He said, "I'd sure like it if you didn't give him anything else to do in this movie or nobody's gonna notice me." He was kidding . . . I think. But he didn't have to worry. If anything, Jimmy was so strong in that picture that most of the other young actors, except I think for Doug McClure, were kind of lost. And the girls [Rosemary Forsyth and Katharine Ross] did well too.'

Shenandoah provided Jim with his best performance of the 1960s, although the critics failed to notice it at the time, in 1965. Andrew V McLaglen noted, 'To me, his performance in *Shenandoah* was one of the most underrated performances ever. There was a *tour de force* and Jimmy didn't get the recognition he should have gotten. Universal should have put him up for an Oscar nomination.'

If anything, much of the fault lies with McLaglen. Despite the fact that he made several successful films in the 1960s, including five with John Wayne, his work lacks any real style. His direction of *Shenandoah* was unremarkable, despite a superior screenplay. Although the film did well and has some fine moments, mostly provided by Jim, it is never as good as it should be.

Jim, however, said, '*Shenandoah* was kinda nice. Now, I know it was anti-war and all that, but . . . but when you make a film with a touchy subject and turn it into propaganda . . . waall, I'm against that, because the important thing is dramatic quality. And *Shenandoah* had some real dramatic quality to it, thanks mainly to the script by Jimmy Barrett.'

To Jim's delight and surprise, he was still steadily working, although not as much as he used to. This suited him well as age crept up on him. In 1965 he was in another good film, *The Flight of the Phoenix*, heading a fine cast that included Richard Attenborough, Peter Finch, Ian Bannen, Hardy Kruger, Christian Marquand, Ernest Borgnine, George Kennedy and Dan Duryea. Except for Jim and Attenborough, they all played oil-field workers being flown across the Sahara. Jim played the pilot and Attenborough his alcoholic navigator who leads them a hundred miles off course, as a result of which the plane crashes in the desert. Directed by Robert Aldrich, the film concentrated on the tension among the survivors, and the audience was made to feel the blistering heat of the desert. For the actors, conditions were not as bad as they looked; the film was shot in Yuma, Arizona.

Robert Aldrich was aware that when filming began, Jim was a little concerned. 'He'd worked with European actors, including British actors, before, and found them a bit precious,' said Aldrich. 'He came into the film wary of a heavyweight cast largely made up of Brits and Europeans.' (Peter Finch was, of course, Australian, but to a lot of Americans, including Aldrich and Jim, he was one of the British contingent.) Aldrich continued: 'So for the first couple of weeks he was kind of distant from them. I had the British actors asking me what was wrong with him. They hadn't noticed that he wasn't mixing all that much with the American actors either. It wasn't that Jimmy ignored everyone. He just liked to be on his own a lot. So the British actors decided they were going to have fun, and they'd make sure Jimmy had fun with them.

'I think Jimmy thought the British actors were drunk because they clowned around a lot – really doing childish things sometimes. Then we'd do a scene and they'd all be stone cold sober – which they had been all the time anyway. Jimmy couldn't figure them out.

But in the end he got silly right along with them.'

Jim told me, 'I'd heard a lot about some of the European actors and how they'd be trying to steal every shot from us Americans. But that wasn't the case. In fact, Dick Attenborough, Hardy Kruger, Ian Bannen and the others were all just a little . . . *insane* . . . and by that I mean, they liked to have a good time. They were like kids out to have a good time . . . and they *did* have a good time. They were raising a little hell back there in Yuma . . . and I wondered if their antics would ruin the picture. But before I knew it, I was having a good time too . . . right along with them. I'd never really raised hell before . . . but there I was, having a ball.'

Ian Bannen explained to me the kind of antics they got up to. 'We had several dummies to stand in – or lie down – for the dead guys after the plane crashes in the desert. Dickie, Peter and myself stole the dummies and put them in a car. We went driving around Yuma with these dummies and threw them out while the car was moving. The onlookers thought we were throwing real people out of the car. We were just like kids.

'Jimmy didn't know what to make of us at first, but he got into the spirit of the thing, and pretty soon he was riding around with us, throwing dummies out of cars. He'd find a prop machine gun and he'd get out of the car and make out he was shooting them gangland style. Then the cops gave us a talking to, but when they saw it was Jimmy Stewart, they just gave us a caution. Peter Finch, who was actually quite drunk, thought they'd throw us in jail. Finchie gave me the responsibility of keeping him sober as much as I could, and Jimmy took it upon himself to try and keep Finchie sober too. It was so much fun.'

But there was tragedy too. Stuntman Paul Mantz flew the plane for the climactic take-off, but due to an imbalance of weight, the plane's wing hit the sand and brought it crashing down. Mantz was killed.

Released in 1965, *The Flight of the Phoenix* was a big hit with the critics and the public. But good scripts that would suit Jim were now hard to find. Andrew V McLaglen came up with *The Rare Breed*, a comedy Western. Jim played a cowboy who is persuaded by Maureen O'Hara and her daughter, Juliet Mills, to transport a Hereford bull to a rancher for crossbreeding with a longhorn.

Jim said he enjoyed working with McLaglen: 'Andy gets on with the job. He doesn't spend hours setting up shots and then doing retake after retake. I like to work that way.' Apparently, unlike on *Shenandoah*, Jim was eager to get on with the filming without doing many retakes. Ben Johnson, who was in the cast, told me, 'The problem with Andy is, he wants to do everything in a hurry – like it's some kind of virtue. Doing it quick is fine for television, which is where Andy came from, but if you want to get it good, take your time. I like Andy. He's a good man and a good friend, but he doesn't get the best results. He just finishes on time and on schedule, and the film turns out quite ordinary.'

And that's what *The Rare Breed* was – just ordinary. It does not rank along with the great James Stewart films.

There was a problem with American films during the 1960s. Many of the great directors had had their day, and many of the current directors, like Andy McLaglen, came from television. So too did Vincent McEveety, who made his big-screen debut with a James Stewart Western, *Firecreek*, in 1968. The fact that there was a two-year break between *The Rare Breed* and *Firecreek* demonstrates how difficult it now was for Jim to find the right vehicle for him. At least *Firecreek* had something a little special about it: it was the first time Jim and Henry Fonda had appeared on screen since *On Our Merry Way* twenty years earlier.

Fonda played the villain for a change, bringing his gang to the town of Firecreek. Jim played a farmer who tries to defuse the town's problems with reason and humour. Inevitably, the film leads to a showdown in which Fonda tries to kill Stewart. But Fonda is shot and killed by a woman (Inger Stevens) he has been dallying with.

Fonda was full of praise for director McEveety, saying, 'He may have been new to the movies, but he did something few directors have been able to do in recent years. He really pushed Jim, and got a great performance out of him. Jim had become a little too used to giving the same performance around that time, but McEveety didn't let him get away with any of it. And it's one of Jim's best performances. I think I was pretty good in it too. It's a shame that the studio [Warner Brothers] didn't know what to do with it, and they just kind of dropped it unannounced into theatres, and nobody went to see it.'

While *Firecreek* was in production, Andrew McLaglen was putting together another Western, *Bandolero!* James Lee Barrett, who wrote the screenplay, told me, 'The film was a package which Darryl Zanuck at Fox dreamed up. He had a story outline about two outlaw brothers. One is going to be hanged, the other brother impersonates the hangman and frees his brother. They kidnap a girl and cross into Mexico, where they bump into bandidos and all get killed. Zanuck told Andy McLaglen he wanted him to direct the film, he wanted me to write it, and he wanted Dean Martin and Jimmy Stewart to play the brothers, and Raquel Welch to play the kidnapped widow.

'I think we came up with a good first half of the story, where Jimmy rides into town, having taken the hangman's place, and saves Dean from the noose. It was all very tongue in cheek. Then it got serious after they escaped, and it was difficult making Jimmy Stewart into an outlaw. You just didn't believe it. So I had to be on set, writing funny lines or typical Jimmy Stewart lines, to try to make it work.'

As far as films were concerned, with most if not all of his pictures ranging from adequate to very good, it was Jim's last successful decade. As for his private life, it became a time of unbearable grief.

In 1968 Jim retired from the Air Force Reserve. By that time, Gloria's sons, Ronald and Michael, had left home. Michael had found himself at Mercersburg. Ronald, insisting he didn't like schools in the east, talked his parents into letting him go to school in Orme, because it was close to the ranch Jim owned in Winecup, Nevada. From Orme, Ronald went to Colorado State University where he majored in business studies. Michael attended Claremont in California to study political science. Jim would have liked both boys to go to Princeton, but he did not want to force them into it the way Alex had forced him.

The two boys were growing to be very different people. Michael grew his hair long and protested against right-wing policies, and especially against the war in Vietnam. Ronald was more like his stepfather, being of a conservative nature. He saw it as his duty to join the Marines when his draft call came through. It was inevitable that he would be sent to Vietnam.

Jim, like a lot of old-time Republicans, was bemused by the many campus protests against the Vietnam war, voicing his disapproval of anyone who dodged the draft. He told me, 'Our country was at war, and when your country is at war, you can't refuse to serve your country.' Gloria insisted that Ronald did not enlist just to satisfy his stepfather. 'Ronald did what he thought was right, and we were proud of him. Just because Michael had his opinions didn't mean we loved him any less. Some people have suggested that Jim drove Ronald into enlisting. But that isn't true. Ronald did what *he* believed was right.'

Jim had supported the war in Vietnam, and he had visited southeast Asia a couple of times. On one tour, he even accompanied a bombing mission near the border with Cambodia. Early in 1969 Gloria accompanied Jim on a USO tour to Vietnam where he shook hands with thousands of soldiers, collecting messages to deliver when he got back home. They even had the chance to visit Ronald, and Jim took a photograph of Gloria with their son, who was now a lieutenant.

Shortly after returning to America, Jim went to work on the comedy Western *The Cheyenne Social Club*. It started out as a joy to make because Jim was working again with Henry Fonda, and this time they were playing friends. Jim played a cattleman who suddenly inherits what he thinks is a saloon called the Cheyenne Social Club. He travels from Texas to Wyoming to claim his inheritance, only to find that it's a brothel. Fonda, as his good friend with nothing else to do, accompanies him.

Directed by Gene Kelly (yes, *the* Gene Kelly of all those MGM musicals) and written by James Lee Barrett, it was a curiously gentle, charming comedy Western. It's still fun to watch, if only to see Stewart and Fonda in action together. They had some wonderful banter, and the opening titles are accompanied by Jim singing a song while Fonda endlessly relates one story after another. Once again, it was a good idea with a good screenplay, but something was not working. Barrett believed he knew what it was:

'I think the only problem with the picture was the choice of Gene Kelly to direct it. Not every director can make a Western but some directors can make fabulous musicals. John Ford and Anthony Mann couldn't make an adequate musical, but they made great Westerns. And even Gene Kelly couldn't make a *great* musical out of *Hello Dolly!*, so what's he going to do with a Western?

'You'd think that with two actors like James Stewart and Henry Fonda a director would find it hard to make a poor Western. I don't say it was a poor film, because I think it had its virtues. But as a Western it pretty much stank. The trouble was, even with those stars, they knew they were in trouble. Fonda was concerned about the script; my department. Usually Fonda would have gone to the director, told him his troubles, and the director would have said, "Leave it with me," and he'd get the writer to sort it out. But Fonda didn't have faith in Kelly, so he complained to Jimmy Stewart, and Jimmy came to me. Fonda's problem was that he felt his part was just a little too secondary to Stewart's. The way Jimmy put it to me was to say, "Hank hasn't got enough to say."

'So I rewrote the entire opening sequence – which was really only for the credits to roll over – where Stewart and Fonda ride a hundred miles or so, and I had Fonda talking the whole way. Stewart finally says to him, "Do you realise you've been talking all the way from Texas?" and Fonda says, "I was just trying to keep you company."

'And Fonda loved that, and we worked that idea into the film where he talks a lot at first, and gets Jimmy so upset, he doesn't say more than he has to the rest of the film.'

The problems on the set paled into insignificance when Jim suffered the worst nightmare of all: Ronald was killed while leading a five-man patrol in Quang Tri on 11 June 1969. Gloria recalled that she was at home at North Roxbury Drive that evening. Kelly and Judy were preparing for their graduation prom at Westlake, when she saw a military contingent coming towards her front door – and at that moment she knew that Ronald had been killed.

Jim came straight home and a memorial service was arranged. A few days after Ronald's death, a representative from the Pentagon arrived to discuss plans to publicise Ronald as a hero, in order to supply propaganda for President Nixon. Jim's anger almost boiled over, but he contained himself, grabbing the representative by the arm and saying through gritted teeth, 'Let me take you to the door now.' Gloria told me, 'I thought he would actually punch the fella out, but he controlled his temper, which is all to his credit.'

Gloria admitted that she was 'a total wreck' following Ronald's death. 'I just cried myself to sleep every night for weeks.' She explained it was a difficult time because Jim really didn't allow himself to mourn, and she felt it prevented her from mourning her loss. 'It wasn't because Ronald was my son and not his,' she said. 'Ronald, as was Michael, was as much Jim's son as anybody could be.' It seems that Jim could never allow himself to show his deepest emotions.

Fonda told me, 'I could see that Gloria wanted to grieve, but Jim just never did show those kinds of feeling, although he was breaking up inside. What was so sad was that Gloria felt that Jim didn't allow her to grieve. The thing is, he was trying to deal with the loss as best he could, and it got in the way of Gloria's needs. That's what happens when people you love die. You tend to blame others – mostly each other – for some strange reason. In some way, they blamed their other son, Michael, because they thought he had somehow turned his back on the family – but he hadn't. He just didn't believe in the war and he didn't believe his brother's loss was worthwhile.'

In September 1969 Ronald was posthumously awarded a Silver Star. Jim and Gloria attended the ceremony to receive the honour, held at the Marine base at El Toro in California.

Long before he should have been ready, Jim went back to work on *The Cheyenne Social Club*. But while he didn't appear to mourn, he was, without doubt, struggling to keep himself from falling into the depths of despair. Barrett recalled, 'Ronald's death just tore Jimmy apart, and he lost all interest in the film. It's to his credit that it doesn't show on screen in his performance, but he didn't have the heart to tackle Gene Kelly on what were Kelly's failings, and Fonda was far more concerned about his friend to worry about the film too. I think with the right director, say Henry Hathaway, that film might have been at least a *good* Western. Hathaway would have roared at Jimmy, "Don't dwell on your loss. Concentrate on the damn film." He would have sounded like the bully he could be, but he would have done it all out of love for Jimmy.

'Kelly thought he was helping Jimmy by shooting around him whenever he saw that Jimmy was depressed, or he'd just cancel the day's work, which I don't think did anyone any good. Gene's heart was in the right place. But frankly they needed a Henry Hathaway to bully Jimmy, or Kelly should have cancelled all further filming until Jim was up to continuing. To be fair to Kelly, I'm sure he just didn't know what to do for the best. And he's a sweet guy. But his biggest sin was not owning up to not having a clue how to make a Western in the first place.' And, as Fonda remembered in 1976:

'When Jimmy told me about Ronald, I saw my friend looking older and more wizened than ever. He'd aged during the [Second World] war, and he aged there and then with the arrival of that devastating news.

'You just don't know what to say when something like that happens. I tried to cheer him with yarns about the "good ol' days" until I suddenly realised how foolish it all sounded considering what he was going through. I said, "Sorry, Jim, I'll just keep my mouth shut." He said, "No, Hank, *please*, just keep talking. You know . . . just then . . . when you were talking about the time Duke [John Wayne] wrapped a boa constrictor around your head while you were asleep in that bar in Mexico . . . it reminded me of the time you and I were back in New York, and we found a rat in our apartment, and it turned out it was living in your shoe . . . and you put that shoe on, and that rat shot out, more frightened than you were." And he started laughing, and we just kept on reminiscing, and that helped Jim to shut out the despair for a short while.

'He said to me, "Hank, if you see me getting low, just tell me a story. It really helps." And so that's what I did. But I had the feeling that his attempts to lift himself out of despair were more for my benefit than for his, because he could see that *I* was struggling to keep *my* spirits up while trying to keep *his* up. As if *I* were the one who needed help. And that's what kind of a friend I have in Jimmy Stewart. The best kind of all. He looks out for you when *he's* suffering.'

There was another sad footnote when Jim's favourite horse, Pie, proved too old to endure the filming. Jim told me, 'That horse had to be twenty-seven . . . twenty-eight years old . . . which is getting on for a horse. The last picture I did with him, *The Cheyenne Social Club*, was in Santa Fe, New Mexico, at an altitude of almost 6,000 feet . . . and it was too much for ol' Pie. I couldn't use him . . . I had to use his double. And he died not long after.'

Fonda said, 'Jimmy loved ol' Pie. And when it proved too much for Pie to work at that altitude, Jimmy said, "Let Pie rest. Get me another horse." I decided to surprise Jimmy by sneaking up to Pie with my sketchpad, and whenever Jimmy wasn't around, I'd sketch Pie a little. After the film was over, I produced a painting of Pie and gave it to Jimmy. It meant all the more to him because two weeks after we finished the film, Pie died. Jimmy had lost his stepson and now his horse, and it was just more than he could bear.'

Stewart recalled, 'Hank is an excellent artist, and his portrait of Pie is just beautiful. Hank really captures his personality. I hung the picture in my library, and it will always be there. In a way, it makes me feel Pie is with me still. I believe there's a place we go to when we die. It's devastating when we lose someone in this life, but they're there waiting for us when we pass on. Pie'll be waiting for me. In the meantime, I have something of his spirit with me still . . . in that painting of Hank's . . . hanging in my library.'

The Cheyenne Social Club was produced and released by National General, a short-lived company that made a handful of films and then failed to give them a proper release. Consequently the picture, which is actually an easy, enjoyable view, bombed in 1970. (In the UK all the company's films were inherited by the releasing arm of the Cinerama production company – where I worked – but it was too late to save any of them from disaster.)

Following Ronald's death, life had to go on for the Stewart family. The twin daughters, Judy and Kelly, went their separate ways after attending Westlake, although both had acquired a taste for other cultures from touring such places as Africa with their parents. Judy went to Nepal to work as a jungle guide, then transferred to Tanzania to work on a coffee plantation. When a cholera epidemic broke out, she returned to California and married, thereby becoming Judy Merrill.

Kelly received a BA in anthropology from Stanford, and a PhD in zoology from the University of Cambridge in England, where she would meet her future husband. She then went to East Africa to study gorillas in Rwanda and Kenya.

Three weeks after his brother's death, Michael got married. He found himself at odds with his mother and stepfather; he believed they felt that he had not been sympathetic to their views on Vietnam.

Back on North Roxbury Drive, the death of Ronald seemed to echo through every room in the Stewart house. 'We were just getting on each other's nerves,' Gloria told me. Jim tried to stay out of Gloria's way by playing golf each morning with Fred MacMurray at the Bel Air Club. He also flew his Super Piper Cub plane at weekends. But the rest of the time, said Gloria, 'he just seemed to be in a state of shock – like he was in a trance and wouldn't let anyone permeate an invisible barrier. That was his way of grieving. I was still given to bursting into tears. I actually began to fear for our marriage. But I guess a lot of people go through troubles like that when there has been a bereavement. But to lose a child is something no parent should go through. It's not supposed to be that way. I think we felt like we had lost both sons in a way, because Ronald was dead, and Michael was off studying law and keeping away from us. It was the worst of times.'

It was, in fact, even worse for Gloria than for Jim; within fifteen months of losing Ronald, she also lost her mother, her sister and her brother. She survived all this only because of her amazing resilience and a determination to live each day to the full for the rest of her own life.

21

The Television Years

While Gloria was dealing with her immeasurable trials, Jim was thrown a lifeline by a desperate New York producer, T Edward Hambleton. Financial problems threatened to close Hambleton's Phoenix Theatre, so to combat closure the producer came up with the idea of resurrecting Mary Chase's play *Harvey*. Hambleton heard that James Stewart would love the chance to play Elwood P Dowd again, and so an offer was made to Jim.

'I thought it was a wonderful idea,' said Jim. 'I figured that I was finally at the right age to play Elwood. Actually, I'd thought about reviving the play myself numerous times over the years . . . but film commitments had always prevented me. Or maybe I was just a little too scared to take the plunge.'

Surprisingly, he didn't exactly take the plunge wholeheartedly when Hambleton made his offer. Helen Hayes, who had agreed to be in the play (being a Phoenix Board member), told me, 'When Jimmy learned that we would be trying out the play first before the students of the University of Michigan, he backed away. He said, "None of those kids have probably heard of me. And if they have, they probably only know me as someone who didn't oppose the war in Vietnam, and they'll just *hate* me." So I told him, "The kids who protest are only against war, not you. And if they don't know who

271

you are, they certainly won't know who I am, so we'll be company for each other." That put an end to his dithering. So we did the play [in February 1970].

'Gloria came out to be with Jimmy, and they were put up in the best hotel, but they said they didn't like the food there, so they started eating in the university restaurant. All these students kept coming up to him in the restaurant asking for his autograph because, of course, they knew who James Stewart was, to his surprise and delight. Someone thought he was being bothered by these students and suggested they should be banned from coming up to him. He said, "When they *don't* come up to me . . . that's when I'll start worrying."'

Jim said that doing the play again made him realise that 'you can't play Elwood as a crazy man. The trick is to convince the audience that this big white rabbit is really your friend. You have to make the audience wish *they* had a big white rabbit friend of their own.' He also believed that what America needed at a time when it was split into divisions by the war in Vietnam was 'another dose of Elwood P Dowd'.

When the play transferred to the Phoenix Theatre in New York, Jim won rave reviews. *Variety* said, 'He's a genuine star, with the presence, projection, feel of an audience and the personal magnetism to take command of a theatre. He gives the impression of not acting at all.' The *New York Daily* wrote, 'Stewart offers a master class of acting with each performance.' 'His garrulous, genial presence is a delight,' wrote the *New York Times*. 'You feel that apart from Harvey himself, there is no one that you would rather encounter in your favourite neighbourhood bar [than Stewart].' (Having had dinner with Jim and Gloria several times, I can attest to that.)

Harvey was to present Jim with a new phase in his career, taking him back to the stage where he began, even as his film career was coming to an end. In fact, there was to be only one more starring role in a major film in Jim's career. In *Fool's Parade* (also known as *Dynamite Man From Glory Jail*), directed by Andrew V McLaglen, Jim, Strother Martin and a very young Kurt Russell played convicts released from prison, determined to start a new life. But a crooked cop (George Kennedy) and a corrupt bank president

(David Huddleston) are intent on getting their hands on the $25,000 that Jim has earned in prison and with which he and his pals intend to open a store. McLaglen recalled:

'When I first talked to Jimmy about the film, and I told him he'd have Strother Martin as his co-star, Jimmy said, "Who's Strother Martin?" I said, "You had a scene with him in *Shenandoah*. You said he stole the scene." He rubbed his chin and said, "Yeah . . . I think I remember him. Waall . . . you'd better let me think about that." And he spent the next four days thinking about whether he wanted to do a whole film with Strother Martin. People think of Jim as being slow because he does things slow-like, taking time to think things out. But he's very sharp. And finally he said, "Tell Strother Martin he's got the part." Jim knew he'd have a tough time keeping from being upstaged by Strother, but I think he saw it as a challenge.

'Jim knew when to draw the line though. He checked out the call sheet one day and saw that Strother was to be holding a pencil, a pad and a piece of string. Jimmy said to me, "Look, Andy, you got Strother with a pencil, and that's all right. He's also got a pad, and I can live with that. But there's no way in hell that you're gonna get me in front of a camera with that fella and a piece of string." So we got rid of the string. It may not seem like much, but Jimmy knew that Strother Martin playing with a piece of string is going to steal the entire scene. But Jimmy really liked Strother. They had a lot of fun together.'

Released in 1971, *Fool's Parade* suffered again from McLaglen's indifferent direction, and it quickly came and went without fuss. Jim couldn't have known it then, but his career – except for a few cameos – had almost gone the same way as the film.

There were suddenly no movie offers, or none Jim thought worth considering, so he contemplated what he thought was a radical idea – a regular TV show. He'd actually been appearing on television for several years on Jack Benny's annual show. Benny, one of the Stewarts' neighbours and a good friend, had persuaded Jim and

Gloria to appear on his once-a-year show – playing a Hollywood actor and his wife who are forever scheming to escape from the comedian's miserly ways yet who always end up in his unsolicited company. Their appearances on his show convinced NBC that a situation comedy staring Jim might well work. And so in 1971 *The Jimmy Stewart Show* was born. In it, Jim would play a professor with problems at work and at home.

The series needed a leading lady, and Jim was quick to suggest Gloria. NBC had no intention of considering Mrs Stewart as they wanted Julie Adams. The show's producer, Hal Kanter, had the unenviable task of breaking the news. He cunningly suggested to Jim that he ought to consider whether he wanted to get up every morning at the same time as Gloria, work long days on a sound stage with Gloria, and then go home with Gloria every day for at least twelve weeks. 'I thought that made a lot of sense,' said Jim. 'That was a sure way to end a marriage. I didn't know then that NBC had already decided they didn't want Gloria, or I might have told them what they could *do* with their show.'

Two seasons – for 1971 and 1972 – of *The Jimmy Stewart Show* were shot. Gloria knew that Jim had quickly begun to hate it. Each thirty-minute episode was rehearsed in four days and shot in two. 'That was *too* quick for Jim, but that's the way they worked in tele-vision,' she said. 'And he was frustrated as an actor. Everybody just loved seeing him be himself, but he didn't want to be just himself. That was the strength of the show, but that was the weakness in Jim. He wanted something to challenge him. I told him to relax and enjoy being himself, but I think it was the pace of the show that finally got to him.'

During the filming of the first season in 1971, Jim's long-time friend Leland Hayward died. Jim sank into a depression, but hauled himself out of it.

Then something happened that Woody Strode believed proved Jim's racist tendencies. Strode explained, 'A black actor called Hal Williams had been cast as an FBI agent in one episode, but Jimmy Stewart got confused with another episode in which a cop was supposed to have a go at Jimmy's character. He thought Hal was playing the cop who has a go at him, and he called for the producer and ranted about how blacks were pushing the white folks around all across the country, and now they had this black cop pushing *him* around, and he wasn't having any of it. It was pointed out to him that Hal wasn't playing the cop – who would be white – but was playing an FBI agent in another episode.'

When I asked Jim about the episode, he said, 'I wasn't chewing out black people. I was chewing out the fact that there were all these black Americans complaining all over the country and bossing politicians about, as if nothing else was more important.' Gloria told me away from Jim's ears, 'We don't talk about black people. Jim has an uneasy time about race and civil rights.'

In 1971, director Peter Bogdanovich had wanted Stewart to co-star in *The Last Picture Show* but the TV series made him unavailable. So the part went to Ben Johnson, who won an Oscar for it. Nevertheless, Bogdanovich still had another idea for Jim, as well as for John Wayne and Henry Fonda. Jim recalled:

'There was this idea which Peter Bogdanovich had to make a Western with Duke, Hank and me. He was a great admirer of the works of Ford and [Howard] Hawks.

'He told me about it first, taking me to lunch. And he told me his idea. There was no script . . . just an idea. It was a sort of "If we did it, we could do this and that." I liked his ideas and told him to get a script so we could explore it some more. You can't do anything without a script. So he went off and he came back some weeks later with a script. I was disappointed. There wasn't much of a story, and the jokes were largely about how old we all were, and I felt that you could make the joke once and it would be funny, but to make a whole film about it . . . waall, I felt like we were being kinda lampooned.

'So I called Duke and asked him if he'd seen the script, and he had, and he said, "Jimmy boy" – I always liked it when he called me Jimmy *boy* 'cos he's younger than I am – he said, "Jimmy boy, they're trying to make three old fogies out of us." I agreed, and so did Hank, and that was that. But we were all disappointed because we would have loved to have made a film together . . . all three of us. We'd never all been in a picture before. And Bogdanovich was disappointed. If he'd come up with a better script, we could have done something.'

There was more sadness for Jim when, in April 1972, his sister Virginia died from a strangulated hernia. Jim typically held back his tears at the funeral, and when he saw Virginia's grief-stricken husband Alexis crying, Jim told him, 'Don't cry in front of all these people. If you hafta cry, do it in private.' Gloria told me, 'Jim was really angry with Alexis. I thought Jim was wrong, but I understood.'

After just two seasons, *The Jimmy Stewart Show* ended. Jim blamed himself for the show's failure: 'They gave me too much authority. I had script approval and cast approval. I had approval over everything, like I was the producer . . . and the trouble is, I'm just an actor. I had no right to make all those decisions. I made some bad choices.'

There was still a little work. In 1972 Jim narrated *Pat Nixon: Portrait of a First Lady*, a documentary about President Nixon's wife. He agreed to do the job because he was a dedicated Republican.

It was also in 1972 that J Edgar Hoover died. Tales about the FBI director's homosexuality had already been circulating for some time, and within a few years of his death came stories of the many secret files he'd kept and ordered destroyed when he died. Among those files was one about Jim and Henry Fonda. Fonda was quite vitriolic when he spoke in 1976 about Hoover's secret files: 'Hoover investigated anyone who was rumoured to be engaged in what might be termed "immoral acts", and that ranged from criminal activity, to promiscuity, and homosexuality.

'I don't think there was a star in Hollywood from the 1930s through to the 1950s who didn't have some kind of an FBI file on them. Jim really admired and liked J Edgar Hoover, although I never cared for Hoover. So it didn't hurt me like it hurt Jim who, for a long time, thought Hoover was one of the great heroes of our country. They were even friends. But Jim was able to forgive Hoover because he felt he understood Hoover's reasons. That's the Republican in Jim. But to me it was an indication that Hoover was the worst thing that ever happened to law and order in America.'

During the 1980s, it became clear that Jim no longer felt forgiving about Hoover. Gloria told me, 'It really hurt Jim to think that J Edgar Hoover, for whom he'd performed all those secret activities, had had a file on him and Hank Fonda. Jim used to talk about Hoover a lot. Now we don't mention his name.'

In 1972, Hallmark Television proposed a new film version of *Harvey* to Jim, and he accepted. He found it an improvement on the original film version, but he felt that it was better as a stage play than a film. Henry Fonda understood Jim's reasoning: 'When I did *Mister Roberts* on stage all those years and then did the film version, the movie failed to capture something that was the essence of the play. That's why plays are plays and films are films, and a film version of a play is never going to be as *right* as the play, in the same way a film never works as well as a play. So I understand when Jim says *Harvey* is a better play than a film. But I tell you this: when Jim plays *Harvey* on stage or on film, nobody can play the part better.'

Jim was tempted back to do another TV show, *Hawkins on Murder*, a full-length CBS television movie in which he played a lawyer. The role won him the Hollywood Foreign Press Club Best Actor award, and the success of the first *Hawkins* film led to seven more.

'I liked that series of films,' Jim said about *Hawkins*. 'I did them because I'd always wanted to play a lawyer since doing *Anatomy of a Murder*. I was a defence lawyer, and I liked the way my character played the game trial lawyers play. When the facts were against him, he argued the law. And when the law was against him, he argued the facts. And when both the facts and the law were against him, he banged his hands on the table.'

His scene-stealing co-star from *Shenandoah* and *Fool's Parade*, Strother Martin, was his regular co-star in *Hawkins*. Jim had no objections about Martin, feeling that he 'might well need someone to help carry the load . . . as I'm not getting any younger'. He also stipulated, 'I don't care too much what Strother does . . . just don't let him carry a piece of string.'

Making *Hawkins* proved too gruelling for Jim: 'I made eight of those films for television . . . in just *two* years . . . but in the end I had to give it up. It was all too *hectic* for me. I'd been in films that were made in a hurry, but they were never shot as fast as they do with television. I just couldn't keep up. I had so many lines to learn and not much time to learn them, and when you're not a young man anymore, you don't remember lines as easy as you used to. One time, I said, "I can't do this. I can't remember my lines." The director said, "You know, Jim, it's okay for you to use cue cards. A lot of actors do." I said, "But I can't *see* the cue cards."'

There was another loss in 1973 when one of his oldest friends from the MGM days, Bill Grady, died. Then, during production on one of the *Hawkins* films, John Ford died. Jim attended the funeral and went back to work. But he was uncharacteristically bad tempered, and after getting into a rage about something trivial, he suddenly stopped and asked, 'What am I doing?' Said Gloria, 'He felt lost. All his friends were dying. He often said to me, "I'm losing all my old friends, and I'm not making any new ones."' (Apparently, according to Gloria, this was why Jim readily accepted me as a welcome guest at their hotel whenever they came to England.)

On a happier note, Jim and Gloria put aside their differences with Michael who, in 1973, gave Jim and Gloria their first grandchild. 'A grandchild can do a lot for healing the wounds in a family,' said Gloria.

In 1974, MGM released *That's Entertainment*, a fabulous compilation film looking back on its many musicals. Jim was one of the star narrators. But he lost another friend that year – Jack Benny. With each death, Jim went through a period of depression, but always pulled himself up again. 'It's remarkable that he finds the strength,' Gloria said to me, in the early 1980s. 'He'll tell you his strength comes from God – but I believe it's simply the mettle of the man himself.'

As if to dust off the webs of melancholy, Jim decided on a London production of *Harvey* in 1975, and it was at the Prince of Wales Theatre that I first met him. 'It was Sir Bernard Delfont who suggested I come and do the play,' Jim told me. (We were able to talk a little about Sir Bernard as I had worked for him. Our experiences were vastly different because Jim was a big star and I had been just a member of staff!)

Jim had pretty much concluded that his film career was over. He said, 'I don't think I'll be making any more movies. I just don't fit in. I just get bewildered by some of the scripts that still get sent to me. I don't seem to have a place in today's movies. Producers and directors don't know what to do with me, and I wouldn't know what to do in their pictures. Everything is so violent. Films seem to be *mean*. They're depressing. They're cynical.

'I don't understand all these Clint Eastwood films. I don't . . . I just don't understand why Fonda had to make one of those *spaghetti* Westerns [*Once Upon a Time in the West*]. They're the films which wrecked the Western with their violence and . . . and . . . their cynicism.'

'But Jim,' I said, 'it was the films you made with Anthony Mann that had those very elements. Those films changed Westerns for ever. The successful Westerns today are the direct result of those films you and Anthony Mann made. Clint Eastwood was inspired by *you*. Today's few good Western directors were inspired by Anthony Mann.'

That made him sit back in silence, as though he had never considered it. Finally he said, 'Then I guess I'm just getting too damn old. It's just that . . . all the scripts I read – and there aren't that many these days – feature some grouchy old grandfather, and I think, "Golly, I wonder who they're thinking to get for that part," and then I realise it's *me*. I don't *want* to be a grouchy grandfather. I want to play something a bit more interesting than that. But they don't write parts like that anymore.

'I have to make way for the new fellas . . . like Eastwood and Redford and Newman. I don't mind. My life has been a good one . . . a *wonderful* life. Right now I'm just enjoying playing *Harvey*. I have no idea what next year will bring.'

As it turned out, the next year brought Jim back to the screen. He guest-starred in the last John Wayne movie (and one of the Duke's best), *The Shootist*, playing the doctor who confirms the ageing gunfighter's illness as cancer. Don Siegel, who directed *The Shootist*, recalled, 'Our first scene, an interior, was the doctor's office, and there I met James Stewart who was worried about his old friend, Duke. Jimmy was very funny. He said, "Are you shooting the left side of my face?" I said, "Yes. Is anything wrong with that? Do you have a better side?" Jimmy just smiled and said, "Nope. Whichever side the camera points is my best side."

'Then Duke came on the set and he and Jimmy embraced. I said, "Gentlemen, this scene is very touching. But I hope you agree we should play against that. If you play the scene very matter-of-factly and don't allow the sentimentality to creep in, all the pain, the suffering and the pathos will be there." And Duke said to Jimmy, "Don't you hate it when the director's right?" And Jimmy said, "I just hate it."

'They did their scenes perfectly. The only problem was that Jimmy was rather deaf so I found myself shouting directions at him. And Jimmy said, "What are you shouting for?" Duke just laughed.'

That year, Jim played another cameo in *Airport '77* (so-called because it was released in 1977). Appearing briefly as the millionaire owner of a luxury jet that is hijacked and then crashes into the ocean, he is mostly seen waiting at home for news of the daring rescue operations.

With little work coming his way, Jim was kept occupied by Gloria's vitality and sense of adventure. By the mid 1970s he was often in places such as Rwanda to promote the conservation of gorillas, accompanied by Gloria and daughter Kelly. He defied his almost seventy years by clambering about at an altitude of 11,000 feet, taking pictures of gorillas. He told me, 'They're scary creatures. My daughter Kelly insists they won't hurt me if I don't pose a threat. But there was this one fella – huge and hairy – and I found myself just six feet away from him. He was just staring at me . . . and I kinda stared back. I got my camera and aimed, and it's a good job the film was fast because I was shaking so much.'

Gloria kept him busier than ever, travelling abroad, attending social functions – 'anything to keep him moving and feeling alive,' said Gloria:

'I know people think I push him too hard, but you can't let age stop you, or you'll stop for good. So I keep Jim going. And he loves it when he starts telling one of his stories. He can make a good story last a long time. Lots of pauses and drawing words out. He'll have a room full of people listening to him, and he's always brilliant. Doesn't always tell the actual truth, but his stories are just wonderful.

'Like the one about Pie. He talks of a scene once where the horse had to walk down the street by himself, and on his saddle is a little bell which tinkles as he walks. The camera had to track along with the horse. Anthony Mann said, "How are we gonna get the horse to walk on cue and keep going until I've got the shot?" So Jim tells him, "Leave the horse to me." Then Jim goes to Pie and says to him, "When you hear the director say 'Action!' you start walking down the street . . . and you don't stop until you hear him holler 'Cut!' Now, you got that?" And Jim makes the story longer each time he tells it. And so when Mann shouts "Action!" the horse starts walking and keeps going until he hears "Cut!"

'I still don't know how true that story is, but it's a tale that gets taller each time he tells it. That's a priceless gift Jim has – to make people happy.'

22

Honoured to the Very End

Jim kept himself busy in 1976 by campaigning in California for Ronald Reagan in the presidential primaries. He also narrated a documentary, *Sentimental Journey*, which commemorated the anniversary of the DC-3, an early civil aircraft that was originally built for the US Army Air Force. Jim had, in fact, narrated a number of documentaries over the years, usually about subjects or causes he personally believed in. They included *Thunderbolt*, a 1947 documentary about fighter-plane support of ground troops during the Second World War, directed by William Wyler, and *How Much Do You Owe?*, made in 1949 in aid of the Disabled American Veterans.

When Jim lost his other sister, Dotie, to cancer in 1977, Gloria kept up the pace. She knew Jim didn't want to lose himself in grief, so she gave him little time to grieve. 'But there are times,' she told me, 'when he suddenly goes off in his mind to some place even I can't reach. I believe he's thinking back on his life, remembering his friends and family who have passed away. I'd hear him say quietly, "It won't be long before I'm with you all." But he doesn't say it in a mournful way. He's very . . . *wistful* about it. Almost saying it with a smile. He believes in God and heaven, and he feels they are all there, waiting for him.' For herself, Gloria said, 'I'm not taking a chance on there being something better after death. I'm making sure I get all I can out of *this* life.'

Jim and Gloria travelled to London in 1977 to attend the marriage of their daughter Kelly to the University of Cambridge lecturer Alexander Harcourt. That same year Jim was back in England to make a cameo appearance in Michael Winner's awful remake of *The Big Sleep*. Jim appeared in just two scenes, playing another millionaire who hires private eye Philip Marlowe (Robert Mitchum) to deal with a blackmailer.

That was followed by *The Magic of Lassie*, playing a vineyard owner who tries to reunite Lassie with his granddaughter. Its producer, Bonita Granville Wrather, who owned all the rights to Lassie, told me in 1977, 'The film is going to bring back Lassie to a whole new generation. It's on television all the time, but there hasn't been a movie about Lassie for years. In this we have a great cast including James Stewart, Mickey Rooney, Alice Faye and Stephanie Zimbalist.' Released in 1978, the film bombed. Popular films for the family were *Star Wars* and *Superman*. Lassie was simply out of date. It was the last Hollywood movie – excluding TV work – Jim made.

In 1979, aged seventy-one, he said, 'Things have changed in movies over the past few years. There are films for the family, but they're all about special effects. Where are you going to put me in outer space? I'll keep looking for something to do, but I don't hold my breath. At my age, you don't want to hold your breath for longer than five seconds anyway . . . just in case the next breath doesn't come!'

The chance of something good finally looked like coming his way in 1979. Joshua Logan told Jim that he was bidding for the film rights to the Ernest Thompson play *On Golden Pond*, with the intention of casting Jim in it. Jim was delighted, but his delight turned to disappointment when Jane Fonda outbid all comers for the rights so she could star in it with her father. It was, in effect, a chance for daughter and father to finally get close. Jim understood, and he called Henry up to congratulate him. 'It was more important for Hank and Jane to make that film than it was for me,' he said. The film would be Fonda's crowning achievement, bringing him a Golden Globe and an Oscar in 1982.

Jim turned up in a bizarre Japanese production called *The Green Horizon*, released in 1981. Jim and Gloria had been visiting a Kenyan game reserve in 1979 where they came across the film-makers, and Jim was persuaded to appear, speaking several lines. 'Never did understand what it was all about,' Jim told me. 'I was just some old fella who loved animals and living in the wild. I did it on a whim . . . thought it would help to promote wildlife conservation.'

In 1980 the best work Jim could find was a thirty-minute TV film called *Mr. Krueger's Christmas*. He played the janitor of an apartment block who is alone at Christmas time. But his Christmas becomes complete thanks to the intervention of a little girl. The film was actually produced by the Church of Jesus Christ of Latter-day Saints (the Mormons) and was an uplifting story about the true meaning of Christmas. Jim and Gloria stayed in Salt Lake City and socialised with the Mormon hierarchy, much to the displeasure of the Presbyterian Church. But as Jim said, 'It was just about faith in God and knowing what Christmas is really about – and that's the same in any Christian faith.'

What Jim probably never knew was that the Mormons stuck a five-minute epilogue on the end to invite people to join their church – although this version was purely for use by Mormon missionaries and was not seen when the film aired on American television.

In February 1980, the American Film Institute (AFI) honoured Stewart with its Life Achievement Award. The cream of Hollywood turned out for the occasion: Gene Kelly, Jack Lemmon, William Holden, Charlton Heston, Stefanie Powers, Walter Matthau, Richard Widmark, Karl Malden – and, of course, Henry Fonda in the role of Master of Ceremonies. Among the younger generation of actors was Dustin Hoffman.

A montage of scenes from Stewart's films opened the proceedings, including the box-office flop that became a legend, *It's a Wonderful Life*, the always-loved *Harvey*, the once derided but now revered *The Spirit of St. Louis*, and the previously reviled *Anatomy of a Murder*. Then Henry Fonda stepped to the podium. Two years earlier, Fonda had been the AFI's Life Achievement recipient. He waved to Stewart and said, 'Glad it's you, Jim . . . in the hot seat!

Gloria, hold his hand and *make* him enjoy it.' Some of Stewart's co-stars had their say, including Widmark, Malden and Ruth Hussey, as did some of Hollywood's most legendary directors including Henry Hathaway and Mervyn LeRoy.

Next, Dustin Hoffman took the stage. He talked of how his own father had worked at Columbia Studios when *Mr. Smith Goes to Washington* was being filmed. Telling Stewart, 'My father grew up with you,' he continued, 'I only saw *It's a Wonderful Life* two days ago. I'm the only one up here representing my generation of actors. When I saw you on screen in that performance, you made me laugh, you made me cry, and you made me wish for a country which perhaps we haven't seen for a while. Let me just say in closing that you made my parents very happy, you have made me very happy and I'm sure you're going to make my children very happy. And if this world has any Capra luck, you're going to make my children's children very happy.'

Gloria told me, 'Although Jim was delighted to have all his friends there – all his *surviving* friends – the tribute from Hoffman meant more to him than anything else said – well, *almost* anything. The thing about Jim is, he would show his appreciation with his usual warm and honest smile, but he would never betray the sense of overwhelming emotion he was fighting to keep from bubbling to the surface.'

Finally, AFI chairman George Stevens Jnr invited the guest of honour up to receive his award. Bottling his emotions, Stewart began by saying, 'Thank you all for sharing such a wonderful evening . . . which is about to go downhill as I . . . fumble around for the right words to express my appreciation.' Of course, Stewart wasn't fumbling at all. He knew exactly what he was going to say, and every word delighted the audience. 'I know it's late and I promised myself to talk fast so as not to keep you up any longer than is necessary. The problem is . . . I don't know *how* to talk fast!' He summed up his life, his career and his Life Achievement Award by calling himself 'Jimmy Stewart, a remarkably fortunate fella'.

By 1980 Jim's age was beginning to catch up on him. He was hospitalised for five days with an irregular heartbeat. That same year he was stricken with sciatica, preventing him from attending a photographic exhibition in New York in aid of conservation causes in Africa.

In 1981 Jim had to give up one of his life's greatest loves. He explained, 'I had to give up flying, and that was a huge disappointment because I loved flying just about more than anything. I loved being at the Piper Club, which I used to own. I could go out there and take off in my little plane, fly up over the mountains, land on the tiny strips ranchers had laid down for me. But my hearing got so bad that I couldn't understand anything the tower was communicating to me. They got kind of tired of having to keep repeating themselves, and I got tired of having to ask them to repeat things. So I had to give it up . . . after forty-five years.'

Gloria said, 'It just got too dangerous to have him flying around up there, cut off from the world. He could never drive a car but he could always fly a plane. But when he couldn't hear what anyone said to him over the radio, he was a danger to himself and to others . . . and to my nerves.'

By the time Henry Fonda was awarded his Best Actor Oscar for *On Golden Pond*, he was too ill to leave his Bel Air home, so his daughter Jane collected it for him. Jim went to see Fonda regularly; Hank lay in bed, Jim sat beside him, and for long periods of time they just stayed in silence. Jim later told me, 'I just couldn't believe I was losing my very best friend.'

Gloria said that both men were so hard of hearing that when they did speak, they had to shout at each other. 'That made Hank laugh,' she said. 'Yeah, it sure did,' Jim said, so softly I could hardly hear him.

Fonda died on 11 August 1982. Jim went straight to Fonda's home to be with the family, including Jane and Hank's widow Shirlee. Gloria later heard how Jim sat quietly in an armchair and said nothing, lost in thought, even though others were talking. After a long while, he suddenly said, 'It was the biggest kite we ever flew.' Then he related to the Fonda family how he and Hank had flown kites, and when he finished his story, he fell into silence again.

In 1982, Jim was offered what he hoped would be a chance to deliver a really great performance – 'much like Hank did in *On Golden Pond*,' he said. A TV film for Home Box Office (HBO) called *Right of Way*, it was based on a play by Richard Lees (who co-produced the film version) about an elderly couple who decide to commit suicide against their daughter's wishes. Bette Davis was cast as his wife. Gloria said that Jim had been made to feel humiliated because the director, George Schaefer, and co-producer, Philip Parslow, insisted he take a physical 'to prove he wouldn't drop dead halfway through production'.

Filming began in October 1982. As well as hoping to achieve a highlight of his own career, Jim was also paying tribute to Henry Fonda in his own way. After finishing certain scenes that stretched him physically as well as emotionally, he would look to the sky and say, 'That's for you, Hank.'

But *Right of Way* was destined not to be the experience Jim had hoped for. Although he would never publicly admit it, he hated working with Bette Davis. 'She thought the film was only about *her*,' said Gloria. 'She didn't give Jim a chance.' While filming a scene where they lie in bed, Jim had to kiss Davis on the cheek. Gloria told me, 'When Jim went to kiss her, she turned her head away. Everyone was shocked, especially Jim. So in the next take he just hugged her. I could have slapped the . . ! But Jim kept his anger in check. The way she treated him was appalling, and I know the director thought so too. There should have been the chemistry that Hank Fonda and Katy Hepburn had in *On Golden Pond*. But there was no chemistry. She just froze him out, and the film suffered.'

Two endings were shot. In one, which was referred to as the 'happy ending', the couple succeed in their suicide bid; in the other, the 'unhappy ending', the police arrive in time to arrest them. Jim had always insisted that the 'happy ending' was the only correct one. Gloria recalled, 'We saw the film for the first time at a private screening. The first thing we noticed was that the picture had been edited around Bette Davis, and so much of Jim's performance was lost. Then when the film got to its end – it wasn't the ending Jim wanted. He was just devastated because this was his last chance to shine as an actor, and it had been taken away from him. I stood there with him and cried. For once he didn't say, "Don't cry in front of everybody."'

HBO were also unhappy about the ending, and while the station argued with the director, the film was shelved. A year passed and finally Jim suggested that they insert a shot of the daughter smelling gas and realising that her parents had died. The battle lines had been drawn for so long that nobody on either side much liked the idea, but to get the film shown, the insert was done. That was the version that was finally seen in 1983. But despite the change in the ending, the film, as far as Gloria was concerned, was ruined by Bette Davis' behaviour on the set and 'her bullying of the director into making it *her* film'.

During the 1980s Jim received all manner of awards and honours – from the Cannes Film Festival, the United Service Organizations (USO), the Boy Scouts of America, Indiana University and New York's Museum of the Moving Image. In 1982 he was invited to the Berlin Film Festival to be honoured along with Joan Fontaine. The following year, in May, he celebrated his 75th birthday in his home-town of Indiana, where he and Gloria rode in a motorcade down Philadelphia Street and witnessed the unveiling of a statue of Jim outside the courthouse. The statue gazed in the direction of the former hardware store where the Savings & Trust Bank now stood.

Also in 1983, Jim was honoured for his career achievements by the Kennedy Centre in Washington. Jim told me a few years later, 'I don't seem to make movies any more. I just get a lot of awards and ceremonies for making 'em.'

That year the irregular heartbeat returned, and this time Jim was fitted with a pacemaker. But only a few weeks later, he was back in hospital to receive radiation treatment for skin cancer. The treatment was successful.

There was another honour in 1985, when the Academy of Motion Picture Arts and Sciences presented him with an honorary Oscar. Cary Grant invited him on to the stage to collect his statuette. Thanks were given to Frank Capra and other directors for 'so generously and brilliantly guiding me through the no-man's-land of my own intentions'. That same year he was also awarded a Medal of Freedom, while the decade's awards were topped by an honour bestowed on him by the Lincoln Centre in 1990.

Jim had one final TV appearance to make, in the Civil War mini-series *North and South, Book 2* in 1986. It was just a cameo, playing a Southern lawyer. Then the scripts stopped coming in altogether. Jim spent much of his time reading books and magazines. He stopped playing golf, telling his golfing friends, 'Look, fellas, the truth is, I don't *like* golf.'

One friend, Gloria told me, thought Jim might like to try flying a glider. But during his one and only flight, Jim found he couldn't control the glider the way he could an aeroplane, and the friend had to take control quickly before they crashed. Gloria felt that the real reason Jim panicked was because he was frustrated by not being able to fly a *real* plane.

For years Jim had been scribbling down little poems, and in 1989 a selection of them were published by Crown Books, simply called *Jimmy Stewart and His Poems*. Published in time for Christmas 1989, Jim and Gloria embarked on a tour of New York, Washington, Chicago and Dallas to promote the book. The tour was gruelling for the 81-year-old actor. Many remarked that he looked frail and thin, but Gloria, now seventy, saw it as her duty to keep him going as long as she could.

Jim was delighted when he was asked to work on an animated feature film in 1991. In *An American Tail: Fievel Goes West*, he provided the voice of a lawman called Wylie Burp. It was the last time that famous voice would be heard in a cinema – except for revivals of old films.

The biggest shock in Jim's life came when Gloria was diagnosed with lung cancer in 1993. I remember her giving me the news over the telephone; typically, she refused to allow the situation to sound too melodramatic: 'You know me, Michael. If I didn't have two packets [of cigarettes] a day, I'd die.' She told me that Jim had been urging her to undergo chemotherapy, and I suggested she should too.

She finally had a course of chemo; almost immediately her hair began to fall out and she was violently sick. She told me that she asked her doctors if the chemo was actually going to save her life, and they finally admitted that, at best, it would only prolong it. She told me, 'I'm not going to lose all my hair and be sick all the time just to live a few more months, so I told them there would be no more chemotherapy. I want to enjoy what life I have left. Jim understands and supports me.'

On 16 February 1994, Gloria died. She was seventy-five. She had always seemed so much younger to me. Over the years, whenever I called the Stewart home, Gloria had always answered. When I tried calling to give my condolences, nobody answered. So I sent a message and arranged for flowers to be delivered.

I never heard from or spoke to Jim again. He slipped into the life of a recluse. Few people saw him, except his family. I eventually heard that Jim was not even seeing his old friends. Gloria had been the very centre of his life, and she was gone. Jim had once told me, 'If the time comes when my life has no more purpose, I won't hold on to it. I won't fight God if he wants to take me.'

On 20 May 1995 Jim was again honoured by Indiana with the opening of the Jimmy Stewart Museum. This took up the entire top floor of the municipal library on Philadelphia Street. Jim declined to join in the festivities, maintaining his reclusive life; instead, his twin daughters represented him. He was, in effect, honoured in some way or another almost to the very end. He said to me once, 'Awards and honours are wonderful things . . . but I sure wish they'd given them to me when I was younger. It gets hard for an old fella like me to go from one ceremony to another.'

During the Christmas holiday of 1995, Jim slipped at home and banged his head. The newspaper stories made it seem worse than it was, and after a few days in hospital for observation, he was allowed home. All of this paints a somewhat pathetic picture of such a much-loved man. I think he was not a sad recluse, but a contented one. He had always had the ability to be alone. If he stayed at home all the time, it was partly because Gloria was no longer there, virtually forcing him to get up and go out. It was also the fact that the man was nearly ninety years old.

He had known for some time that his God would eventually call him, and He did, on 2 July 1997. Jim died peacefully in his sleep. The whole of Hollywood mourned, as did his family, along with much of the world. The funeral at the local Presbyterian Church came complete with a small military guard of honour. Afterwards his remains were interred at Forest Lawn Memorial Park in Glendale, California.

It was sad to lose a man so much admired and loved. He would be much missed, not just by those who knew him personally, but by everyone who enjoyed watching films. And yet, like all great movie stars, he provided a legacy of films – some excellent, some good, some not so good, but all imbued with that special magic which made James Stewart a star – for coming generations to enjoy.

But to Jim, it wasn't so much the films that he felt would be his lasting gift after he had gone, but what he called 'little pieces of time'. When I asked him once how he would like to be remembered, he didn't take too long to think of an answer – as though he had known it for many years. He said, 'I hope people will say things like, "I remember there was this film and Jimmy Stewart was dancing with some girl, and the floor opened up and underneath was a swimming pool, and they fell in."' (This was a scene from *It's a Wonderful Life*.) He continued, 'It doesn't matter if they can't remember the name of the film, just that it made them happy for a couple of minutes, and they always remembered it. It's a wonderful thing to have been able to give people little pieces of time that they can remember. I want people to say, "Yeah, Jimmy Stewart, he gave us little pieces of time."'

Jimmy Stewart gave us all a whole lot of little pieces of time.

Filmography

The abbreviations are as follows: *D* director; *P* producer; *S* screenplay; *C* Cinematographer (director of photography); *Lp* leading players. Studios and production companies are named in brackets. The date of each film is the year it was released.

The Murder Man (MGM) *D* Tim Whelan. *P* Harry Rapf. *S* Tim Whelan & John C Higgins, from a story by Tim Whelan and Guy Bolton. *C* Lester White. *Lp* Spencer Tracy, Virginia Bruce, Lionel Atwill, Harvey Stephens, Robert Bruce, James Stewart. 1935.

Rose Marie (MGM) *D* W S Van Dyke. *P* Hunt Stromberg. *S* Frances Goodrich, Albert Hackett & Alice Duer Miller, based on the musical play by Otto Harbach and Oscar Hammerstein. *C* William Daniels. *Lp* Jeanette MacDonald, Nelson Eddy, James Stewart, Reginald Owen, Allan Jones, George Regas (and further down the list, David Niven). 1936.

Next Time We Love (Universal) *D* Edward H Griffith. *P* Paul Kohner. *S* Melville Baker, from the story 'Say Goodbye Again' by Ursula Parrott. *C* Joseph Valentine. *Lp* Margaret Sullavan, James Stewart, Ray Milland, Anna Demetrio, Grant Mitchell, Robert McWade. 1936.

Wife vs. Secretary (MGM) *D* Clarence Brown. *P* Hunt Stromberg. *S* Norman Krasna, Alice Duer Miller & John Lee Mahin. *C* Ray June. *Lp* Clark Gable, Jean Harlow, Myrna Loy, May Robson, Hobart Cavanaugh, James Stewart. 1936.

Small Town Girl (MGM) *D* William A Wellman. *P* Hunt Stromberg. *S* John Lee Mahin, from the novel by Ben Armes Williams. *C* Charles Rosher. *Lp* Janet Gaynor, Robert Taylor, Binnie Barnes, James Stewart, Lewis Stone, Elizabeth Patterson. 1936.

Speed (MGM) *D* Edwin L Marin. *P* Lucien Hubbard. *S* Michael Fessier. *C* Lester White. *Lp* James Stewart, Wendy Barrie, Ted Healy, Una Merkel, Weldon Heyburne, Patricia Wilder. 1936.

The Gorgeous Hussy (MGM) *D* Clarence Brown. *P* Joseph L Mankiewicz. *S* Ainsworth Morgan & Stephen Morehouse Avery. *C* George Folsey. *Lp* Joan Crawford, Robert Taylor, Lionel Barrymore, Melvyn Douglas, Franchot Tone, James Stewart. 1936.

Born to Dance (MGM) *D* Roy Del Ruth. *P* Jack Cummings. *S* Jack McGowan, Sid Silvers & B G DeSylva. *C* Ray June. *Lp* Eleanor Powell, James Stewart, Virginia Bruce, Una Merkel, Sid Silvers, Frances Langford. 1936.

After the Thin Man (MGM) *D* W S Van Dyke. *P* Hunt Stromberg. *S* Frances Goodrich & Albert Hackett, from a story by Dashiell Hammett. *C* Oliver T Marsh. *Lp* Myrna Loy, William Powell, James Stewart, Elissa Landi, Joseph Calleia, Jessie Ralph. 1936.

Seventh Heaven (20th Century-Fox) *D* Henry King. *P* Darryl F Zanuck. *S* Melville Baker, based on the play by Austin Strong. *C* Merritt Gerstad. *Lp* Simone Simon, James Stewart, Gale Sondergaard, Gregory Ratoff, Jean Hersholt, J Edward Bromberg. 1937.

The Last Gangster (MGM) *D* Edward Ludwig. *P* J J Cohn. *S* John Lee Mahin. *C* William Daniels. *Lp* Edward G Robinson, James Stewart, Rose Stradner, Lionel Stander, Douglas Scott, John Carradine. 1937.

Navy Blue and Gold (MGM) *D* Sam Wood. *P* Sam Zimbalist. *S* George Bruce, based on his novel. *C* John Seitz. *Lp* Robert Young, James Stewart, Lionel Barrymore, Florence Rice, Billie Burke, Tom Brown. 1937.

Of Human Hearts (MGM) *D* Clarence Brown. *P* John W Considine Jnr. *S* Bradbury Foote, from the story 'Benefits Forgot' by Honore Morrow. *C* Clyde DeVinna. *Lp* Walter Huston, James Stewart, Beulah Bondi, Guy Kibbee, Charles Coburn, John Carradine, Ann Rutherford. 1938.

Vivacious Lady (RKO) *D & P* George Stevens. *S* P J Wolfson & Ernest Pagano, from a novelette by I A R Wylie. *C* Robert De Grasse. *Lp* Ginger Rogers, James Stewart, James Ellison, Charles Coburn, Beulah Bondi, Frances Mercer. 1938.

The Shopworn Angel (MGM) *D* H C Potter. *P* Joseph L Mankiewicz. *S* Waldo Salt, from the story 'Private Girl' by Dana Burnet. *C* Joseph Ruttenberg. *Lp* Margaret Sullavan, James Stewart, Walter Pidgeon, Hattie McDaniel, Nat Pendleton, Alan Curtis. 1938.

You Can't Take It With You (Columbia) *D & P* Frank Capra. *S* Robert Riskin, from the play by George S Kaufman and Moss Hart. *C* Joseph Walker. *Lp* Jean Arthur, Lionel Barrymore, James Stewart, Edward Arnold, Mischa Auer, Ann Miller. 1938.

Made For Each Other (United Artists) *D* John Cromwell. *P* David O Selznick. *S* Jo Swerling. *C* Leon Shamroy. *Lp* Carole Lombard, James Stewart, Charles Coburn, Lucile Watson, Harry Davenport, Ruth Weston. 1939.

The Ice Follies of 1939 (MGM) *D* Reinhold Schunzel. *P* Harry Rapf. *S* Leonard Praskins, Florence Ryerson & Edgar Allan Woolf. *C* Joseph Ruttenberg. *Lp* Joan Crawford, James Stewart, Lew Ayres, Lewis Stone, Bess Ehrhardt, Lionel Stander. 1939.

It's a Wonderful World (MGM) *D* W S Van Dyke. *P* Frank Davis. *S* Ben Hecht. *C* Oliver T Marsh. *Lp* Claudette Colbert, James Stewart, Guy Kibbee, Nat Pendleton, Frances Drake, Edgar Kennedy. 1939.

Mr. Smith Goes to Washington (Columbia) *D & P* Frank Capra. *S* Sidney Buchman, from the story 'The Gentleman From Montana' by Lewis R Foster. *C* Joseph Walker. *Lp* Jean Arthur, James Stewart, Claude Rains, Edward Arnold, Guy Kibbee, Thomas Mitchell. 1939.

Destry Rides Again (Universal) *D* George Marshall. *P* Joe Pasternak. *S* Felix Jackson, Gertrude Purcell & Henry Myers. *C* Hal Mohr. *Lp* Marlene Dietrich, James Stewart, Mischa Auer, Charles Winninger, Brian Donlevy, Una Merkel. 1939.

The Shop Around the Corner (MGM) *D & P* Ernst Lubitsch. *S* Samson Raphaelson, from the play *Perfumerie* by Nicholaus Laszlo. *C* William Daniels. *Lp* Margaret Sullavan, James Stewart, Frank Morgan, Joseph Schildkraut, Sara Haden, Felix Bressart. 1940.

The Mortal Storm (MGM) *D* Frank Borzage. *P* Sidney Franklin. *S* Claudine West, Andersen Ellis & George Froeschel, from the novel by Phyllis Bottome. *C* William Daniels. *Lp* Margaret Sullavan, James Stewart, Robert Young, Frank Morgan, Robert Stack, Bonita Granville. 1940.

No Time For Comedy [aka *Guy With a Grin*] (Warner Brothers) *D* William Keighley. *P* Hal Wallis. *S* Julius J & Philip G Epstein, from the play by S N Behrman. *C* Ernst Haller. *Lp* James Stewart, Rosalind Russell, Genevieve Tobin, Charles Ruggles, Allyn Joslyn, Clarence Kolb. 1940.

The Philadelphia Story (MGM) *D* George Cukor. *P* Joseph L Mankiewicz. *S* Donald Ogden Stewart, from the play by Philip Barry. *C* Joseph Ruttenberg. *Lp* Cary Grant, Katharine Hepburn, James Stewart, Ruth Hussey, John Howard, Roland Young. 1940.

Come Live With Me (MGM) *D* & *P* Clarence Brown. *S* Patterson McNutt. *C* George Folsey. *Lp* James Stewart, Hedy Lamarr, Ian Hunter, Verree Teasdale, Donald Meek, Barton McLane. 1941.

Pot o' Gold (United Artists) *D* George Marshall. *P* James Roosevelt. *S* Walter De Leon. *C* Hal Mohr. *Lp* James Stewart, Paulette Goddard, Horace Heidt and his Musical Knights, Charles Winninger, Mary Gordon, Frank Melton. 1941.

Ziegfeld Girl (MGM) *D* Robert Z Leonard. *P* Pandro S Berman. *S* Marguerite Roberts & Sonya Levien. *C* Ray June. *Lp* James Stewart, Judy Garland, Hedy Lamarr, Lana Turner, Tony Martin, Jackie Cooper, Ian Kelly. 1941.

It's a Wonderful Life (RKO) *D* & *P* Frank Capra. *S* Frances Goodrich & Albert Hackett. *C* Joseph Walker & Joseph Biroc. *Lp* James Stewart, Donna Reed, Lionel Barrymore, Thomas Mitchell, Henry Travers, Beulah Bondi. 1946.

Magic Town (RKO) *D* William A Wellman. *P* & *S* Robert Riskin. *C* Joseph Biroc. *Lp* James Stewart, Jane Wyman, Kent Smith, Ned Sparks, Wallace Ford, Regis Toomey. 1947.

Call Northside 777 (20th Century-Fox) *D* Henry Hathaway. *P* Otto Lang. *S* Jerome Cady & Jay Dratler. *C* Joe MacDonald. *Lp* James Stewart, Richard Conte, Lee J Cobb, Helen Walker, Betty Garde, Kasia Orzazewski. 1948.

On Our Merry Way (United Artists) *D* King Vidor & Leslie Fenton. *P* Benedict Bogeaus & Burgess Meredith. *S* Laurence Stallings,

Lou Breslow & John O'Hara. *C* John Seitz, Ernest Laszlo & Joseph Biroc. *Lp* Paulette Goddard, Burgess Meredith, James Stewart, Henry Fonda, Dorothy Lamour, Victor Moore, Fred MacMurray. 1948.

Rope (Warner Brothers) *D* Alfred Hitchcock. *P* Sidney Bernstein & Alfred Hitchcock. *S* Arthur Laurents, from the play by Patrick Hamilton. *C* Joseph Valentine & William V Skall. Lp James Stewart, John Dall, Farley Granger, Joan Chandler, Cedric Hardwicke, Constance Collier. 1948.

You Gotta Stay Happy (Rampart/Universal) *D* H C Potter. *P & S* Karl Tunberg. *C* Russell Metty. *Lp* Joan Fontaine, James Stewart, Eddie Albert, Roland Young, Willard Parker, Percy Kilbride. 1948.

The Stratton Story (MGM) *D* Sam Wood. *P* Jack Cummings. *S* Douglas Morrow & Guy Trosper. *C* Harold Rosson. *Lp* James Stewart, June Allyson, Frank Morgan, Agnes Moorehead, Bill Williams, Bruce Cowling. 1949.

Malaya (MGM) *D* Richard Thorpe. *P* Edwin Knopf. *S* Frank Fenton. *C* George Folsey. *Lp* Spencer Tracy, James Stewart, Valentina Cortese, Sydney Greenstreet, John Hodiak, Lionel Barrymore. 1949.

Winchester '73 (Universal) *D* Anthony Mann. *P* Aaron Rosenberg. *S* Borden Chase & Robert L Richards. *C* William Daniels. *Lp* James Stewart, Shelley Winters, Dan Duryea, Stephen McNally, Millard Mitchell, Charles Drake (further down the list, Rock Hudson, Anthony Curtis). 1950.

Broken Arrow (20th Century-Fox) *D* Delmer Daves. *P* Julian Blaustein. *S* Michael Blankfort, from the novel *Blood Brother* by Elliott Arnold. *C* Ernest Palmer. *Lp* James Stewart, Jeff Chandler, Debra Paget, Basil Ruysdael, Will Geer, Joyce MacKenzie, Arthur Hunnicutt. 1950.

The Jackpot (20th Century-Fox) *D* Walter Lang. *P* Samuel G Engel. *S* Phoebe & Henry Ephron. *C* Joseph LaShelle. *Lp* James Stewart, Barbara Hale, James Gleason, Fred Clark, Alan Mowbray, Patricia Medina, Natalie Wood. 1950.

Harvey (Universal) *D* Henry Koster. *P* John Beck. *S* Mary Chase & Oscar Brodney, from the play by Mary Chase. *C* William Daniels. *Lp* James Stewart, Josephine Hull, Peggy Dow, Charles Drake, Cecil Kellaway, Victoria Horne. 1950.

No Highway in the Sky [aka *No Highway*] (20th Century-Fox) *D* Henry Koster. *P* Louis D Lighton. *S* R C Sherriff, Oscar Millard & Alec Coppel, from the novel by Nevil Shute. *C* Georges Perinal. *Lp* James Stewart, Marlene Dietrich, Glynis Johns, Jack Hawkins, Janette Scott, Kenneth More. 1951.

The Greatest Show on Earth (Paramount) *D* & *P* Cecil B DeMille. *S* Frederic M Frank, Barry Lyndon & Theodore St John. *C* George Barnes. *Lp* Betty Hutton, Cornel Wilde, Charlton Heston, Dorothy Lamour, Gloria Grahame, James Stewart. 1952.

Bend of the River [aka *Where the River Bends*] (Universal) *D* Anthony Mann. *P* Aaron Rosenberg. *S* Borden Chase, from the novel by Bill Gulick. *C* Irving Glassberg. *Lp* James Stewart, Arthur Kennedy, Julia Adams, Rock Hudson, Lori Nelson, Jay C Flippen. 1952.

Carbine Williams (MGM) *D* Richard Thorpe. *P* Armand Deutsch. *S* Art Cohn. *C* William Mellor. *Lp* James Stewart, Jean Hagen, Wendell Corey, Carl Benton Reid, Paul Stewart, Otto Hulett. 1952.

The Naked Spur (MGM) *D* Anthony Mann. *P* William H Wright. *S* Sam Rolfe & Harold Jack Bloom. *C* William C Mellor. *Lp* James Stewart, Robert Ryan, Janet Leigh, Ralph Meeker, Millard Mitchell. 1953.

Thunder Bay (Universal) *D* Anthony Mann. *P* Aaron Rosenberg. *S* Gil Doud & John Michael Hayes (& Borden Chase uncredited). *C* William Daniels. *Lp* James Stewart, Joanne Dru, Gilbert Roland, Dan Duryea, Marcia Henderson, Jay C Flippen. 1953.

The Glenn Miller Story (Universal) *D* Anthony Mann. *P* Aaron Rosenberg. *S* Valentine Davies & Oscar Brodney. *C* William Daniels. *Lp* James Stewart, June Allyson, Henry Morgan, Charles Drake, George Tobias, Barton MacLane. 1953.

Rear Window (Paramount) *D* & *P* Alfred Hitchcock. *S* John Michael Hayes. *C* Robert Burks. *Lp* James Stewart, Grace Kelly, Wendell Corey, Thelma Ritter, Raymond Burr, Judith Evelyn. 1954.

The Far Country (Universal) *D* Anthony Mann. *P* Aaron Rosenberg. *S* Borden Chase. *C* William Daniels. *Lp* James Stewart, Ruth Roman, Corinne Calvet, Walter Brennan, John McIntire, Jay C Flippen, Henry Morgan. 1955

Strategic Air Command (Paramount) *D* Anthony Mann. *P* Samuel J Briskin. *S* Valentine Davies & Bernie Lay Jnr. *C* William Daniels.

Lp James Stewart, June Allyson, Frank Lovejoy, Barry Sullivan, Alex Nicol, James Millican. 1955.

The Man From Laramie (Columbia) *D* Anthony Mann. *P* William Goetz. *S* Philip Yordan & Frank Burt. *C* Charles Lang. *Lp* James Stewart, Arthur Kennedy, Donald Crisp, Cathy O'Donnell, Alex Nicol, Aline MacMahon, Wallace Ford, Jack Elam. 1955.

The Man Who Knew Too Much (Paramount) *D* & *P* Alfred Hitchcock. *S* John Michael Hayes & Angus McPhail. *C* Robert Burks. *Lp* James Stewart, Doris Day, Brenda de Banzie, Bernard Miles, Ralph Truman, Daniel Gélin. 1956.

The Spirit of St. Louis (Warner Brothers) *D* Billy Wilder. *P* Leland Hayward. *S* Billy Wilder & Wendell Mayes, from the book by Charles A Lindbergh. *C* Robert Burks & J Peverell Marley. *Lp* James Stewart, Murray Hamilton, Patricia Smith, Bartlett Robinson, Marc Connelly, Arthur Space. 1957.

Night Passage (Universal) *D* James Neilson. *P* Aaron Rosenberg. *S* Borden Chase, from the novel by Norman A Fox. *C* William Daniels. *Lp* James Stewart, Audie Murphy, Dan Duryea, Dianne Foster, Elaine Stewart, Brandon de Wilde. 1957.

Vertigo (Paramount) *D* & *P* Alfred Hitchcock. *S* Alec Coppel & Samuel Taylor, from the novel *D'Entre Les Morts* by Pierre Boileau and Thomas Narcejac. *C* Robert Burks. *Lp* James Stewart, Kim Novak, Barbara Bel Geddes, Tom Helmore, Henry Jones, Raymond Bailey, Ellen Corby. 1958.

Bell, Book and Candle (Columbia) *D* Richard Quine. *P* Julian Blaustein. *S* Daniel Taradash, from the play by John Van Druten. *C* James Wong Howe. *Lp* James Stewart, Kim Novak, Jack Lemmon, Ernie Kovacs, Hermione Gingold, Elsa Lanchester. 1958.

The FBI Story (Warner Brothers) *D* & *P* Mervyn LeRoy. *S* Richard L Breen & John Twist, from the book by Don Whitehead. *C* Joseph Biroc. *Lp* James Stewart, Vera Miles, Murray Hamilton, Larry Pennell, Nick Adams, Diane Jergens. 1959.

Anatomy of a Murder (Columbia) *D* & *P* Otto Preminger. *S* Wendell Mayes, from the novel by Robert Traver. *C* Sam Levitt. *Lp* James Stewart, Lee Remick, Ben Gazzara, Joseph N Welch, Kathryn Grant, Arthur O'Connell, Eve Arden, George C Scott. 1959.

The Mountain Road (Columbia) *D* Daniel Mann. *P* William Goetz. *S* Alfred Hayes, from the novel by Theodore H White. *C* Burnett

Guffey. *Lp* James Stewart, Lisa Lu, Glenn Corbett, Henry Morgan, Frank Silvera, James Best. 1960.

Two Rode Together (Columbia) *D* John Ford. *P* Stan Shpetner. *S* Frank Nugent, from the novel *Comanche Captives* by Will Cook. *C* Charles Lawton Jnr. *Lp* James Stewart, Richard Widmark, Shirley Jones, Linda Cristal, Andy Devine, John McIntire. 1961.

The Man Who Shot Liberty Valance (Paramount) *D* John Ford. *P* Willis Goldbeck. *S* Willis Goldbeck & James Warner Bellah. *C* William H Clothier. *Lp* James Stewart, John Wayne, Vera Miles, Lee Marvin, Edmond O'Brien, Andy Devine, Woody Strode. 1962.

How the West Was Won (MGM-Cinerama) *D* Henry Hathaway, George Marshall & John Ford. *P* Bernard Smith. *S* James R Webb. *C* Joseph LaShelle, Charles Lang Jnr, William Daniels & Milton Krasner. *Lp* Carroll Baker, Lee J Cobb, Henry Fonda, Carolyn Jones, Karl Malden, Gregory Peck, George Peppard, Robert Preston, Debbie Reynolds, James Stewart, Eli Wallach, John Wayne, Richard Widmark. 1962.

Mr. Hobbs Takes a Vacation (20th Century-Fox) *D* Henry Koster. *P* Jerry Wald. *S* Nunnally Johnson, from the novel by Edward Streeter. *C* William C Mellor. *Lp* James Stewart, Maureen O'Hara, Fabian, Lauri Peters, Lili Gentle, John Saxon. 1962.

Take Her, She's Mine (20th Century-Fox) *D* & *P* Henry Koster. *S* Nunnally Johnson, from the play by Phoebe & Henry Ephron. *C* Lucien Ballard. *Lp* James Stewart, Sandra Dee, Audrey Meadows, Robert Morley, Philippe Forquet, John McGiver. 1963.

Cheyenne Autumn (Warner Brothers) *D* John Ford. *P* Bernard Smith. *S* James R Webb, from the novel by Mari Sandoz. *C* William H Clothier. *Lp* Richard Widmark, Carroll Baker, Karl Malden, Sal Mineo, Dolores del Rio, Ricardo Montalban, James Stewart, Edward G Robinson. 1964.

Dear Brigitte (20 Century-Fox) *D* & *P* Henry Koster. *S* Hal Kanter. *C* Lucien Ballard. *Lp* James Stewart, Fabian, Glynis Johns, Cindy Carol, Billy Mumy, John Williams (cameo appearance by Brigitte Bardot). 1965.

Shenandoah (Universal) *D* Andrew V McLaglen. *P* Robert Arthur. *S* James Lee Barrett. *C* William H Clothier. *Lp* James Stewart, Doug McClure, Glenn Corbett, Patrick Wayne, Rosemary Forsyth, Phillip Alford, Katharine Ross, George Kennedy, Strother Martin. 1965.

The Flight of the Phoenix (20th Century-Fox) *D & P* Robert Aldrich. *S* Lukas Heller, from the novel by Elleston Trevor. *C* Joseph Biroc. *Lp* James Stewart, Richard Attenborough, Peter Finch, Hardy Kruger, Ernest Borgnine, Ian Bannen, Ronald Fraser, Christian Marquand, Dan Duryea, George Kennedy. 1965.

The Rare Breed (Universal) *D* Andrew V McLaglen. *P* William Alland. *S* Ric Hardman. *C* William H Clothier. *Lp* James Stewart, Maureen O'Hara, Brian Keith, Juliet Mills, Don Galloway, David Brian, Jack Elam, Ben Johnson. 1966.

Firecreek (Warner Brothers) *D* Vincent McEveety. *P* Philip Leacock. *S* Calvin Clements. *C* William H Clothier. *Lp* James Stewart, Henry Fonda, Inger Stevens, Gary Lockwood, Dean Jagger, Ed Begley. 1968.

Bandolero! (20th Century-Fox) *D* Andrew V McLaglen. *P* Robert L Jacks. *S* James Lee Barrett. *C* William H Clothier. *Lp* James Stewart, Dean Martin, Raquel Welch, George Kennedy, Andrew Prine, Will Geer. 1968.

The Cheyenne Social Club (National General) *D & P* Gene Kelly. *S* James Lee Barrett, from the novel by Davis Grubb. *C* William H Clothier. *Lp* James Stewart, Henry Fonda, Shirley Jones, Sue Ane Langdon, Elaine Devry, Robert Middleton. 1970.

Fool's Parade [aka *Dynamite Man From Glory Jail*] (Columbia) *D & P* Andrew V McLaglen. *S* James Lee Barrett, from the novel by Davis Grubb. *C* Harry Stradling Jnr. *Lp* James Stewart, George Kennedy, Anne Baxter, Strother Martin, Kurt Russell, William Windom. 1971.

The Shootist (Paramount) *D* Don Siegel. *P* M J Frankovich & William Self. *S* Miles Hood Swarthout & Scott Hale, from the novel by Glendon Swarthout. *Lp* John Waync, Lauren Bacall, Ron Howard, James Stewart, Richard Boone, Hugh O'Brian, Bill McKinney, Henry Morgan, John Carradine. 1976.

Airport '77 (Universal) *D* Jerry Jameson. *P* William Frye. *S* Michael Scheff & David Spector. *C* Philip Lathrop. *Lp* Jack Lemmon, Lee Grant, Brenda Vaccaro, Joseph Cotton, Olivia de Havilland, Darren McGavin, Christopher Lee, George Kennedy, James Stewart. 1977.

The Big Sleep (ITC) *D & S* Michael Winner, from the novel by Raymond Chandler. *P* Elliott Kastner & Michael Winner. *C* Robert

Paynter. *Lp* Robert Mitchum, Sarah Miles, Richard Boone, Candy Clark, Joan Collins, Edward Fox, John Mills, James Stewart, Oliver Reed. 1978.

The Magic of Lassie (International Picture Show/Lassie Productions) *D* Don Chaffey. *P* Bonita Granville Wrather & William Beaudine Jnr. *S* Jean Holloway, Richard M Sherman & Robert B Sherman. *C* Michael Margulies. *Lp* James Stewart, Mickey Rooney, Pernell Roberts, Stephanie Zimbalist, Michael Sharrett, Alice Faye. 1978.

The Green Horizon (Sanrio Communications) *D* Susumu Hani & Simon Trevor. *P* Terry Ogisu & Yoichi Matsue. *S* Shintaro Tsuji. *C* Simon Trevor & Tsuguzo Matsumae. *Lp* James Stewart, Philip Sayer, Cathleen McCosker, Eleonora Vallone, Hakuta Simba. 1981.

An American Tail: Fievel Goes West (Universal) *D* Phil Nibbelink & Simon Wells. *P* Steven Spielberg & Robert Watts. *S* Flint Dille. *Voices* Dom DeLuise, James Stewart, John Cleese, Amy Irving, Phillip Glasser, Cathy Cavadini, Nehemiah Persoff. 1991.

Television Work

The Windmill (CBS) James Stewart, Barbara Hale, Donald MacDonald. 1955.

The Town With a Past (CBS) James Stewart, Fredd Wayne, Walter Sande. 1957.

The Trail to Christmas (CBS) James Stewart, Richard Eyer, John McIntire. Directed by James Stewart. 1957.

Cindy's Fella (NBC) James Stewart, George Gobel, Lois Smith. 1959.

Flashing Spikes (Avista) James Stewart, Jack Warden, Pat Wayne. Directed by John Ford. 1962.

The Jimmy Stewart Show (NBC) James Stewart, Julie Adams, Jonathan Daly. 1971–2.

Harvey (NBC/Hallmark) James Stewart, Helen Hayes, Marian Hailey. 1972.

Hawkins on Murder (CBS) James Stewart, Strother Martin, Bonnie Bedlia. 1973. Followed by *Hawkins: Murder In Movieland* 1973; *Hawkins: Die, Darling Die*, 1973, *Hawkins: A*

Life For a Life, 1973; *Hawkins: Blood Feud*, 1973; *Hawkins: Murder in the Slave Trade*, 1974; *Hawkins: Murder on the 13th Floor*, 1974; *Hawkins: Candidate For Murder*, 1974.

Mr. Krueger's Christmas (The Church of Jesus Christ of Latter-day Saints) James Stewart, featuring the Mormon Tabernacle Choir. 1980.

Right of Way (Home Box Office) James Stewart, Bette Davis. Directed by George Schaefer. 1983.

North and South, Book 2 (ABC/Warner) James Stewart appeared in a cameo. 1986.

Sources

I have listed below the people I have interviewed and who have been quoted in this book, along with the year (as best as I can remember it), the location or if the interview was conducted by transatlantic telephone (as I told James Stewart, 'You don't often catch me up in an aeroplane').

Foremost among these names are, of course, **James Stewart**, whom I interviewed and met with socially several times over a dozen or so years from 1975, and **Gloria Stewart**, with whom I also socialised and to whom I spoke on numerous occasions by transatlantic telephone.

Robert Aldrich: London (1977).
Carroll Baker: her London home (1978 or 1979).
Ian Bannen: on location in London for the film *Sweeney!* (1975 or 1976).
James Lee Barrett: by telephone (1979).
Julian Blaustein: by telephone (1989).
Frank Capra: by telephone (1980).
Jose Ferrer: London (1981).
Henry Fonda: London (1976).
Bonita Granville Wrather: London (1977).
Helen Hayes: Pinewood Studios (on the set of *Candleshoe*), England (1976 or 1977).
Charlton Heston: from a number of interviews conducted in London (1977–81).
Rock Hudson: Twickenham Film Studios, on the set of *The Mirror*

303

Crack'd, England (1979 or 1980).

Ben Johnson: by telephone (1979).

Van Johnson: Norwich, England, filming *Tales of the Unexpected* (1981 or 1982).

Jack Lemmon: by telephone; this was not a formal interview but was related to my theatrical work – we spoke a number of times (1998).

Mervyn LeRoy: by telephone (1981).

Joshua Logan: London (1976 or 1977).

Doug McClure: EMI offices, London (1978).

Andrew V McLaglen: Pinewood Studios, England (1979).

Lee Marvin: on location in England for *The Dirty Dozen: The Next Mission* (1984).

Ralph Meeker: by telephone, as I happened to know his cousin (1985).

Burgess Meredith: London (1980).

Ray Milland: on location in England for *The House in Nightmare Park* (1972).

Kenneth More: Pinewood Studios, England, on the set of *A Tale of Two Cities* (1980).

Kim Novak: London (1980).

Donna Reed: by telephone (1984).

Lee Remick: on location in London for *The Omen* (1975).

Aaron Rosenberg: London (1974).

George C Scott: on location in England for *The Last Days of Patton* (1985).

Don Siegel: Pinewood Studios, England (1979).

Woody Strode: London (1976).

William A Wellman: by telephone (1974).

Richard Widmark: Pinewood Studios, England, on the set of *Bear Island* (1979).

Shelley Winters: London (1981).

Bibliography

Bessie, Alvah, *Inquisition in Eden*, Macmillan (US), 1967.

Ceplair, Larry and Englund, Steve, *The Inquisition in Hollywood*, University of California Press (US), 1979.

Carpozi Jnr, George, *The Gary Cooper Story*, W H Allen (UK), 1971.

Christensen, Terry, *Reel Politics*, Basil Blackwell (US), 1987.

Dietrich, Marlene, *Marlene*, Grove (US), 1987.

Douglas, Kirk, *The Ragman's Son*, Simon & Schuster (US), 1988.

Eames, John Douglas, *The MGM Story*, Octopus Books (UK), 1975.

Finler, Joel W, *The Movie Directors Story*, Octopus Books (UK), 1985.

Ford, Dan, *The Unquiet Man: The Life of John Ford*, William Kimber (UK), 1979.

Gabler, Neal, *An Empire of Their Own*, W H Allen (UK), Crown (US), 1988.

Hardy, Phil, *The Western (Aurum Film Encyclopedia)*, Aurum Press (UK), 1983.

Hepburn, Katharine, *Me, Stories of My Life*, Viking (UK), Alfred A Knopf (US), 1991.

Hirschhorn, Clive, *The Universal Story*, Octopus Books (UK), 1983.

McBride, Joseph, *Frank Capra: The Catastrophe of Success*, Faber & Faber (UK), Simon & Schuster (US), 1992.

McClure, Arthur F, Jones, Ken D and Twomey, Alfred E, *The Films of James Stewart*, A S Barnes (US), 1970.

Navasky, Victor, *Naming Names*, Viking (US), 1980, John Calder (UK), 1982.

Pickard, Roy, *James Stewart, The Hollywood Years*, Robert Hale (UK), St Martin's Press (US), 1992.

Place, J A, *The Western Films of John Ford*, Citadel Press (US), 1970.

Robinson, John, *A Reason to Live*, Castle Books (US), 1988.

Shipman, David, *The Great Movie Stars: The Golden Years*, Hamlyn (UK), 1970.

Willis, Donald, *The Films of Frank Capra*, Scarecrow Press (US), 1974.

Index